MAKING TRUE LOVE

HEALING RELATIONSHIP PATTERNS THROUGH PAST LIFE REGRESSION

Bad relationship? Again?

Why do you repeatedly attract the same type of partners? What blocks you from finding true love?

Karen Kubicko, hypnotherapist, past life regressionist, and psychic intuitive, gives insight on how to heal these patterns so you can find true love.

Since 2004, Karen has worked with numerous people to help them feel comfortable remembering their own past lives. Since 2013, she's provided in-depth psychic intuitive readings comprised of seeing someone's whole soul experience (past lives, current lifetime, and more).

Most people who come for a session are interested in relationships—whether it is family, friends, or lovers.

Heart closed? Bedroom issues? Do you feel wanted? Perfectionist? Do they cheat on you? Is your partner a narcissist? Is it you?

If you suspect you're in an abusive relationship, please read, "Chapter 18, Warning! Danger! Signs of Abusive Relationships."

Common root causes stemming from past lives can continue to penetrate someone's current lifetime. 11 typical relationship patterns, 25+ past life examples, their root causes, and ways to heal—all based on spiritually provided information through past life regressions and readings.

How do you heal so you can find true love? Karen provides her angelically channeled induction script to help you find your root cause in a past life, plus additional healing modalities to continue your healing.

Bonus—learn what Archangel Chamuel, angel of relationships, provided to Karen on soulmates and twin flames.

MAKING TRUE LOVE

HEALING RELATIONSHIP PATTERNS THROUGH PAST LIFE REGRESSION

KAREN ANN KUBICKO

Karen A.B. Kubicko
Pittsburgh, Pennsylvania U.S.A.

Copyright ©2021 Karen Ann Kubicko

All rights reserved. No part of this book may be reproduced by any mechanical, photographic, or electronic process, or in the form of phonographic recording; nor may it be stored in a retrieval system, transmitted, or otherwise be copied for public or private use—other than for "fair use" as brief quotations embodied in articles and reviews without prior written permission of the publisher.

The author of this book does not dispense medical advice or prescribe the use of any technique as a form of treatment for physical or medical problems without the advice of a physician, either directly or indirectly. The intent of the author is only to offer information of a general nature to help you in your quest for emotional and spiritual well-being. In the event that you use any of the information in this book for yourself, which is your constitutional right, the author and the publisher assume no responsibility for your action.

Please note, all names and identifying information in the examples provided has been changed to protect their privacy. Any resemblance to actual events, locales, or persons, living or dead, is entirely coincidental.

Author's Photograph: Tom Pierce

Library of Congress Cataloging-in-Publication Data

Kubicko, Karen Ann
Making True Love—Healing Relationship Patterns Through Past Life Regression
Karen A.B. Kubicko
p. cm.
ISBN-13: 979-8531147769
1. Spirituality. 2. Reincarnation. 3. Reincarnation—Case studies
4. Relationship. 5. Self-Help. 6. New Age. 7. Spiritual Healing.
8. Shamanism. 9. Angels. 10. Spirit Guides 11. Sexuality.
12. Self Help. 13. Marriage. 14. Hypnotherapy.

Library of Congress Control Number: 2021913819

ISBN-13: 979-8531147769

U.S.A.

DEDICATION

To all my beautiful, loving spiritual beings here and to all my spirit guides, angels, and passed over loved ones on the other side that have inspired me, supported me, and helped me bring this book to fruition.

I deeply appreciate all of your love, knowledge, time, support, and patience. Thank you for being part of this lifetime with me—again.

Lots of love to you all. XOXOX

To the warm-hearted ladies at the Hays-Caldwell Women's Center in Texas for providing me with the knowledge to heal.

Please donate to your local shelter.

Contents

	The Rag Doll by Karen Kubicko	ix
	Introduction	xi
1	A Few Near-Death Experiences Spark My Journey to Find True Love	1
2	Feeling Loved—Healing Through Past Lives	11
3	How to Remember a Past Life	25
4	Sex. Sex. And More Sex.	35
5	Closed Heart—Blocking True Love Due to Death of a Loved One	51
6	Abuse is Not Love	65
7	Doing Your Duty	77
8	The Need to Feel Wanted	87
9	Perfectionism and Being Type A	97
10	Silent Partner. No Voice. Not Being Heard. Be Quiet!	107
11	Are You Drained?	113

12	The Victim and The Martyr	123
13	Mothering A Narcissist. I Can Change Them. I Can Save Them	131
14	Cheaters Always Cheat	141
15	Chakras—How I See Them	151
16	Tools to Help You Heal	155
17	Making True Love Affirmations	181
18	Warning! Danger! Signs of Abusive Relationships	187
19	Inspiration from Archangel Chamuel On Soulmates & Twin Flames	205
	Bibliography	215
	Index	217
	About the Author	221
	Connecting	222

THE RAG DOLL

The rag doll has a permanent smile sewn on her face
Always appearing happy
She lets you touch her, squeeze her, and hold her without complaint
Inside, her stuffing is turning moldy and grey
Yet her smile continues
She listens intently to all you say
Hears all the harsh words that you pour out
Keeping her lips sealed
Unable to open her tightly stitched smile
Slowly, day after day passes
She is easily forgotten
Pushed outside in the cold, bitter rain
Her little piece of love
Her heart-shaped piece of material
Long ago placed inside
Begins to be crumpled
Broken
Emotionally thrown about
Torn and tattered
Finally, it becomes guarded
Protected
She becomes stronger
Tired of the loneliness
She musters up all her courage
Takes a deep breath
Rises to the challenge of knowing one's true self
The rag doll limps away, outside
Knowing that there is more
There is unconditional love
Somewhere, out there

The rag doll learns
Learns that there is so much more to life
Remembering love
Deserving of unconditional love
She travels far, far away
Out into the beautiful forest
Filling her senses with all that nature offers
Healing
Connecting
Feeling the wind flowing through her yarn hair
She grows
She learns and grows some more
Her heart heals and glows with selflove
She knows that someday she will be found in the world
Reconnected to unconditional love
A shimmer of hope glistens in her eyes at the vision
A tear gently rolls down her cheek
One day, the thread between her lips becomes loose
Her lips begin to move
The smile becomes genuine
Soon the threads that sealed her lips completely unravel and open up
She utters her first word
She blushes
She sings
She yells in delight
Someday she will scream,
"Love"

by Karen Kubicko

INTRODUCTION

Think of all the bad dates and bad relationships you have had.

Now, thank each and every one of them for showing you what you do not want in this lifetime. These relationships are part of the learning lessons that you chose to go through to grow on a soul level.

This book is meant for those who are serious about healing themselves and reflecting deeply within to find the root cause of their relationship issues, with the intent to resolve them to find true love.

You have decided to make a change in your life.

Through free will, we decide to incarnate. We choose our lessons to learn, we choose our parents, our city, and even our closest friends and lovers. Each aspect of our life assists us in fully understanding our lessons. Some lessons are hard, and some are easy.

Here, in our Earth classroom, we see and sometimes experience things that can be hard—physically and emotionally. If our life on Earth were easy all day, every day, we would not learn. Sometimes we must learn things the hard way. How often have you heard that said to you in your life?

Ultimately, these hard experiences help us learn and grow. Some experiences help us identify what we really want out of life. Every person we pass by on the street lives in the same classroom. We all learn in the same school but focus on different subjects. Some students focus on charity, some on relationships, and others learn to be their true self. We chose these lessons long before we started incarnating.

When you work with your past lives, you can step out of your current lifetime and look at your whole soul journey to gain clarity on your current relationship trials and tribulations. This knowledge can bring understanding, forgiveness, and healing into your current lifetime. Which in turn, brings you greater love connections within yourself and with others.

I believe the goal for any true love relationship should be a mutually supportive, respectful, and loving one.

The intent of this book is to help you use past life regression to recognize and understand root causes so you can heal and release any relationship patterns preventing you from experiencing a true love relationship.

As most of my clients are heterosexual females, a majority of the examples provided are from their perspective. All information provided will help you with your relationship goals, whether it is to find true love with a male or female, in any type of relationship including heterosexual, lesbian, transgender, bisexual, or gay. It is truly about a soul loving a soul.

To heal through releasing patterns found in this lifetime and through past lifetimes, there are a few simple steps:

1. Understand how past life regression therapy can provide healing.
2. Find the pattern within these chapters that you would like to resolve.
3. Work to find and remember one past life or more to start your healing process.
4. Allow healing to occur. Replace your old pattern with a new positive affirmation.

~ BUT FIRST—WHERE DID WE COME FROM AND WHO ARE WE REALLY? ~

Through my own past life regressions and near-death experiences, I fully believe that our true selves are our souls. When we are born, we take a small part of our soul and lower its energetic vibration so that it can come down to the vibrational level of Earth. This conscious part of us is now focusing on this human life we chose. Earth, to me, is a classroom. Once here, we take the class of life. Most importantly, when we awaken to this knowledge, we remember that we have actually stayed connected to our whole soul.

The energetic part of us is incomprehensibly large. This energy, essentially our whole soul, extends throughout many dimensions or planes of existence. The whole soul part of us is often called our higher self. One small piece of our whole soul resides in our human body here in this Earth plane or dimension. Today, you are here, living in the Earth plane of existence because this is where you have chosen to focus your conscious attention.

I believe most of us spiritually reside in the multi-dimensional space we refer to as Heaven. Heaven is our home. Heaven to me is the land of love where everyone and everything is beautiful in every way. It is filled with unconditional love. Telepathy is used for communication—thoughts transmit to others easily. Plus, there is instant manifestation—thoughts can turn into anything instantly. There is no pain, jealousy, trauma, or fear in Heaven, so our spirits need to come to Earth to experience them, thereby collectively accumulating knowledge for the greater good.

Pure unconditional love is the highest vibration. This vibration resides on the highest plane of existence which is Source or God. We can connect to or raise our energy towards this higher vibration through gratitude and positive affirmations. The healing energy of unconditional love is available for everyone, anytime, or anyplace.

This whole soul part of us, stays connected to Source—and all that is—through our line of energy that flows through all of our chakras. There are a core group of seven chakras within our physical body. I have been psychically shown numerous additional chakras that energetically connect throughout all of the dimensions both above and below, including connecting to Source. Knowledge of your chakras and how you can deeply heal them is mentioned throughout this book. For basic chakra information, please see, "Chapter 15, Chakras."

~ 1. CAN PAST LIFE REGRESSION HELP ME HEAL? ~

Through your free will choice, your spiritual being has had several human experiences. I believe that each life we have is a class. Think of the thousands of lifetimes as thousands of classes you have taken on your soul growth journey. This one human life you have now is just one part of your whole soul life. When you choose a lesson for your human class, it may take you several lifetimes to learn the lesson. It may just be for the experience, it may be for learning how to overcome, it may be for enlightenment, or even being able to help someone else learn a life lesson.

Do you know what it feels like to truly be in love and to be deeply loved? "Chapter 2, Feeling Loved," provides you with hope and the motivation to remember something you may never have experienced in your current life—true love. Once you remember a loving lifetime, you realize you are worthy of that type of deep love.

Then, read through "Chapter 3, How to Remember a Past Life." With a basic understanding of past life therapy healing, as you read through the rest of the book, you recognize how deep a relationship pattern can go. I have also included my angelically channeled past life regression induction script to help you get started.

Through past life memories, you begin to realize that you travel through these lifetimes with a soul group. You have spent many lifetimes with so many loving beings. This knowledge will help explain several relationships—good or bad.

Working through a past life can heal so much more than just relationships. Since there are too many to list, I will share a few. Fears can be released. Releasing past life trauma can help improve your health. It explains why you love a certain part of the world or a certain thing. Past lives can explain déjà vu. You can remember whole lifetimes where you had amazing talents and skills and through remembering them, you can bring that knowledge into your current life.

~ 2. FIND YOUR PATTERN ~

There is a reason for every pattern. When someone comes to me for a past life regression or a reading, my intent is to always get to the root cause of the issue—to find the instigator, the start, the beginning of the pattern that holds a person back from something. This could explain why they have a fear of water, fear of flying, or exactly what is preventing them from finding true love.

After an initial trauma happens, then consecutive lifetimes (including this one) intensify the issue. This creates the pattern. You repeat this pattern until healing occurs. Make it your goal to heal in your current lifetime.

Let us say, for example, that you realized your heart is closed off to love. In this lifetime, you subconsciously chose relationships that were unloving. They may have been abusive. You remembered a few past lives and found more unloving relationships. You set the intent to find the root cause and asked your spirit guides for help. Then you remembered a past life where someone you deeply loved was killed in front of you. At that point you created the pattern, "I don't want to feel deep love like that again, it hurts too much."

Maybe you realized that you are stuck in the pattern of doing your duty to your partner, parents, and job while not taking care of yourself. You remember a few past lives that provide more examples of you doing your duty. Then you set your intent to find the root cause and go back to a past life that explains your pattern. You remember a past life where your spouse died while you were out having fun with friends one afternoon. You were overcome with guilt since you believed that had you been home, you would have prevented his death. Then, you realize the pattern you set into place was, "Other people's needs are more important than mine and if I am not taking care of them, they die."

When you remember a past life, you can locate the root cause to heal a relationship pattern. The root cause is the first traumatic occurrence that started the pattern.

Why is a root cause so important? When you find the root cause of a pattern or uncomfortable issue you have in this life, you can have what is called catharsis, a fancy word for putting a past trauma into perspective which then elicits deep healing. The root cause may be found in this life, but it has been my experience that it is often found in past lives and the issue has compounded over time. Once you recognize and do the healing work that connects to the root cause in that past lifetime, then healing can easily occur in your life now.

Knowing the root cause, you can begin to see the connection that trauma has in your current life. You gain a deep understanding on how it might have affected you in other lifetimes. Finding and healing any past life trauma can be the path to address a similar trauma in this lifetime. This begins your healing process to remove the pattern.

Each time you heal and remove a relationship pattern, you are loving yourself more. Increased selflove brings so much healing on so many levels—emotional, physical, energetic, and spiritual.

Awareness of the root cause is always an important first step to healing a pattern. Awareness of any problem is always the first step to any healing. You pull that problem out by the root when you find the root cause.

~ 3. TRY A PAST LIFE REGRESSION ~

Working with your past lives can bring you deep healing.

Choose one pattern that you would like to heal and set that as your intent during a past life regression. Maybe you would like to understand why you cannot tell your partner you want to leave them.

Ask your spirit guides and angels to help you in this process. They are there to help us more than we can comprehend. Due to the free will rule; they cannot interfere in our lives unless we ask. Please ask for their help. The more specific, the better. For this example, you can ask your spirit guides and angels to help you find the root cause to your block in communication or for issues with your Throat chakra.

Utilize the past life regression induction script found in "Chapter 3, How to Remember a Past Life," with a trusted friend or listen to it on a recording. There are many avenues to remember a past life.

Working with all your intuitive senses, trust whatever comes to you during a past life regression.

For this example, you might remember a few past lives that have to do with trauma to your throat. Maybe you remember one in which you were running from an angry mob of people who then cut your throat. In that past life, you learn you had caused their taxes to increase due to something you said.

Keep in mind, your true spiritual being is neither male nor female. You will come across lifetimes as a male or a female, various sexual orientations, as well as numerous ethnicities. Be open to anything.

While you are remembering a past life, your spirit guides are there helping you. During the regression, you can ask for them to show you the connection of that past life to your current lifetime. You can ask them to show you how to heal and release any patterns, traumas, pent-up emotions, and more. You can ask them to help you with forgiveness.

In that example of a past life with the throat trauma, you forgive the mob, their anger, the ax that cut your throat, yourself, your voice, the words you said, the tax collector and more. Your spirit guides help you recognize that you set the pattern of, "I cannot speak out or I will die," in place.

~ 4. ALL HEALING IS LOVING YOURSELF ~

Our nature is to heal, adapt, and overcome. When we get a cut, our whole body, including the immune system, comes to the rescue with white blood cells, fibrin, microphages, and antibodies to stop the bleeding and heal the wound. Emotional and spiritual wounds are not always as obvious—as blood gushing out of our skin—as a sign of pain.

We are energetic beings having a human existence.

Everything in the Universe is comprised of atoms in a constant state of motion or vibration. Depending upon the speed at which these atoms are vibrating, it turns them into a solid, liquid, gas, or plasma. The energetic part of us is much larger than the human body part of us. Our body is only one aspect of the multi-dimensional being that we truly are.

When an energy healer, like myself, psychically sees a trauma or pent-up emotion in someone's energy, it appears as a dark or grey area. This dark area prevents your spiritual energy from easily flowing. These dark areas can be the energy of the cause of your blocks or patterns in your life. It can be as simple as forgiving someone (or something) to release a dark area or block on your heart. You can choose to see or feel this trauma, (pent-up emotions, resentments, etc.) release from your energy as you simultaneously allow the healing angels to pour pure love and light into you. You can choose to rewrite or reprogram the old pattern with a new one.

All energy is mutable. A lump of coal can be formed into a diamond. The energy of old patterns and trauma can be healed (transmuted) into love and light energy.

So, in the examples given above, you can replace the energy of these patterns with a positive loving affirmation. You can find a long list of affirmations in "Chapter 17, Making True Love Affirmations."

Replace, "I don't want to feel deep love like that again, it hurts too much," with, "It is safe to love again."

Replace, "Other people's needs are more important than mine and if I am not taking care of them, they die," with, "I know how to take care of my needs, plus all my relationships support me in my lesson of learning deep love, support, and trust."

Replace, "I cannot speak out or I will die," with, "I speak clearly and with confidence."

In all healing modalities listed in, "Chapter 16, Tools to Help You Heal," the bottom line is that you are releasing the dark, grey energy of patterns, traumas, or emotions and replacing it with pure unconditional love. I have included lots of other energy healing modalities in addition to past life regression. You might resonate with Reiki, EFT, or soul retrieval to help further your healing.

As we heal, our energy becomes more whole, vibrant, and loving. It is at that point when we attract someone as equally healed and vibrant. When you love yourself and respect yourself, other people in your life have no choice but to reflect that love and respect back to you. The more you love yourself, the more you open the door for someone else to love you fully.

The reward is true love.

Your angels and spirit guides provide lots of insight to helping you. Frequently angels and spirit guides recommend six months to two years of selfcare to rebuild a solid sense of loving and healing yourself before starting a new relationship.

Selflove, self-confidence, self-respect, and selfcare all fit hand in hand. As you rebuild and heal yourself deeply, inherently you learn to love yourself. Always easier said than done but know that it is possible. When you try something new, like a healthy relationship pattern, it will feel uncomfortable at first.

You can do it. Do not give up on yourself. You have already started your selflove healing journey. You are ready for change; you picked this book because you chose to truly love yourself.

I believe in you.

CHAPTER 1

A FEW NEAR-DEATH EXPERIENCES SPARK MY JOURNEY TO FIND TRUE LOVE

I fucking hate men.

Such a strong statement.

I am sure some of you are thinking the same exact thing.

So, do I hate men? When I left a loveless marriage, I felt this way and as I worked my way through a divorce, I thought I did. In reality, I was sad that someone truly did not want to be with me, even though I had given up my whole self in the hopes of pleasing them and somehow thinking I could get them to love me if I did.

I do not feel that way anymore, thank goodness! I do want to share my life with a man. I adore touching a man's body, kissing them, holding endless intellectual conversations, smelling their scent, holding their hand, and enjoy time with them in all kinds of ways.

Everyone wants to feel loved and appreciated. How we were raised (and how we interacted with those around us while growing up) shaped us, and how we relate to others, more than we realize.

Our relationships are the most important thing in our lives, often affecting us the most. When I regress others into a past life, no one ever cares much about how much money they had, their job, or how big a house they owned, but they do care about the relationships they had with spouses, children, parents, friends, pets, and other loved ones that were in their life. It is also evident that even their own past life death pales in emotional response when remembering a loved one dying in a past life.

We are humans. We crave relationships. Good, solid, trusting relationships. How can you shift to a life filled with mutually supportive and loving relationships?

The Law of Attraction dictates that you will attract those who are as healed as you. The more healed you become, the better the connection you will have with the people in your life. So, if you have done some healing work and go on a bad date, do not blame them. Ask, "What more do I need to heal?" This way you can connect to someone with whom you can maintain a mutually supportive and loving relationship.

The PRIZE for doing all this self-healing work is TRUE LOVE because, in fact, you are learning to truly love yourself in the process. You are, in a sense, making true love.

A relationship was built over time and integrated in many ways, so it will take time and many ways to heal from a relationship, create new patterns, and learn to deeply love.

~ JOURNEY TO FIND HEALING ~

I grew up Catholic, even attending a Catholic high school for a few years. I had some faith during this time, but it mostly felt reverent and dutiful. The priests and nuns taught us that we were not good enough to talk to angels or God. Then one night, I lost my faith in everything and became atheist. How could a loving God let anything this bad happen to me?

One trauma can cause a lot of changes in your life. Quite a long time ago, while I was sleeping, I woke up to being raped. The next day, I moved into a women's shelter and lived there for a month until I found my own apartment. This experience and the group therapy sessions I attended while there, brought you most of the information provided in "Chapter 18, Warning! Danger!" It was during these therapy sessions when I first learned about patterns in abusive relationships.

This rape affected me in a variety of ways—ways I did not fully realize until twenty years afterwards. A year after the rape, I had cervical cancer removed. Looking back at this psychically, I now realize that the traumatic energy of this experience manifested into cancer.

I created lots of weird new rules to prevent triggers to the traumatic event. I found I stopped wearing similar nightgowns like the one I wore at the time. A mirror could not be in a similar place in my bedroom.

During one of my first aided past life regressions (someone helped me remember the past life), the rape was brought up in connection to a past life trauma. A lot of PTSD (post-traumatic stress disorder) triggers in connection to the rape were healed that day.

The rape also brought on a fear of being awoken while sleeping by a person or even a pet cat. During the end of my last long-term relationship, I dressed in sleep pants, shirt, and a housecoat tied at my waist to prevent easy access to raping me while I slept. I did not even realize the connection until after I left him. It took me a long time to be able to deeply sleep, even when alone.

Piece by piece, each aspect of this rape healed as if chipping away at an immense boulder. One 15-minute experience caused me decades of issues, now thankfully resolved. Motivation to heal from it all, was part of the inspiration for this book.

This experience now helps me feel comfortable working with others who have had sexual trauma too. Sometimes, having a trauma that allows you to relate to others, is referred to as a wounded healer.

One of the counselors at the shelter mentioned that abusers had common traits. The other ladies in the shelter and I were told we could use this knowledge as a tool to learn how to recognize abusive behavior patterns and thus helping us prevent an abusive relationship. We had to read through lists (these lists, and more are located in "Chapter 18, Warning! Danger!") of abuse traits and we were taught ways to reclaim our confidence and love for ourselves by setting boundaries. See "Human Rights in Intimate Relationships" and "Bill of Personal Rights" in "Chapter 16, Tools to Help You Heal."

Later, I found myself in another relationship pattern.

~ AWAKENING ~

Around the age of four, I remember being able to see and talk to two of my main spirit guides, Lena and Daniel. When my parents told me that there was no such thing as ghosts, I told my guides I had to stop talking to them.

Prior to 2001, I only had a passing interest in anything New Age or metaphysical. That year, I gave birth to my second child. Both of us nearly died that day. During my near-death experience, I saw and talked to several other spiritual beings on the other side while watching over my newborn baby. The spirit part of me did not fully reenter my body until my baby came home from the hospital eleven days later.

Three months later, I visited a local psychic with some friends. He told me that my newborn had a strong Third Eye (I had no idea what that meant at the time). The psychic went on to say that unless I helped my child understand and be okay with their psychic talent, life would be hard.

So, I read some books about psychic abilities. The books were so intense and over my head, I stopped researching the subject.

During a trip to West Virginia in 2004, I found Carol Bowman's book, *Children's Past Lives*, in a metaphysical store. That book inspired me to read everything I could find on past life regression.

In early 2005, I started listening to a self-hypnosis past life regression recording. After a month of trying, I saw glimpses of a few past lives. In May of 2005, I re-experienced some very intense past lives with the help of a local hypnotherapist.

Inspired by such deep personal healing, I wanted to learn more.

I trained under Dr. Brian Weiss in 2007, so I could help others remember and heal through past life regression too. I was lucky enough to be the subject on stage for a quick induction (the fastest way to go under hypnosis) by Dr. Weiss himself.

My inner fire ignited as I learned more about past life regression therapy and soon realized this is part of my life's path. As I read and researched more about the topic one late night, I was overcome with bliss and grace as I regained my faith in a higher power. Tears still come to my eyes remembering that moment.

I mostly kept my interest in past life regression to myself and only regressed friends and others by word of mouth.

In 2010, as I laid in a hospital bed, unable to breathe, I realized that my current relationship was not supportive, and it felt unloving. This Heart chakra trauma had caused my asthma, exacerbated to a point that triggered this hospital stay. It dawned on me that my issue with asthma started not long after we moved in together.

One afternoon, in the hospital, I experienced a lucid dream with information on a past life. I realized that my breathing issues were connected to feeling unwanted in a past life as well as my current life. I healed on many levels that day, more than I recognized at the time. My asthma issue went away altogether a few short months later.

I realized I was giving and not receiving. I realized I lived my life for everyone else and not for me. I realized I had given up most everything I loved to do. According to the doctors, I could have died that week in the hospital. This was a wakeup call.

I began altering my life at that point. I began to care about me. I began doing things that made me happy. I started writing and researching past lives for my first book, *Life Is Just Another Class—One Soul's Journey Through Past Life Regression*.

In late 2011, I remembered a past lifetime in which I realized, no matter how many times I get killed, I am never dead. Prior to this, I did not have any social media or even a website. That changed too.

As I wrote and worked on that book, it was acutely obvious that I was repeating a few bad relationship patterns throughout my past lives, and they had leaked into this lifetime. Since then, I became determined to release, resolve, forgive, and heal from any and all relationship patterns. I had healed many of my minor and major phobias as well as healed my asthma through remembering past lives, so past life regression work—clearly—was the perfect place for me to start.

As I healed and collected myself, by late 2012, I realized I needed to make a major relationship change. No easy task with little kids involved. However, I could not bring myself to say anything—and what I did say, went unheard.

So unhappy in the relationship, I thought about driving over the edge of a bridge. (Suicide does not solve anything. You just repeat the challenge again in the next life.) At that point, I knew I needed help. I found a counselor. When you focus on personal healing, you are loving yourself.

I took various metaphysical and intuitive training classes. A friend attuned me in Reiki. I started meditating.

I felt more awakened intuitively. As you work with past life regression, you become more connected to your true spiritual self. This clear knowledge inherently awakens your intuitive abilities. A huge benefit of deep spiritual healing is that it can clear blocks to your intuition too.

I also learned that having faith and trust in asking spirit guides for help will bring amazing results.

~ CONVERSING WITH SPIRIT GUIDES ~

I remember the day I was guided to ask questions to spirit guides. Mind you, I was in a hypnotic state, in the midst of recalling more past life information to further refine my book.

Tears filled my eyes during the memory of a past life death. I saw my spirit guide, Lena, by my side the whole time. I entered The Light, met loved ones in the greeting room, and had just completed an amazing angelic healing session. I felt so loved.

These are the notes from right after the angelic healing session that day:

Someone is telling me, "You can ask us anything."

I go off to bed now. It seems funny to have a bed there.

"Heaven is yours; you can make with it what you want." I am hearing a voice, but not seeing anyone though. Jamie [my friend helping me remember this lifetime] wonders aloud, "Is it possibly God?"

I hear, "Information is key."

If I go to the right, I can walk out of the healing room. The passageway is like a short walkway/tunnel with a curved ceiling and glistening walls. Everything glistens, it is pretty. I see a light at the end of the tunnel.

I hear, "The why."

I walk out of the tunnel and see gardens, pathways, and buildings. There are many people walking around. No one is hurrying.

I hear, "Open your heart before you die."

Lena, my spirit guide, told me during a later past life regression that I was having a conversation with her. I had only spoken with her a few times during previous past life regressions, plus we had kept the conversation to the information occurring in a past life. (No doubt my Catholic upbringing caused my reverent view of her.)

She was standing near me moments prior to this interaction, but since she was not standing next to me in the healing room, it was not clear who spoke. I had not fully understood telepathy yet.

That January day in 2013 set me on a journey to explore everything to do with trusting my intuition and what I could do to achieve personal healing. Her message, "Open your heart before you die," sounded ominous.

Lena had said I could ask them anything. At this point in my spiritual development, I had no idea what to ask a spirit guide. It felt like I would be imposing.

I asked a friend if she had any questions for my spirit guide. She wanted to know about someone who had passed. The next time I went into a hypnotic state, I went back to that same death scene (seemed like the way to do this) and asked the questions. Lena had incredibly beautiful in-depth answer. I was in awe. My friend cried hearing the healing information.

Lena asked me to include this message from her, "You can be blind and still receive knowledge. You can be sighted and ignore it all."

~ BREAKING PATTERNS ~

A month later, I found an energy block in my Throat chakra that equaled to, "I have no say," during a soul retrieval class. That night, as I healed through soul retrieval; my voice actually changed how it sounded. That was a life-changing Throat chakra healing for me. It was the day I reclaimed my voice; lost because of the trauma of the rape.

Days later I was able to tell my partner of 20 years our failing relationship needed serious work, or it was over. I told him I would give him a year.

At this point in my life, I worked part time and stayed home with my two children. A few weeks after this ultimatum, I knew I needed a real job. Feeling as though I had no way out, through tears in my eyes, I asked my spirit guides, "Please help me find a monetary way out of my relationship."

The very next day, I received a call from my current boss. He asked me if I would like to get back into marketing at a place I used to work. I almost fell off my chair. I had worked there well over a decade ago.

Since my husband was uninterested in counseling or working on the marriage, I left a year later.

I continued my intuitive training and attending other metaphysical classes. I received my certification in hypnotherapy. I read more and studied anything on metaphysics. I practiced my psychic reading skills, taught past life experiential classes to groups, and continued helping more people remember past lives to heal.

In late 2014, I published my book, *Life Is Just Another Class—One Soul's Journey Through Past Life Regression*.

I took a hard look at each of the nearly fifty past lifetimes I had remembered thus far and noticed that I barely had any mutually supportive and loving relationships in them. Something had to change, and I knew it would have to be me that did the changing and healing.

Clearly, I had a long-standing pattern of loveless relationships—through many lifetimes. Remembering those other lifetimes helped me to come to realize that I needed more profound healing for me to have the deep, mutually supportive, and loving relationship that I deserved.

I knew there were connections to issues in a current life to past lives, but now I began seeing patterns through many lives and the root cause to help a person heal. These patterns and the root causes were not always obvious, but always brought healing.

~ GROWING INTO HELPING OTHERS ~

I barely remember 2016 and most of 2017. In 2016, I sustained a head injury during a car accident. This caused me to have severe post-concussion syndrome plus a second near-death experience. According to my spirit guides, I had gotten off my life path and I added this wreck to my timeline to get me back on course. While I could not easily drive or do much of anything, I was able to talk to spirit guides and angels even better than before.

I soon realized this wreck granted me a gift during this near-death experience. I spoke in depth to Archangel Jophiel. As I left my unconscious body and looked up (in spirit), I saw her hand reaching towards me through The Light.

She said, "Come with me."

I took her hand and she showed me many things including some of my future. She is so loving.

Since I started my journey to speak to spirit guides and angels, my faith and trust in my intuition grew. I now see a person's whole soul experience. This includes from the time one seemingly separates from Source (we are never apart) through all past lives, this lifetime, and more. I see their whole team including all spirit guides, angels, and past over loved ones throughout all lifetimes.

Spirit guides show me the root cause of relationship patterns for others. They show me stagnant energy left behind by trauma along with information about the trauma and what to do to help them heal. They show me connections of everything to help the person to heal on several levels—physical, emotional, energetic, and spiritual. I am honored to help a person heal by releasing a relationship pattern that has plagued them in their current life and past lives.

~ MAKING TRUE LOVE ~

I love connecting with someone's spirit guide and angel team. We have an entire team helping us in this life including passed over loved ones. When I start one of my readings, I hear a number for how many spirit guides and a number for how many angels are standing there with a person that day. Then I tune into a few of them to see and talk to them on behalf of the person who would like a reading. It is truly an honor to be able to introduce their spirit guides and angels to them. Passed over loved ones visit too (they are truly next to you the moment you think of them).

The main reason I love helping people in this way—literally by connecting with someone's spirit guide and angel team—is so others can deeply feel the love that their team has for them. The warmth, the goosebumps, the raise in positive energy, the glow they have when our session is complete ... It is awe inspiring.

Helping so many involved in an abusive relationship inspired me to produce this book. I have had so many women and men come to me for readings who have been abused in some way. My heart goes out to them. My hope is to reach more people who could be helped by going deep within their past lives to heal. I encourage everyone to read through "Chapter 18, Warning! Danger!" and to, in turn, help others in abusive situations to learn about the signs of abuse. Awareness is the first step to healing.

As I typed and collected examples for this book, it dawned on me that while the goal is finding a true love partner, in reality, it is about truly loving yourself. Taking the time to heal yourself IS loving yourself.

When you truly love yourself, then someone who truly loves you will find you.

Chapter 2

Feeling Loved—Healing Through Past Lives

What does it feel like to experience deep love from someone and what does it feel like when you experience love for someone else? You might think that you have felt love for someone or from someone, but maybe you found out it was not real love.

Real love is hard to describe. It is like trying to explain the color green to a blind person or music to a deaf person. How do you know if you have felt deep love?

It includes a calm knowing that you can be your true self. They accept you for who you are, and you accept them the same way. You both look forward to seeing each other every day. The sex is fantastic because you feel at ease, accepted, and wanted by them and vice versa. You both support each other in nearly everything each of you do. You never think about being with another person. So, maybe you are not sure what that feels like to have someone look into your eyes and feel exactly how much they care about you. They want to be with you. They want to share your day with you. To some reading this book, all this might feel like a fantasy.

I personally do not know that I have ever truly, deeply experienced romantic love in this lifetime—yet. The day I remembered a few very loving past life moments including amazing, loving sex, I knew I was definitely missing out on something wonderful. That sparked my search to understand what blocked me, why did I have these relationship patterns, and what steps do I need to take to heal?

I definitely screamed, "What the FUCK?!?" I am pretty, educated, successful, and healthy—why has dating been so seemingly hard?! (The divorce process, car wreck trauma, and COVID did not help.)

It has been a long journey. Finding your true self usually is. The journey to selflove is completely worth it. Here I am writing this to hopefully help you, too.

"All for your healing. This time has a purpose," my spirit guide, Lena, said to me on one of my darkest days.

I am open to heal. I participated in a lot of healing, soul searching, and more, during the last several years. and Sure, I have gone on dates, but not many lasted past the first date. Most men were swiped left on the dating app and avoided all together. I even dated a few for a short while. A few of them were nice.

I am determined to never settle for mediocre love again. This book became part of my healing, but ultimately, I hope you find the courage to love yourself and ultimately find love through your own healing within these pages, too.

A few failed relationships and, as of the publishing of this book (now nearly eight years after I left my ex), I am still single, and it is ok. My spirit guides remind me that, "I signed up for this. I signed up to go through these experiences. I signed up to write these books, provide readings, and help others heal through past life regression and more."

I also know that I will not remain single for long.

My spirit guides told me repeatedly, "You will meet the person of your dreams after you publish your relationship book." I have been working on this book for over seven years. One would think I would have rushed to finish this book years ago. Clearly, it was not my time for true love. Time will tell. "Divine timing," they say.

For my own personal healing, I did what I do best, I turned to past life regression. I have experienced some serious healing through recognizing relationship patterns during a past life regression and using that knowledge to heal my current life. Plus, I have witnessed numerous healings for others while providing readings and past life regression sessions.

For example, I used to have asthma and take several medications each day. Five years after remembering my very first past lifetime as Od, I laid in a hospital bed with death knocking at my door. I could barely breath to utter a complete sentence. During that hospital stay, I realized that my now ex made me feel unwanted. The afternoon of the third day in the hospital, I woke up from a lucid dream in which I saw that how I died as Od (pneumonia—I could barely breath) was also connected to not feeling wanted in my current lifetime. The day I made this Heart chakra trauma connection of feeling unwanted in a past life to this current life, I started a complete recovery. A few days later, I left the hospital. A few months later, I eliminated all the asthma medications I had taken for well over a decade. I have not taken them in the ten years since that experience. (Od's complete story is found in my book, *Life Is Just Another Class—One Soul's Journey Through Past Life Regression*.)

One day, I became inspired to experience a truly romantic and loving past lifetime. This inspiration came to me during a reading I gave to a young woman. Her spirit guides showed me several seriously abusive patterns from her past lives as well as how she continued this abusive pattern in this lifetime. After relaying the third abusive past lifetime to her, her guides said, "You need to show her that not all of her past lives were terrible. Let us show you a few of her happy, loving lifetimes now. Tell her about them in depth. Give her hope. This will help her heal more than you realize."

The spirit guides explained that when you find a point in a lifetime before a relationship issue occurred, you can bring that healed, loving feeling forward into your current lifetime. This helps heal the energy of the unhealthy relationship pattern when you replace it with the feeling of knowing there are loving people, and it is healthy to receive authentic love. It is like overwriting a bad line of code (or energetically imprinted rule) in your programming. Also, if you are like me and have no frame of reference in having a deeply loving relationship experience, now you can add the new line of code enhanced with the feeling of true love.

After I finished the reading for this young woman, I worked to find my own happy, loving lifetimes so I could experience deep, romantic love.

Prior to this, I completely believed, as I was taught, that deep healing comes from catharsis in remembering the trauma in a past life. In a majority of my past lifetimes that I remembered (well over 150 at this point); the first memory shown to me is normally the most traumatic scene. I do know that was my personal intent I set in place a long time ago when I first started learning about past life regression healing. Proof for me that setting an intent works.

Now, I have taken many people to a memory of a loving, wonderful past life to offset or counteract a traumatic past life.

Knowing that you have had true love before and actually remembering every aspect of feeling that deep love is incredibly healing. As the spirit guides have said, it provides you with the hope, plus the experience to know what it actually feels like to love and be loved.

Please be aware of a few things about remembering or being told you had a past life with someone. Just because you had one or several past lives with someone you are involved with does NOT necessarily mean they are a good match in this lifetime. You might feel comfortable with them because of the subconscious past life familiarity. It could have been abusive, but you feel like you know them because of some subconscious reason. Unfortunately, the relationship repeats the past life abuse pattern, until you heal it. Some people get all excited if their abusive partner shows up in another lifetime. Most of the time, they were abusive in a past life too. It does not mean they showed up again for a healthy, loving relationship in this lifetime.

Beware, it is entirely possible that you are completing a learning lesson or karma from that past life too. I am sure you can name quite a few people you have dated that were learning lessons in this lifetime. Really understanding what is healthy and what is not healthy in a relationship is extremely important.

Set the intent (like—state it right now) that, in this lifetime, your next serious relationship is all about the lesson of deep love, support, and trust. Say: All my relationships support me in my lesson of learning deep love, support, and trust.

In "Chapter 5, Closed Heart," I recounted my past life as Alexandria with Victor. That is an amazing example of what true love feels like. That past life was one of the first deeply loving lifetimes I remembered.

Here are a few of my past lifetimes that provided me with examples of true love. These past lives gave me a deeper understanding on how to recognize what love should feel like in my current lifetime. These memories also gave me hope that true love is real and confirmation that I am worthy of deep love.

~ CURRENT LIFE EXAMPLE: KAREN ~

I love Paris, the Eiffel Tower, the French language, the Fleur de Lis—the list goes on for days.

In chatting with one of my intuitive friends, he said, "Don't you think it is weird to love a city and its culture like you do? I would bet there is a loving past life connection there." I responded, "So, take me there. Help me remember it then."

My love of Paris is connected to this romantic Parisian lifetime with Olivier.

~ ROOT CAUSE EXPLORATION ~

"I sit at a table in an outdoor café, laughing, drinking tea, and eating with two of my female friends. There should have been a third friend, but she could not make it.

We take time to discuss all the details of the world around us through the use of all of our senses. We hear the rhythmic splash at the water's edge in the nearby Seine River and the birds chirping overhead. We admire the large grey cobblestone in the adjoining street—the rectangle-shaped stones have a smooth, curved top. The smell of fresh baked bread wafts in the breeze. We marvel at how the metal table reflects the sunshine into a spray of rainbows. It helps us all relax when we immerse in our surroundings.

Even though I do not have a ton of money and am in a lower social status, my friends do not adhere to normal social status discrimination. The four of us have been close friends since childhood. I am thankful they accept me for who I am and not for my income.

I wear an older style dress with a loose corset underneath that is terribly uncomfortable, since I need to get the stays fixed. I never seem to make the time to deal with fixing them, which reminds me of the perpetual illusion of lack of time I seem to have in my current life. I wiggle my toes inside my old, but comfortable brown leather shoes. I sigh inwardly as I look at their stylish clothes.

Even so, I feel happy. We are having fun, laughing, and talking. We chat endlessly about boys, which is funny since the intent of this past life regression is to find an example of true love with a man. What a fun coincidence. Remembering fun with close friends in this past life demonstrates love and support, even within friendships.

I move forward in time in that life.

Still single at 32 years old, I keep myself busy working.

My aunt gifted me her townhouse plus enough money to get settled in this new home. The place needed completely redone. I already cleared away the cobwebs and cleaned. My aunt left her home sit empty during the last year of her life due to her illness. She passed away last month.

I decide to freshen the entire place with new wallpaper. Remodeling interiors and helping with interior design is my career so I look forward to decorating my new home. I always worked since my parents passed away long ago. I did not have a lot growing up.

A deliveryman arrives with all the new wallpaper in his carriage. He refuses to help me when he realizes we must take several trips up a tall flight of stairs. His bad leg kept him from walking that much, he said.

I smile in excitement about the wallpaper delivery, then I look at the large stack and sigh. I can only carry a few of the big, thick, long rolls of wallpaper at once—they are cumbersome and heavy.

After my third trip back down the steps for a few more, the deliveryman becomes openly impatient with me since he has other deliveries to do. We could not lay them on the muddy sidewalk.

A cute upper-class man, wearing a dark green shirt, hears the deliveryman's insults and stops.

He said to me, "I can help you."

I look up from my new bundle of wallpaper, smile and say, "Thank you ever so much."

Sweat drips from my brow. I am sure I looked like hell in my work dress, but he did not mind. I am clearly winded from carrying several loads of wallpaper up the steps. The dress and all the underlayers did not help in this task. Plus, the warm sun finally beat down on us today. He knew I needed help.

He smiled, confirming his commitment to help, looked at the stack and said, "I can help for a little while." He introduces himself as Olivier. I tell him my name is Emée. I take great delight in meeting a well-mannered gentleman.

Olivier's eyes widened in disbelief when he first looked up at the tall, steep set of narrow stairs. The 30 stairsteps seemed to grow in each consecutive trip. He now knew why the deliveryman saw it as such a chore to lug the wallpaper inside.

He helps me carry it all upstairs even though the stack seemed endless.

By the second load, he took off his long brown coat with rounded brass buttons. The buttons look funny to me—like little golden mushroom caps. The coat was unnecessary on a warm day like today.

By the time we finished, his dark brown hair is a mess. I notice how adorable he is.

We both sat down on the bare floor exhausted afterwards, laughing about the impatient deliveryman. I found us a glass of water. I talk excitedly to him about my home improvement project. He listens and flirts with me. He makes me giggle and laugh. We have fun talking and flirting. Hours pass. I took my shoes off, so he rubs my feet. I am impressed with how nice he treats me. We really connected and felt completely at ease with each other so quickly.

Neither of us paid attention to the time. As it became dark, I lit a candle. This prompted him to look outside. He laughed at how much time had passed. He missed his business meeting. He said it was more fun to stay and talk with me today. He told me how fortunate he felt to meet me. My parents would have loved Olivier and his genuinely nice personality.

I move forward six years later in that lifetime.

Olivier and I are happily married and we now live in a new home that looks like a brownstone.

I watch our 4-year-old daughter play with our little grey, short-haired dog while I breastfeed our new baby girl. The girls are so precious. I smile, watching them play. The baby wears a sweet, exceedingly long dress that doubles as a blanket for her naps.

Olivier works a lot, but the children keep me busy while he is gone for the day. I look forward to him coming home in the evenings. I have not worked since we married five years ago, but I still offer interior design advice to my friends.

Our dog often is constantly underfoot, as it follows me all around the house. It makes it hard to walk holding the baby. That is my only stressor. Olivier pays for a maid and a cook to help us around the house.

I do not get the opportunity to meet with my girlfriends as often, but we visit when we can. I feel more aligned with their social status now since my clothes and shoes appear much more stylish.

When Olivier arrives home, we both look forward to talking about our day and to relax with the children together. We reminisce about one memory of us dancing together with other couples before the children—it makes us smile. I feel special when we look into each other's eyes.

Our relationship remains stable, loving, and committed until he passes much later in life."

~ HEALING STEPS ~

As this past life memory started to fade, I brought forward the feeling of being deeply loved by Olivier into my current lifetime.

I was relieved to remember this past life—which is an amazing, supportive experience the whole time—as one with no serious trauma. For once, I experienced no suffering, no pain, or trauma in one of my past lifetimes.

My past life personality as Emée was intuitive and confident; she had no qualms about much of anything. I see her chakras extending below the Root and well above the Crown. It is funny—I hear, "Thank you for the present of time," like remembering this was a present, a gift.

Remembering this lifetime raised my self-image with all relationships too.

Finding a lifetime before any relationship trauma occurred was healing in and of itself. I brought that deep, loving feeling forward into my energy in this lifetime to help replace the energy of any unhealthy, unwanted, unworthy-feeling relationship patterns. It felt amazing.

~ CURRENT LIFE EXAMPLE: KAREN ~

Through past life work, I remembered a lifetime where I was a young girl abused by my mother. Even her father did not speak up about the abuse, or he would have been verbally accosted. She experienced a life of strict control in a large, upper class household. Children were to obey, be seen, and not heard, and only do as they were told. She was forbidden to talk to boys or even consider them as a future mate. Sex was not discussed.

As a young teenager, this girl met a young boy from a much lower class. She would sneak out late at night, on full moons, to travel for hours on horseback to see the boy. They fell in love and wanted to marry. The girl knew that would not be permitted by her mother or society.

The mother found out about their relationship the moment she realized her daughter was pregnant.

Enraged, the mother beat the daughter with a silver candlestick even after the burning hot wax disfigured her face. She did this, all in the name of punishment. Eventually, an older brother helped her escape and even though permanently disfigured, she was able to be loved and accepted by the poor boy's family. She never saw her rich family again.

Even though this lifetime started with abuse, it soon became acutely obvious that this lifetime proved that you can be loved, cherished, and supported unconditionally. In this past lifetime, I am shown much love and devotion by two men, a brother and a lover.

~ ROOT CAUSE EXPLORATION ~

"I race against time. The lowering of the sun tells me it is the downside of the day. The spring sun will set in a few hours. I push my horse, Cary, to run faster. I pat his grey speckled backside in assurance.

I ride alone through the woods on a well-traveled horse trail through England's countryside. I hurry so I can watch the sunset with Mitchell. I have limited time to escape away to meet with him.

I wrap the skirt of my dress around my legs to prevent it from flapping in the wind. My white bloomers peek out at my ankles. I dress in three layers to abide by the clothing rules of the day—a petticoat, grey dress, and an overcoat. I dread the chore of getting dressed. I do not own the proper male-styled clothing for horseback riding. However, I refuse to ride sidesaddle.

For safety, I make sure I buckle every latch on my black boots with my buttonhook tool before I leave. This feat took an inordinate amount of patience to buckle up to my knees.

I take a short break with my horse near a berry bush. We both stop to eat. I eat triangular-shaped thick and flaky bread.

I think about my life.

My father, a baron or duke, often travels to take care of "affairs of the state." My mother accompanies him if there is a ball to attend. I love when they take these long trips together. It gives me the opportunity to sneak away from it all and feel free.

My parents left the five of us behind at the large estate. A nursemaid, governess, and others all tend to our needs. A tutor taught us daily lessons including language and etiquette. I fully realize the deep importance of being taught a variety of knowledge and skills, especially as a female.

I live without responsibilities at the estate but feel trapped.

Mother rarely attended to us. Occasionally she ordered me and my two sisters to crochet with her. Even though I am the eldest daughter and in my early twenties, she still treated me as a child and expected me to be subservient.

Thankfully, Mother let the five of us learn horsemanship together. My sisters and I learn how to ride like a lady along with some other basics, while my brothers learn so much more. It felt unfair. My older brother and best friend, Joseph, taught me much more in secret. He taught me how to use a knife and other essential knowledge of skills, too. I now comfortably carry a knife in my stockings while riding.

My brothers learn many more skills than the rest of us. I enjoy watching my two brothers receive instruction in swordsmanship. My younger, 6-year-old brother allows me to practice with his sword in secret. He laughs at my novice form but helps me learn too.

I hate the subservient role I must play.

Mother despises us all, but she remained loyal and doting to my father. She likes him a lot, but only pretended to care about us when he is nearby. Our caretakers corroborate by pretending everything is wonderful for Mother when Father is around too, otherwise Mother permanently dismisses them. My two sisters remain mousy, silent, and show their subservience by keeping their heads down. While we were spoiled with things, we were deprived of affection.

I felt unwanted as a female. Normally, my two sisters and I were kept under lock and key. I never understood why. Often Mother locked my sisters and I in our rooms when Father travels. One time, she definitely forgot about us. We stayed locked in our rooms for three days during the heat of summer until I pounded on my door for help. We live in a large stronghold, but it seems more like jail to me.

I overheard one maid say that my mother and her sister acted too good for their britches.

When I can, I ride off on my horse to feel the freedom and love in the world around me. My mother stifles me beyond frustration causing so much sadness and anger within me. When I get away from it all, I smile endlessly and feel blissful.

During one of my adventures riding across the countryside, I meet Mitchell. Mitchell happens to be nearby when I need help with my horse's shoe. His muscular build is in stark contrast to the thin or flabby men who live and work at the manor. He is handsome with his long sandy brown hair and mesmerizing hazel eyes. He treated me with respect and loving kindness from the moment we meet. We make plans to meet at night under the light of the full moon. My interest in astronomy grew.

I always lock my bedroom door before I leave, so they think I am asleep in there. I always head back before the sun rises so I am not found missing.

One disastrous night, while spending time with Mitchell, my parents came back home a day early. They unnaturally check on the five of us, only to find me missing. It became a big 'to do.' They form a search party thinking the worst. They accuse others of kidnapping me. Mother yells at nearby subordinates living just outside our compound. She had one uncooperative underling's farm burned down. People residing in the area hate her as much as I do.

I had told Joseph about Mitchell months ago. He felt heartened by my happiness. My patient and kind brother knows where I go to see Mitchell. He had helped me make the necessary preparations to ride my horse that night. He adores me. The night I went 'missing' Joseph traveled to the lake, found me, and warned me of the search party. We had Mitchell leave quickly so as not to be found or harmed. Joseph and I agree I should say I became lost while out practicing riding. Without judgement, Joseph helps me get redressed in the multiple layers of clothes. I need to be presentable before heading back home. Even though Joseph found me only in my chemise, he still liked Mitchell.

On another evening, I travel about an hour to meet him down by the lake I love. As I arrive, I watch Mitchell swimming in the lake to cool off from the heat of the day. He smiles as he sees me and walks out of the water. He builds a fire and shares some of his dad's homemade wine from a jug with me. We eat the baked treats, fruits, and cheese I brought. People of his status do not normally get these types of food. Using my overcoat as a blanket, we lay together all night talking, napping, kissing, and listening to the insects make music. My long brown hair, usually perfectly done up, becomes a disarray by morning.

I thoroughly enjoy these rare occasions we meet. I appreciate his honest, loving, caring nature. He exudes a genuine concern for the well-being of those around him and of all other living things.

One special night, Mitchell whispered, "Regina, I love you." We talk seriously about spending our lives together.

Mitchell described to me how animals make love. He shows me gentle passion. Status disappears completely when naked.

Several months later, my mother suspects pregnancy because the nursemaid told her I have not had 'the bloods.' She yells at me and the nursemaid.

I suffer humiliation during the doctor's examination. Yet, he remains kind to me. I smile when I learn I am pregnant. He talks to me about what is happening and what to expect for my pregnancy.

I heard Mother say to the doctor, "I told you not to help her." My mother is a nasty bitch.

Mother immediately thinks I am pregnant to the fat boy who lives down the hall. His father is severely lambasted. I never answer who could be the baby's father, but I know Mitchell is of an unacceptable status. My mother was so quick to accuse the fat boy, I did not have time to correct her.

By spring, my growing stomach became hard to hide. The accused boy has no idea how to impregnate a girl. They prep him to be my husband anyhow. I have zero respect or affection for him. The boy pathetically tries to get acquainted with me. I cannot go through with the wedding. It would be a farce.

I spend all my time in my room and have been unable to see Mitchell for months.

I decide to abandon my current lifestyle to be with Mitchell. He would be considered a servant by my mother and probably killed for having had sex with me.

During the regression, I hear the words, "An investment in standing up for myself."

That night, I tell my mother I cannot marry the fat boy. My furious mother, worried more about her reputation than my emotional wellbeing, grabs a nearby silver candlestick and repeatedly hits my face, breaking my jaw and hurting my eye. My brothers pull Mother off me, but it is too late. The hot wax splashed and severely burned my face. My mother yelled, "Good. Now no one will want you," and left my room. The nursemaid bandaged my wounds. She and Joseph take turns watching over me in case Mother returns.

I worry Mitchell would stop loving me. My right eye is damaged from the trauma. My vision is cloudy now, but I can still see. The doctor considers sewing my eye shut. They confine me to bed to both heal my face and to hide my growing stomach. I look around my elegant bedroom—it validates how wealthy we are, but emotionally poor. I am tired of being in bed. I have them remove all the mirrors from my room. My eye shriveled up. With my face permanently scarred, I am sure I look like a monstrosity.

I tell Joseph to find Mitchell LaBaron and speak with him about my situation and intentions. I worry endlessly about what Mitchell will do or think. He has no idea what happened to me since we last met. He probably wonders why I have not shown up at our standing full moon dates, especially since we spoke of marriage on our last meeting. I worry.

Mitchell professes unconditional love for me to Joseph. They both travel back to the estate. He sneaks Mitchell in as a kitchen servant. Then, Joseph insists he needs his help to serve me dinner.

I cry tears of joy when I see him enter my room. Mitchell gives me flowers and immediately puts me at ease. I overcome my embarrassment as soon as he kneels beside me, takes my hand, and asks me to marry him.

My younger brother stands guard for me at my door, so I give him my sweets from dinner. I trust my brothers with my life.

We plan my departure from this hell and set a date for me to leave. The eve of the next full moon, which is in a few days, aligns perfectly with when I see the doctor next. The doctor was scheduled to check on my pregnancy and burns. After that, I cannot stay any longer. I no longer care about status anymore.

My younger brother knocks two times to warn us that someone is coming. Mitchell quickly hides under my bed as I pretend to sleep. I smile in relief that it is Father, he is loving but rarely home enough to know what truly occurs. Father holds my hand and draws back my hair to look at me. I tell him I love him and to let me get some healing sleep. I memorize his face, knowing this will be the last time I see my father. He kisses my forehead and responds, "You are still as beautiful as the day you were born," and leaves. Mother told him my facial disfigurement was caused by accidently falling out of bed.

Hours later, Mother commands my brother to go to bed. Without warning, Mother enters my room to find Mitchell kneeling at my bedside. Mitchell stands and confidently professes his love to me. "There is no wrong in love," I added when I saw her grimace and grab her wooden switch. She snaps the air with it and says, "I do not care about love," and whips us both. Mitchell protects me until Joseph arrives moments later. He tells Mother he will get the guards to remove Mitchell from the estate. This calms our mother, so she leaves my room. My mother keeps Father in the dark about everything.

After Joseph saw what Mother did to me and Mitchell, he knew my time here grew short. He helps me leave. Joseph prepared a few of my things, my horse, and several provisions for me and the forthcoming baby. He had already helped Mitchell after our beating. Joseph saved Mitchell's life by telling the guards he would take care of him personally. Joseph had already secretly dropped off several things with Mitchell by the time I left. He packed many of my things and helped me find Mitchell's house. I had never been there before. Joseph packed a lot of gold and silver coins in a satchel to help us have a better life. I agree to meet my brother at the lake in three moons, he said he would bring more provisions and coins.

Mitchell genuinely loves me and worries more about me, than what my mother did to him.

His parents accept me into their family without question. His mom sang as she worked around the house and land. She showed great kindness to me. She demonstrated more love to me in a few days than my own mother did in my whole life. I give my fancy skirts to Mitchell's mom after she admires them. I felt relieved to get rid of a reminder of my broken heritage.

We marry that week. A few months later I give birth to our little girl. His mother helps deliver the baby.

I learn that love brings happiness, things do not.

I move ahead in time. Our little girl is five years old now. My brother Joseph still visits me, but not as often. He never told anyone where I live. He shares that our mother still pretends to mourn my loss—all for attention.

I give birth to two more children. Our daughter loves her little brothers just as I loved my brothers.

I grow old with Mitchell. My brother Joseph moves away from the estate—finally—and now lives closer so we can visit. Mitchell's parents help with the kids and live to an old age.

I never see any of my other family members again aside from Joseph. One meeting, I gave my brother a note from me to Father. Father framed it and placed it in his chamber. My mother hated that he did that, she considered me dead.

I live a long, happy life complete with grandchildren. My jaw and eye were never the same, but Mitchell never minded.

Our lives end in a housefire. In shock, I had a heart attack and died. Mitchell died a few hours later of smoke inhalation. We enter The Light together. It was our time to go from this lifetime. We had chosen, before entering this lifetime, in spirit, to die together. I reflect on our loving lifetime together.

Once in spirit, I learn that someone branded my mother's stomach as a child. The extensive mistreatment my mother endured contributed to her emotional issues and abuse. I never knew of her sad circumstances. This knowledge helped me forgive her.

My lesson in this lifetime is to choose love. Both Joseph and Mitchell showed me unconditional love."

~ HEALING STEPS ~

The healing angels focus on my eye, right side of my face, and jaw. They help clear unresolved emotions from my energy.

I work on forgiving my mother and her abuse. I forgive the silver, the candlestick, the burning, the wick, and wax that marred my face. I forgive my father for not seeing the truth and for not rescuing me from the abuse by my mother.

I felt unworthy of a loving relationship. In my current life, I thought love like this was impossible. I thought it was fake. Once I recognized this pattern of belief, it needed removed and replaced.

True love with mutual respect, support, and intimacy—is a positive, loving pattern. I take that pattern and feel and see it integrate it into my energy in this lifetime. I bring it forward completely to the present moment and send it fully into my body and integrate it with emotions and feelings. I ask the angels to help me continue to integrate it, continue to manifest it, and to keep it flowing into my future.

When I moved that new pattern of love into my future, I felt tingly all through my body. I could feel it flow into my current future and into future lifetimes.

Think of it as code written for computers. As you are moving this loving pattern into your energy, it feels like you are receiving a code upgrade overwriting your current computer programing. Delete the pattern that no longer serves you and replace it with the one you deserve.

When I see my past lives (or anyone's), I see them as individual beings. I see mine lined up in front of me. I see them as me from several other lifetimes. I see the loving pattern as DNA coding and bring it forward to this current lifetime. From my perspective, this loving pattern is an energy that came into my Heart chakra, because the heart is my main focus for this regression. I feel the loving pattern come into my heart to heal my current lifetime and then see it move forward into my timeline, into my future—whatever love that may bring.

To help me visualize this healing, I personified that pattern and connected every chakra from the positive, loving pattern into my chakras in my current lifetime.

~ AFFIRMATIONS ~

Hope, faith, and love brings the light within
I am open to receive
I love myself more every day
I genuinely love myself
I am capable of being loved and giving love
It is my life and I can bring what I desire to me
I have love in my life
My heart is open to love
All my relationships support me in my lesson of
     learning deep love, support, and trust

Chapter 3
How To Remember A Past Life

Past life regression can uncover deep-seated emotional trauma from a past life to help you heal, explain many things in addition to relationships, bring forward knowledge, understand loves, remove fears, improve health, and so much more to help you in your current lifetime.

The intent of this book is to help you use past life regression to recognize, understand root causes, heal, and to release any relationship patterns preventing you from experiencing a true love relationship.

A past life can be remembered via a variety of avenues. Each modality has something in common—a relaxed, focused-concentration state of mind. Meditation, self-hypnosis, dreams, and aided hypnosis are the usual ways to re-experience a past life. Work with whatever modality helps you feel comfortable remembering your own past lives.

For me, aided hypnosis offered the most in-depth avenue towards an encounter with my past. Often, aided hypnosis is referred to as a past life regression or regression therapy. Someone trained in past life regression will work with you to help you remember a past life.

To remember a past life, listen to your intuition; it will guide you through the entire process.

Most importantly, TRUST whatever comes through to you. The biggest hurdle to overcome when experiencing a past life is to trust the information you receive. You might receive information by feeling it, seeing it, hearing it, smelling it, or simply receiving a knowing about it. Do not judge or analyze it. Even if it feels like imagination, it is all coming from within you.

For those of you who think that hypnosis is a little scary, here is an analogy to help quell some negative connotations associated with the word hypnosis. Being in a hypnotic state is merely focused concentration. We all go in and out of a hypnotic state (i.e., the theta state - a meditative, drowsy, or focused concentration state) throughout the day.

When you work with a past life regressionist to remember a past life, it will feel like you are having an interesting talk about a memory to a friend, but the only difference is that your eyes are closed. Many people think they should feel completely different when remembering a past life, but that rarely occurs. You are always in control.

Again, the most important thing to remember is to trust what first comes to mind. It is essential to become focused on whatever first information is received; however you receive it, from a past lifetime. Once you begin to describe more about this initial memory, this is called grounding into a past life.

Allow yourself to be open to whatever happens. I recommend setting an intent for your past life session, but how you reach that goal might be different than expected.

As you enter a past lifetime, the first type of thing that you experience can be different each time. I have seen colors, heard music, felt pain, visualized the whole scene, and had only a knowing of what I experienced as I ventured into a past life.

Generally, when I enter a memory of a past life, I experience a highly emotional event first, like the death scene. This can be a little scary initially because it feels as though it is really happening—at that moment. However, the re-experience brings healing and a deeper understanding on whatever you can relate to your current life.

Of all the people I have helped remember a past life, normally only about 5-10 percent of them start with remembering their death scene. Most people avoid it altogether. You will only remember what you are ready to during each past life regression.

When you remember a difficult part in a past life, you can experience catharsis, which is just a fancy word for the process of releasing and thereby providing relief from repressed emotions or traumatic experiences. We can heal by simply remembering. The healing is so deep, we heal on the soul level.

The aura is part of the colorful, energetic aspect of our spiritual being. We store difficult past life experiences and deaths in certain parts of our aura.

Forgiveness is essential to healing. When we forgive someone, we release an unseen tether of attached emotion to that person. From this perspective, forgiveness heals everyone involved. Forgiveness is not saying that it is okay that something happened, but that you are releasing your attachment to it—whatever that may be.

At the end of each past life regression, I recommend mentally reviewing each harmful act brought upon you. Offer forgiveness to what or whoever harmed you or caused your death directly or indirectly. This allows for healing spiritually, emotionally, and physically each time you offer forgiveness.

Each injurious act may have contributed to an emotional or physical pain in your current lifetime. By acknowledging it, you can release it from your energetic being. Usually, a particular place in your body correlates with the pent-up pain from a past lifetime. Sometimes it can physically appear as a birthmark. Each time you release the bottled-up energy from a past life experience or death from wherever it was stored in your body, your health can potentially improve in that area.

Some of these bottled-up emotions have been stuck inside of you for thousands of years. They are long overdue for their release! For example, during one regression I released the pain and any associated emotions from my back being sliced by a sword in 610 B.C. I used a visualization process to release the stuck emotions. I visualized pouring the painful energy from where it was stored in my body into the dirt of the Earth outside. I asked the angels to fill this void in my energy with unconditional love (the highest form of positive loving energy) and visualized sealing the open wound shut.

To complete forgiveness work, I recommend sending love to anyone or anything you feel you affected negatively too. Then offer forgiveness to people, happenings, and things. Most importantly, forgive yourself so healing on a deeper level can occur.

Forgiveness is necessary to continue the soul's development and growth. Unseen weights on your shoulders detach each time you forgive. Then you feel lighter, less burdened. Forgiveness can set you free.

We drop our past physical or emotional obstructions so we can better focus on our current lifetime—to live in the now.

An intent to learn more about any aspect of a relationship, even the one you have with yourself, is vitally important. Ask your spirit guides to show you root causes, areas you need to heal, knowledge, career, vows, or contracts you no longer need, life path—really anything.

My spirit guide, Lena, said to me one day, "You can ask us anything." I believe that was meant for anyone, not just for me. Make a list of questions to ask.

During the regression, if you are a facilitator, make sure you ask some helpful questions to dig deeper into the past life connection to this lifetime. What and how someone talks about something will give clues. While someone is in the deepened meditative state during a past life regression, you can ask them to ask their spirit guides to show them the root cause of one of their relationship issues. Be open to what comes up, as it may surprise you.

Healing in this life not only positively affects your current life but also brings your healing forward into your future lifetimes.

Some relationships simply prepare you for the next one ... sometimes preparing you for relationships in your next lifetime.

INDUCTION SCRIPT

~ HEALING WITH THE ANGELS
AS CHANNELED BY KAREN KUBICKO ~

This past life regression induction script was channeled to me by the angels. Record this for yourself or have a good friend read it to you. The important thing to remember is to read this in a relaxed, slow pace while speaking monotonously. Say it with the intent of relaxation and to remember a past life. You can choose to play relaxing music if you desire.

Ask for your spirit guides and angels to guide and protect you throughout any healing process.

If someone is reading it to you, or you are reading it to someone, ask their permission to do so. This solidifies the intent to remember a past life.

Relax ...
Relax your head, the top of your head ...
Relax your cheeks, the back of your head, the sides, forehead ...
Relax your neck ...
Let that beautiful relaxation flow down to your shoulders ...
Release anything that you put there...
Like any burdens, heavy loads, responsibilities, or packages ...
Let them float off your shoulders, letting them feel light and loose ...
Relax ...
Let that relaxation flow down your arms, all the way to your fingertips ...
Relax your chest, all the way down to your abdomen ...
Relax your upper back all the way down to your lower back ...
Feel the relaxation flowing all the way down your sides ...
Allow that beautiful relaxation to flow down through your hips, down both legs and all the way to your toes ...
Relaxing your body completely ...
Now, I want you to begin to feel, see, or become aware of that beautiful chakra energy that flows within your body. This energy flows from the top of your head down to your base of your spine and follows the flow of energy between all of your chakras ...
Let's focus on this beautiful energy starting at the top of your head, at your Crown chakra ...
Notice how the energy flows with ease down to your Third Eye chakra located between your eyes and flows down to your Throat chakra and continues to flow to your Heart chakra moving down to your Solar Plexus located right at the base of your lungs, then continues to flow to your Sacral chakra and then your Root chakra located at the base of your spine ...

And become aware that this beautiful flow of energy moves back up through all of your chakras to the top of your head, then back down again to the base of your spine at your Root chakra ...
It continues to flow with ease ...
This beautiful energy flows within you ...
It is almost as if it is aligned with your breathing ...
Breath in and out. Relaxing even more ...
Allow yourself to breathe and begin to feel or see the flow of energy moving up to the top of your head and back down to the base of your spine ...
It flows down through all of your chakras. Begin to become aware that as it goes down to your Root chakra, it extends through the base of your spine, through the Root chakra, and extends beyond your Root chakra, flowing down through all the dimensions below and connecting your beautiful flow of energy down into the center of the Earth, where you will find the root of creativity and manifestation ...
That beautiful energy now connects on a conscious level, so you can bring that beautiful, creative energy back up to you, here in this Earth plane of existence where we live ...
And that energy flows back up, up through all of the energy within you, and continues to flow up through your Crown chakra at the top of your head, and then continues to flow up through all the dimensions above connecting you to Source ...
Which is pure unconditional love. It is so healing ...
That beautiful energy—you connect to that all the time—but now you are connecting on a conscious level ...
You can bring that beautiful healing energy back down through all the dimensions above, down into your physical being, here, in this Earth plane, where it can heal you in any way that you allow today ...
To help you fully feel that connection in a conscious way, let's connect again ...
Allow yourself to continue to focus upon your breathing, and as you breathe, your energy flows down through all of your chakras, down through all the dimensions below, connecting you to the center of the Earth, and again, allowing that creative energy to come back up, consciously, flowing up to you, allowing that energy to consciously become part of you ...
Then allowing your energy to continue to flow, up through your body, up through all the dimensions above, connecting to Source and bringing that beautiful unconditional loving energy, that's so healing, back down here, allowing it to expand throughout your entire being, helping you to heal in any way you allow today ...
So, I want to take this one step further and allow you to focus or to bring your attention to the center of your being, the seat of your soul, the light being part of you, the conscious part of you, this beautiful, radiant, pulsating ball of light ...
Which is located in the center of you ...
As you bring your focus and attention to this beautiful light being aspect of you, it expands and grows throughout all of your energy, and that in and of itself is healing ...
It is so beautiful ...
You can take this conscious part of you, the light being part of you, and allow it to ride that wave of beautiful chakra energy ...

MAKING TRUE LOVE

Allow that conscious, light being part of you to ride that wave of chakras energy up through the top of your head, through your Crown chakra, up, to a few dimensions above you, to a place of healing, a place of universal consciousness, a place of universal knowledge, a place where your angels and spirit guides can easily be with you …

Allow yourself to go there now, you are worthy of the healing …

Imagine yourself, feel yourself, floating up through the dimensions to this beautiful place …

This is where the healing angels and your spirit guides can meet you, they are there to provide you with any healing that you allow today …

Let yourself become aware that there are at least three healing angels standing around the sides of you now …

Allow them to provide you with healing unconditional love energy …

They have their hands stretched out overtop of you, pouring beautiful energy down throughout your entire spiritual being, raising your vital energy, helping you to release pent-up emotions, resentments, traumas, fears, patterns, and frustrations of any kind throughout all of your energy …

Helping you to heal …

Help the Angels in this task by gathering up all that needs released…

From anywhere in your physical body or in your energy, anywhere that you stored any pent-up frustrations, emotions, sadness, guilt, resentments, anger, anywhere you've stored those emotions, and any other ones that come to mind, visualize or feel them being gathered up, brought together, and then poured out of you like a stream of energy …

It may come out through your navel, or some other place in your body, allow it to pour, just let it pour out a window, out into the ground outside, so it can be transmuted back into positive …

All the while, these beautiful Angels are pouring healing unconditional love energy, it is so beautiful …

This beautiful, bright light love energy pours into those places that you've released today …

Release any traumas, harsh words, things that you've long forgotten, stored within you, allow them to be released now …

We thank the Angels for helping you today, by pouring the beautiful healing energy down through your entire energetic being. They will continue to provide you will the beautiful healing, unconditional love energy while we ask for further assistance …

Now we ask Archangel Michael to help you too …

He comes. Allow yourself to see or feel him standing directly in front of you. He is an expert in helping to release deep traumas, attachments of any kind, and connections that you might have made in this lifetime, or in any other lifetimes that are no longer serving you …

We ask Archangel Michael to release them, to sever any cords of connection …

Allow them to be cut away from you now …

We ask Archangel Michael to release and to remove any and all attachments of any kind, through all time, space, and dimensions, and to remove them from you …

It can be emotional attachments, traumas, vows, contracts, patterns, anything that is no longer serving you in this lifetime …

We now ask Archangel Raphael for his assistance. Raphael is an expert in healing. Raphael holds a special wand that looks like a filament of light energy. With your permission, Archangel Raphael can go down through all of your chakras with this healing filament and transmute even the most miniscule negative energy into love and light, to help you heal, and to release any traumas ...
They are ready to release now. Allow Raphael to go within and to remove and transmute any negative energies, any traumas, any pent-up frustrations and emotions, and resentments. Allow Archangel Raphael to turn those back into the beautiful loving light ...
We ask the healing angels to help you collect and return any pieces or parts of you that you set aside for future healing ...
Bring those pieces of your spiritual being back to you now ...
Allow these pieces of you to come in through the top of your head, through your Crown chakra, and to integrate them down through you, through all time, space, and dimensions and in all directions and to continue to integrate them, now and into the future ...
We thank all these Angels for their help today. They are saying that they will continue to help and provide healing to you for the weeks ahead and that they appreciate your participation, assistance, and openness to receive during this energy healing session ...
The healing angels say that they will continue to work with you, with the spiritual part of you, while the conscious part of you can step forward, walk forward for an experience. Be open to the experience ...
If you look down in front of you, you will begin to see, know,
or feel an illuminated path ...
Allow yourself to step forward now, onto this path ...
As you walk down the path, you will begin to notice interesting things on the sides of the path, you will be able to look ahead and see very far into the distance. You may see one or more of your spirit guides, an angel, a passed over loved one ...
Or simply enter into a memory ...
This beautiful path leads you to a past life, a beautiful experience, a future lifetime, your future in this lifetime ...
A place that will bring you healing of some kind ...
Your spirit guides are leading you on this journey ...
It is all for you, it is all coming from you, it is all for your healing ...
They have known you since you started this journey as a spiritual being, so allow them to help you, let them lead you down this path ...
As you walk along the path, allow yourself to notice the things along the sides ...
Notice, become aware of what type of clothes you are wearing, if you are wearing shoes or simply walking in your bare feet ...
Become aware of your path, what it looks like. It could be sand, rocks, dirt, bricks, grass, stone, or some other kind of material ...
Allow yourself to feel your feet stepping on your path, really feeling your feet touching the path with each step ...
This is your beautiful path ...
Follow your path to the knowledge that is being given to you ...

You might meet people that you have known in this lifetime, a spirit guide, or even walk into a past lifetime ...
Allow yourself to go there now ...
Allow yourself to trust the first thing that comes to your mind ...
In any way that you allow ...
Whether you see it, feel it, smell it, or simply know it ...
Allow this information to become clearer and clearer as you go deeper and deeper into this experience ...
Allow more information to come to you with ease ...
Every detail you remember is important to you in some way ...
Let yourself receive the knowledge of what will help you. Let yourself receive the knowledge of the root cause of the issue you would like to explore today ...
If you have entered a past life or future point in your life ...
Let a date come to mind, it will be the first number that you hear ...
Let the name of the place come to you. Trust the first name that you hear ...
Every detail is meaningful ...
You will remember and receive the knowledge ...
Allow yourself to move to important events ...
And to understand more about that experience ...

<<allow some silence here>>

Let yourself know how this memory is connected to your current lifetime and how you can heal from it ...
If there is any trauma, forgive anyone or anything that was involved ...
Remember you have these beautiful angels with you right now, they will help you when you ask ...
Allow yourself to receive a message from your spirit guide or angel ...
You can ask them any questions in your mind, and they will hear you ...
Be open to receive the answer ...

<<allow some silence here>>

When you have finished, allow your light being, conscious part of you to come back down, fully grounded, centered and whole within your body ...
Feel yourself becoming fully grounded into your body, all the way down to your toes ...
These beautiful angels will continue to provide more healing energy to you in the coming weeks ...
You will remember all that just transpired ...
Allow yourself to become awake, aware, and in full control of your body and mind, feeling confident, secure ...
You can open your eyes, wiggle your toes, as you come back into the present, the now ...

KAREN ANN KUBICKO

Chapter 4

Sex. Sex. And More Sex.

Sex. The fun part of a relationship. Most relationships often start by feeling sexually attracted to the other person.

We are sexual beings with an instinctive drive to procreate. Sex is nature's way we create the miracle of a baby. We all have an inner urge to procreate and to produce more humans to continue our species.

Many people are interested in healing their sexual issues and come to me for a reading or a past life regression to seek deeper understanding. Some examples of sexual problems include men who had performance issues, women who expected their man to pleasure them, couples who barely had sex, women afraid to date because of sexual trauma, and even an 85-year-old who wanted to know if she would ever be able to have sex with her neighbor again.

I have provided readings for far too many women and men who have been sexually traumatized in this lifetime. It is heartbreaking. I am grateful that I can work with their spirit guides and angels to help them heal from their experiences. In addition to providing the root cause in this life and other lifetimes, their spirit guides show me ways to help them heal. All of which are included in, "Chapter 16, Tools to Help You Heal."

Ask yourself a few questions to see where you stand on sex.

- Do I enjoy masturbation?
- Do I enjoy receiving pleasure and orgasms?
- Do I love my body?
- Do I genuinely enjoy sex?
- Do I see sex as fun and not a job?

If you answered, "No," to any of these questions—please keep reading.

There are two kinds of sex. Sex with yourself and sex with another person. Either way, sex is meant to be fun and satisfying. What do you do when sex stops being fun? I recommend asking for help to find the root cause.

A few ways that sexual issues show up in this life can include rape, molestation, loss of a baby, body shame, a narcissist partner, or being in an abusive relationship. Also, there are many signs that someone has endured sexual trauma. I provide a few examples of clues that sexual trauma from this life or a past life might be affecting someone. They include lack of interest in sex, gaining weight, losing weight, and hard to diagnose pain in the groin area.

Traumas that occurred in your current life might have been intensified by a similar past life.

~ SEX WITH YOURSELF ~

Our sexual awareness starts much younger than most realize. Ask any parent. Think about when you realized that touching yourself stirred up a delightful feeling. Masturbation can be a wonderful way to express deep selflove for yourself and your body. Keep it a special act of selflove to be honored and cherished only by you or with a partner. Self-pleasure is not dirty or wrong, but a sacred act of loving yourself. Enjoy masturbation.

Learning how to masturbate has a lot of benefits. Showing love to yourself teaches you to actually love yourself. When you masturbate, you learn what brings you to orgasm, then you can show your partner. Orgasm can naturally release dopamine, serotonin, endorphins, and the hormone oxytocin to produce a wealth of pleasure throughout your body. All this reduces stress, relaxes your body, plus many other health benefits. You can do a quick online search to find numerous studies on this.

Part of masturbation is loving your body. Loving your body is part of loving yourself. Feeling sexy in that new outfit, smiling at your naked body in the mirror, and being comfortable naked with another person all leads back to loving your body just the way it is. If going to the gym and eating healthy make you feel good about your body, then do that, but you do not have to be a model to love your body.

How you feel about your own body has a lot to do with how you feel about being naked in front of someone. Your body image can prevent you from having a partner, sex, or even an orgasm. Loving yourself is not selfish, it is selflove. Lack of selflove can prevent you from receiving attention, love, or even pleasure.

~ SEX WITH OTHERS ~

Sex is an innate part of being human. Sex should be healthy mutual fun.

Enjoy sex. If you have a fantastic relationship or are participating in enjoyable sex, you might not be reading this book. When you find someone who you deeply connect with, it is easy to enjoy sex with them. If you choose to avoid sex, (and nothing physical is impeding sex) then there is something off in the relationship—something needs healed on some level. Think about it, no one wants to get naked and have sex with someone they do not respect, trust, or love. Sex should be a comfortable, mutual, and especially loving experience. If you have sex and cannot wait until it is over, that is a red flag something is wrong.

Make sure sex is fun. Sex is not a job. Sex is not your duty. I have provided readings to several who have sex with their partner because they feel like it is their duty to them. In one reading, a women had sex with her husband just to placate him and not because she wanted to have sex. They are now divorced.

Sex is not about when the hormones are right so conception might happen. When sex becomes your job, the main ingredient of love is forgotten.

I have given a few readings to women who felt as though the only purpose of sex is to produce a baby. In each of these women's cases they forgot about their relationship with their partner, and therefore forgot how fun sex can be. In one woman's case, she came back to me months later to thank me. She said she had, "The best six months of sex in their entire relationship," since having a reading with me. She healed from the pattern of, "Sex is only for trying to have a baby."

Remember to cultivate the relationship with your partner.

~ WHEN SEX STOPS BEING FUN ~

A few ways that sexual issues show up in this life can include rape, molestation, loss of a baby, body shame, a narcissist partner, or being in an abusive relationship.

Rape or molestation to any degree can cause PTSD (post-traumatic stress disorder) in a variety of ways beyond sexual health and happiness. Through my work, I have met a lot of women and men who have experienced sexual trauma in this life. While every person is different, the two areas that seem to need the most energetic healing are the Throat chakra and Sacral chakra areas.

Losing a baby, trying to have a baby, a miscarriage, or a planned miscarriage brings sorrow, guilt, grief, sadness, anger, or frustration to all your sexual organs. Therefore, sending lots of love and forgiveness to your sexual organs becomes vitally important. Forgiveness of yourself, your partner, your baby, or potential baby will help you release those pent-up emotions. These pent-up emotions and feelings could block your creative, artistic abilities, including joy of sex with the intent to create a baby again. See, "Chapter 5, Closed Heart," for much more on loss of a baby.

I have met several women who were subconsciously punishing themselves or their body for losing a baby. A few of them never wanted to have sex again, therefore preventing a pregnancy and avoiding heartache. A few of them had physical issues because of all the anger they stored within their energy. If you have anger towards your uterus or any part of your body, please send love (instead of anger) to that part of you. Make sure to read the section on "Only Positive Loving Words" in, "Chapter 16, Tools to Help You Heal."

Feeling ashamed stifles pleasure. A religious upbringing can bring with it shame of sex, masturbation, etc. Or you might have had strict parents who made anything sexual, your sexual body parts, your thoughts, even masturbation labeled as bad. When you are a child, the words that are said to you become a rule, like computer programming. Mostly, we are unaware that this occurred and spend most of our adulthood re-writing this encoding. Forgive anyone who made you feel ashamed in any way about sex, your body, being aroused, orgasming, etc. Remember, your body is an amazing work of art, a masterpiece in engineering, a multi-tasking chemical factory, that can retain and process unlimited knowledge.

Being with a narcissist sucks. They basically suck the lifeforce out of you, literally. In a one-sided, narcissistic relationship, the user does not notice whether you, their partner, achieved orgasm. The lovemaking is only about their wants and desires, and they will make you feel guilty if you mention your own needs. Hedonistic pleasure—for them—dominates the relationship. When your partner is a narcissist, your pleasure becomes their lowest priority. You probably end sex feeling miserable, used, and unsatisfied. Volumes of books have been written about narcissists. If you think you are in a relationship with a narcissist, please get help. See more information on this in, "Chapter 13, Mothering a Narcissist."

Abusive relationships tend to be like a narcissistic relationship—the abuser does whatever they feel they need to do in order to remain in control and the victim slowly loses all sense of self. Please, please, please read through, "Chapter 18, Warning! Danger! Signs of Abusive Relationships." This chapter is filled with common abusive patterns, warning signs, and specific examples of abusive relationships. About fifty percent of the people I psychically read, have been in an abusive relationship at some point in their life and have had abusive past lives. Many of them had a history of sexual abuse as a child. As an adult, they associated sex with abuse. Their life lesson is always about overcoming the abuse, releasing the codependency, and regaining their self-confidence. Please see, "Chapter 6, Abuse Is Not Love."

~ SEX DOES NOT EQUAL LOVE ~

Sexual attraction is normally the first way we are attracted to someone. While sex might be what brought you together in the beginning, it cannot be sustained as the only part that holds a relationship together. One member of the relationship will start to feel like something is missing, or worse, feel used.

A relationship that is based on sex is like eating a pile of icing without the cake. That would make your stomach hurt, especially in the Sacral chakra area. Think of a beautifully decorated layer cake as an analogy to a relationship. The spongy, flavorful cake layers are the base of the relationship that gives it a solid form. Each aspect of a relationship that is nurtured allows the cake layers to experience exponential growth. The icing is the sweet treat that enhances the flavor of the cake and makes it oh so much more worth each and every bite. The icing is by no means necessary but adds so much beauty to any cake.

If you are looking for a deeply connected, mutually supported, and loving relationship, it cannot be based solely on sex.

Does sex equal love?

When sex equals love, that math never calculates accurately. There are some relationships that are based solely on the sex, for the sex, and when are we having sex again, sex. When you find yourself in a relationship that only sees you as a piece of meat, that is a huge red flag.

Yes, humans are innately sexual beings. However, there are some folks who believe that sex is the only way to feel love. They have forgotten how to feel emotions and rely upon the physical touch to feel love. Remember, you are an amazing human and not just a body to be simply used for sex. Let sex be the icing, the making love, or the extra special touch to a relationship.

Additionally, some individuals may look for any possible way to please their partner, go to great lengths (even purported 'shades of grey') to prove their love through sex. In reality, they are looking for a smidgeon of love from their partner. Please read, "Chapter 6, Abuse is Not Love."

~ CLUES TO SEXUAL TRAUMA ~

Sexual problems, on the other hand, are often rooted in deeper issues. There are so many aspects of sex-related issues in a relationship, it could be a book in and of itself—there probably are a few out there already.

Through all the psychic intuitive readings and past life regression work I have done; sexual issues all boil down to one thing—trauma—emotional or physical trauma that affects mainly the Root, Sexual or Sacral chakra area.

I psychically see an orange-red chakra (between the red Root chakra and the orange Sacral chakra), sometimes called the Sex chakra, illuminated on a person with unhealed sexual trauma. (For more on chakras, see "Chapter 15, Chakras—How I See Them.") Stuck sexual trauma energy in your energetic being can affect one or all chakras in some way. Sexual trauma in this lifetime compounds any similar past lifetime trauma too.

There are some clues that sexual trauma from this life or a past life might be affecting you. Apathy about sex, gaining weight, losing weight (not eating, anorexia), and undefinable pain in the sexual organ areas are a few of them.

Apathy about sex—even hugging, physical touch, kissing or any physically pleasurable thing can be a sign of something blocking you from receiving pleasure. Most of the time, sex tastes like delicious, creamy ice cream—once you get the true experience of it, you want more. Some people just do not want to be touched. When you avoid touching yourself or letting someone touch you, you miss out on receiving pleasure. Some may have an aversion to being touched in certain ways or on certain body parts. That indicates some type of trauma may have happened there.

Please note that children should never be forced to hug or kiss someone hello, goodbye, or otherwise. This tells the child that is it okay for an adult to force them to do something to their body even if they are uncomfortable with it.

Be open to receive. Being open to receive anything, including help getting to an orgasm is part of loving yourself. If you find yourself being the one who provides all the pleasure, foreplay, etc. during lovemaking, let that be a sign that it is time allow your partner to focus on providing you with pleasure too.

Gaining weight. Sexually abused or traumatized individuals can subconsciously gain weight. If they believe they are unattractive, in their mind, it might prevent further molestation. Essentially, (subconsciously) adding padding of protection. As you heal, the padding (i.e., the weight) will come off. Sometimes people eat for emotional reasons. If you eat for emotional reasons, take a moment to ask for a sign to help you find the root cause of why you connect eating food to feeling better. Whether you are hiding (not expressing) your emotions by placating them with food or subconsciously forming layers to hide behind so no one can harm you again, you can dig within to find the root cause and begin to heal.

Losing weight. If you lose weight to the point of anorexia, it can have disastrous effects on your physical body. Controlling what you eat or when you eat is normally the real reason for anorexia. It is all about the control. Therefore, normal control of some aspect of your life was removed. If you were abused, raped, or molested, you might have felt out of control and found that you could control of what you ate, giving your mind some peace. Sometimes, a subconscious belief that you will be safe if you make your body disappear, and if no one can see you, no one can harm you. Anorexia and other eating disorders are normally about being able to control something in your life. Please get professional help too. Getting help is a form of selflove.

Unexplainable pain during sex can be exasperating. Numerous times during readings I have psychically seen an ailment, a rash, or a pain directly related to an unresolved issue stored within a person. Painful intercourse, not explained in any other way (a sexually transmitted disease, physical issue, or anything else), pain or burning during or afterwards or even the inability to get wet if you are a female or to get hard or ejaculate as a male can be signs of an unresolved issue. There may be something holding you back from feeling pleasure.

Additionally, you may already know on some conscious or subconscious level that you do not want to be with your partner. I have provided readings to several people who had been experiencing pain or other issues during sex. One person also had a rash on their hands that would not go away. All of them remarked that their health issues went away right after leaving their abusive partner. Sometimes when you leave the person, physical issues can resolve.

If leaving a partner does not help your health, then finding the root cause could possibly resolve the pain or issue.

It can be completely unrelated to sex. Sometimes a pain can be rooted in the feeling that you deserve to be punished for having pleasure or fun.

I have provided readings for a few who were told, as a child, that they would never be good enough to have a partner. They each had an abusive childhood too. Each of them made the subconscious rule of, "I do not deserve to have closeness with someone."

Sexual trauma can arise at any time in this lifetime and can re-emerge from a past lifetime as well. For example, a past lifetime as a celibate monk, priest, or nun could cause subconscious inhibitions in the bedroom. Past lifetimes involved in sex slavery could bring up feelings of being used each time sex occurs. Inability to orgasm could be rooted in a past life with sexual organ mutilation or one that did not allow for pleasure.

~ CURRENT LIFE EXAMPLE: REBECCA ~

Past life trauma can affect your current sexual nature.

Rebecca recounted her two-year relationship with Zach. They have a great relationship except for in the bedroom. Zach shows her a lot of kindness and understanding. They had sex one or two times a month, but Rebecca never felt sexually satisfied. She felt certain her sexual response should be more exciting, based on what she had watched on videos and heard from her friends. She did not have any direct sexual trauma in this lifetime and wanted to see if we could find a past life that might explain it.

However, in this lifetime, her mother taught Rebecca that masturbation was dirty and against their religious beliefs. Rebecca was yelled at by her mother when she found Rebecca touching herself at the age of ten.

Deep down, Rebecca felt that she was not permitted to feel pleasure or any sexual excitement. Unbeknownst to her, some of the men she slept with over the years felt as though they failed as a partner when they could not bring her to orgasm. Rebecca felt she was missing out on fun in the bedroom.

In this lifetime, her subconscious restriction of sexual pleasure compounded her inability and fear of enjoying sex. Through past life regression, Rebecca experienced a few lifetimes directly related to this issue.

In the first one, she was abducted at the age of fourteen to be used as a sex slave back in 1450AD in Europe. They kept her in a locked room and used her like a whore. She was provided food if she performed sex without complaint. The man in charge beat her if she complained. He abused her during menstruation and expected her to stuff her vagina with rags to stop the flow, so she could continue to perform. He often had sex with her, he said, to keep her obedient. One day he became violently jealous after he heard her orgasm in pleasure with a paying customer. Afterwards, he abruptly removed her clitoris. She died of sepsis due to this genital mutilation. She died believing that she was evil for feeling sexual pleasure.

In the second one, she became her town's sacrificial virgin. She heard the message that this lifetime was the root cause of her sexual issue in her current lifetime.

~ ROOT CAUSE EXPLORATION ~

"Spring is upon us, so the townsfolks in many nearby communities know it is time for the yearly sacrifice of the virgin. This special ceremony helps maintain the fields for a good harvest and to protect the crops.

A small group of leaders are chosen from each of the nearby communities in Europe around 1000 A.D. to participate in this yearly ritual. They are sworn into secrecy to maintain the sacredness. While most saw this ritual enhancing the harvests, it also united their villages to promote peace amongst them all.

Each year, a different community was chosen for the sacrificial virgin. This year, my community was chosen. The leader in my community pointed out the young pre-pubescent virgins to the group. I am one of them. Most believed the young virgin merged into the air, water, and soil to promote fertile crops. Everyone knew the chosen one was never seen again after the ritual.

After a few days of discussions, after interviews with parents and potential sacrificial girls, a few of the men came to my house. I became this year's virgin sacrifice at the age of fourteen. My name is Iona, but they want me to remain nameless.

I am specially chosen because I had not menstruated yet. They gave my mother a small bag of coins and other items. In my house, they began the ritual. They cut a lock of my hair for my mother to keep. There were rumors that my hair, too, would dissipate. My mother knew I would never return but did not argue with the leaders. The last time a family refused, a drought occurred so all the townsfolk shamed them endlessly.

They directed me to cleanse my body in their basin of herbal infused water and I was given a white loose gown to wear. It had many ties down the front of it. As soon as my family said their tearful goodbyes to me, the men gave me a red liquid to drink from a stone cup as a final parting of ways. It tasted terrible. They gave me a second extremely sweet drink immediately afterwards. The ritual preparations took several hours. Night had fallen.

The nighttime sky is filled with stars. I look at the expanse of the sky as they carry me like royalty on a blanket-covered board in a procession over the hillside to a spacious open field. Six men dressed in white robes covered by long, dark cloaks carry me in the procession. Some locals watch somberly as I am transported past the last few houses in the town. The men chant quietly as we walk.

The drugs in the drinks make my body feel tingly all over. I feel like I am hallucinating. My senses are heightened. The farther and farther we walk away from town, the more drugged I feel. It seems like they knew how long the drug took to fully activate.

It feels like I cannot breathe or even talk right, but I do not feel nervous. I feel like a little child, giggly and wide-eyed because of the drugs. My body feels electrified, every touch tantalizing.

We walk up to the center of the large open field where they have prepared a huge stone pedestal for me. They have used this area for these rituals before. Two additional men prepared this space and met up with the processional as they walked towards the center of the circle. These two men seemed to oversee the ceremony.

One large stone has thick layers of dried crops lying on it. I am raised up onto this pedestal and placed in a reclined position, laying back on all the dried herbs and grains. It reminds me of a large reclining chair. The herbs feel soft and smell so good. By this time, my body is limp and motionless from the drugs, but I am still awake and aware of everything.

Large rocks form a circle here akin to Stonehenge. Several small fires burn around the large circle of tall stones. The smoke smells sweet while creating a cloak of privacy. It felt sacrilegious to me to be doing this ceremony here.

Two men stand next to me, stroke my curly brown hair, and softly say loving words about my body and me. The rest of the men begin their promenade around the large circle of stones, now chanting louder than before. An air of seriousness fills the area as the real ritual starts.

They sprinkle an herb-scented powdered substance and essential oils down my entire body. One man smears an oil on my forehead while saying more incantations.

Two men continued to stand on either side of me, saying loving words, and stroking my hair. I am only able to lie there. I receive nonstop sexual attention for what seems like hours. They continue to randomly provide me more of the red liquids. First the bitter, then the sweet one.

I watch the men who stand nearest to me, smile up at them, and listen to their caring, loving words. I trust them. I hear them talk about the need to complete the circle of tribes.

The entire event continued to be highly ceremonious throughout. I never felt dirty or degraded.

Part of me feels guilty for liking this experience. I am unclear whether I should like it or not. I could not speak to ask because of the drugs.

From my perspective in this current lifetime, it seems inappropriate, as if they are taking turns legally raping me.

They finish. A hush fell over the group. The chanting and walking stopped. There seemed to be some sort of discussion happening. I could not hear their conversation. Two men still stood next to me, watching the group prepare for what would happen next.

They again, gave me something strange to drink. This time it tastes different. I started to feel quite altered as well as tired. I wondered how this long night would end.

The chanting resumed. This time they all stood around me, raising their hands to the sky, and asking for blessings. One man stood behind me, put one hand on my chin, took *his curved knife and slit my throat from my chin to my chest. This did not allow me to die immediately. The blood poured from my body. They each now held several long stalks of a variety of grains. They dipped the seed end in my blood and smeared it all over my body, then they smeared it on the tall stones in the circle. It took a while for me to die.*

It was all very confusing since it felt good, yet wrong. Then while continuing to speak kind loving words to me, they kill me.

I watch over my body in spirit afterwards. They bury my body down over the side of the hill in a mound. I see other girls' spirits wandering around the field. Soon I see a few of my spirit guides and transition into The Light.

I learn after I die, that one of the men felt I should stay alive. The rest of the men believed it was best to kill each virgin girl in sacrifice. "Tradition," they said. None of them wanted to be responsible for a drought or worse, a famine."

~ HEALING STEPS ~

Rebecca realized that the entire ritual adversely affected her Heart chakra, Sacral chakra, and Throat chakra. Guilty pleasure, shame, mistrust, and the inability to have a say in the experience along with all the emotions from this ritual become buried in her energy.

She immediately realized that this lifetime was a root cause of her deep mistrust of men. Rebecca said, "They made me feel special and loved. They acted as if they really cared because of the loving things they said to me during the ritual. None of it was true."

After remembering both of these lifetimes, we worked immediately on forgiveness to herself, her mother in both past lives and in this lifetime. I had Rebecca forgive all the men involved in both past lives. I had her forgive the plants that created the drugs. Forgiveness is not saying what happened is ok, but to release her from continuing to have trauma from it.

I had Rebecca forgive herself for feeling pleasure, forgive her sexual organs that brought her pleasure, including forgiving the religious beliefs involved with rules made in this lifetime, plus her sexual trauma and death in both past lifetimes.

I asked the angels to help us by providing her with a deep energetic healing using unconditional love. I had Rebecca visualize the pent-up emotions (including guilt, guilty pleasure, anger, shock, etc.) and trauma stored in her energy be collected and poured out of her body, out the window, into the ground outside so it can transmute back to positive. Then to release any trauma-related energy and emotions from her chakras too.

We asked the angels to help find and return any and all scattered pieces of her soul and to help them reintegrate within her energy.

We asked the angels to replace her pattern of, "Sexual pleasure should be restricted," plus, "Enjoying sex brings fear of death," with, "It is safe and enjoyable to feel pleasure." We asked for help replacing the pattern of, "All loving words are lies," by first enhancing her intuitive abilities to recognize deception, then replacing that pattern with, "I am secure in the knowledge that I love myself and I am open to receive and believe true compliments."

Rebecca's spirit guides told her to start with loving herself through spending time alone in the bedroom, masturbating, and getting to really learn about her own body as a sexual being. She was tasked with learning to enjoy an orgasm.

Her spirit guides also wanted to make her aware that it is safe to receive attention. In that past life she received a lot of attention and liked it, but it was not healthy attention. They asked her to practice being open to receive compliments.

~ CURRENT LIFE EXAMPLE: MARCUS ~

Marcus talked about his relationship with Cara. He loved her but did not feel like a man because he often avoided having sex with Cara. Cara thought he was being a gentleman at first, but now that they have been together for three years, she questioned their relationship and mentioned to him that she felt unattractive and unwanted by him. Marcus wanted to marry Cara, but he knew something deeper affected their sexual relationship. He did not want to lose her.

Even though Marcus was not that old, he had issues with getting aroused enough to perform sexually. We started with a reading before the past life regression to see if we could locate clues to his issue.

His spirit guides pointed out his red-orange Sex chakra to me. They showed me that in this lifetime, starting around the age of ten, a few older boys shamed him into performing various sex acts with them. They often teased him, calling him gay, threatening to tell on him for doing these things if he did not continue. Marcus associated sex with forced pleasure. He showed signs of PTSD (post-traumatic stress disorder) from the repeated rape. He had never spoken to anyone about this trauma, not even Cara.

Now, as an adult, he also has issues speaking about how he feels. His Throat chakra was affected during the sexual abuse he endured when he was ten. He mentioned that he stutters when he speaks in front of a roomful of men at work. His doctor prescribed antidepressants for him to take before a meeting, to help him speak. When he was ten, he did not express that he disliked the sexual acts, tell them, "No," or tell anyone about this experience. This squelched his Throat chakra, thereby affecting his actual voice. Marcus also showed signs of dissociation as he regularly referred to himself in the third person (saying, "Marcus," instead of, "I," when speaking).

Marcus decided to try a reading and a past life regression to help get to the root of his sexual issues. He also hoped he could find something that would help him understand why he stuttered in front of his mostly male co-workers and superiors at work.

First Marcus entered a past lifetime as a woman. In his life as a female, he endured an arranged marriage with an abusive man. He beat her into sexual submission. Behind closed doors, he would have her perform unspeakable, abusive sexual acts for him, otherwise he would beat her. He made her feel like an animal. He dressed her in rags and treated her as such. However, as soon as she walked outside their front door, he expected her to appear prim, proper, and very obedient, only wearing the finest clothes. Her husband forbade her to speak to her family and did not allow her to have friends. She repressed her emotions in that life to endure the abuse. She never spoke up to him and never told anyone of her abuse. She also believed that she had to be dutiful by staying in that relationship and due to brainwashing, she felt dependent upon the husband for everything.

Then, he remembered a second lifetime as a small boy who lived in a monastery.

~ ROOT CAUSE EXPLORATION ~

"I wake up alone one day. My dad has been missing for a long time. My mother normally laid beside me on the floor of our very humble home. I meander around my home to only find a dried piece of bread. After what seemed like several days, a wandering monk found me dehydrated and starved lying on the street nearby. I hear him asking neighbors about my family. My dad had died, and my mother could no longer afford to care for me and chose to leave me behind. When the monk found my sickly mother, she felt I could be better cared for by leading a holy life. I never saw her again. I felt abandoned.

After learning I had been essentially orphaned, he cared for me, nursing me back to health over several days. We traveled a week to get to the monastery. My small, undernourished body made me appear much younger than four years old. The kind monk carried me most of the way. Once there, they made me feel as though it was an honor to be chosen to join them at the monastery. I felt loved.

To settle into life at the monastery, they shaved my head and dressed me in old robes. Once healed, they taught me the rules of living there, how to clean, be obedient, and how to live the holy life. It feels like an honor to be chosen to live at this monastery. I remained small and meek.

The monastery complex towered over the small Chinese town located near Tibet. The name of the city starts with the sound of 'Shoo.'

Life at the monastery turned out to be abusive. The restricted meals, hours of cleaning, plus hours of silence in prayer allowed for zero time to play.

The older boys housed at the monastery verbally and sexually abused me. As soon as I heard them condescendingly call my name, "JeshShuWoo," I would get a pit of pain in my stomach. The older boys would be very obedient in front of the Abbot, but controlling and abusive to the younger boys when the Abbot was away.

The monastery rules forbade and demonized all sexual feelings, masturbation, or any sexual act. The older boys would often force the younger boys to perform sexual acts. If a younger boy refused, they would collectively punish the boy by preventing them from eating the meager meals served at the monastery.

I often starved for days because of refusing to continue to participate. At fourteen, I died of starvation caused by the older boys' directive to give all my food to them as punishment for not performing sexually. The Abbot was clueless of this abuse. If a boy threatened to tattle on them, they were soon found dead.

Consequently, I chose to starve to death to end this life of hidden torment."

~ HEALING STEPS ~

In both sexually abusive past lifetimes and this current lifetime, he felt as though speaking up was not permitted. As the woman, he felt that he had to be dutiful to stay in that relationship because he was dependent upon the husband. In this lifetime, his subconscious restriction of sexual pleasure compounded his inability to sexually perform and fear of enjoying sex. In both past and present lifetimes his Throat chakra was restricted.

We started with forgiveness work to release any connections to those past lives in his current lifetime. I had Marcus forgive the husband in his first lifetime and the people involved with arranging the marriage. I had him forgive his mother, the older boys, the monks, and the Abbot who did not save him from the abuse in the second lifetime. Then we worked on him forgiving himself in both past lives and this current lifetime. Please keep in mind that when you forgive, it is not acknowledging that the abuse was okay, but to release you from the subconscious ties that bound your energy to that trauma.

The pattern of being shamed into submission in this lifetime was compounded by these two past lifetimes of abuse. He recognized that the pattern of submission and the current issue of restriction of sexual pleasure were related.

Next, I asked the angels to provide pure love energy healing. I asked Marcus to locate any pent-up emotions (including guilt, guilty pleasure, anger, depression, horror, etc.) and trauma stored in his energy, be collected, and stream out of his body, out the window, into the ground outside so it can transmute back to positive. I asked Marcus to pay special attention to his Throat chakra and to release any resentments and emotions stored there and allow the angels to replace all of this with their healing love and light. As he released repressed emotions and trauma energy, he saw it leave as if it were a stream of grey-black mucous. His entire energy became brighter.

About a year later, Marcus came to me again for a second session. He happily relayed how the previous session had really helped. He and Cara had set a date to get married. He began to enjoy a hard penis in response to pleasure. Marcus practiced expressing his wants and desires in the bedroom and in other aspects of his life as well. All this brought further healing to his Throat chakra. He had stopped referring to himself in the third person and his stuttering had drastically decreased.

Through forgiveness work, catharsis, and the work to clear and strengthen his Throat chakra, he has now resolved a lot of the issues from before the first session.

~ AFFIRMATIONS ~

I am a sexual being
I feel pleasure and it is okay
I am allowed to feel pleasure
I touch myself with ease
Feeling pleasure is good
Being touched is safe
Sex is natural
Enjoying naked time with myself and others is healthy
Sex is fun
I trust
I only allow truth in my life
Masturbation is selflove
Every part of my body is beautiful
I am secure in the knowledge that I love myself
I am open to receive pleasure

CHAPTER 5

CLOSED HEART—BLOCKING TRUE LOVE DUE TO DEATH OF A LOVED ONE

When you love someone, it is hard to let them go. It is even harder when they die.

Did you ever break up with someone and not miss them at all? Then have another relationship and feel the same way? When you leave a 20-year relationship and feel nothing for that person; that is not normal. Yes, it is relief that the relationship is over, but no feelings whatsoever for them? Do you feel like you settle for the mundane—because it is easy?

Or worse, they might have been abusive somehow too, but you allowed it since on some subconscious level, that meant you would not have to fully open your heart to them.

Why though?

The surprising reason is that, in reality, all this saves you from heartache. Meanwhile, you suffer through all these unfulfilling relationships that are topical, unloving, and downright hurtful or abusive. Somewhere, subconsciously you are avoiding a true love relationship to protect your heart.

This could be because you lost a loved one in this life or in one or more past lives. The trauma of loss from a past life can be compounded by the passing of someone you loved deeply in this lifetime. The pattern of avoiding true love continues to perpetuate. Sometimes it is because of a past life where you saw your loved one die and you were never able to overcome the pain of their death.

The grief and heartache of that person dying might have caused you to make a statement, like a vow, of some kind that became a rule for your life now. It might have sounded like, "I will never open my heart again," or "If I love deeply, I only get hurt so I will avoid love," or "I will never love like that again." These rules are written with high emotions and stick within you on a very deep, subconscious level.

Some had a parent or someone close to them pass suddenly or traumatically in this current life and closed their heart. Some had pets pass when they were a child and for the remainder of their life avoided pets. It is all the same, you do not want your heart to ache again and somewhere, subconsciously, you believe you need to avoid deep love like the plague.

How do you know if this is affecting you?
- Do you feel numb or indifferent to most people you meet?
- Do you find yourself sitting uncomfortably in a room with your partner, only to feel like you are just going through the motions?
- Are you simply roommates sharing time together?
- Does it feel like you are living a life sentence in a long-forgotten jail cell?
- Have you noticed that neither one of you seem to look forward to seeing or talking to each other?

I am sure it did not always seem this way. It might have been fun at first—the sex—the excitement of something new—more sex. Then you remembered that sex is not love, it is lust. A few months later, it is constant drudgery. It feels like you have forgotten how to love.

Puppies and kittens might not even excite you. Some may describe you as closed off, blocked, boxed in, or broken-hearted. Some describe a feeling of being so disconnected from others, it hurts. What is the root cause of this depression-like feeling? Is it from this lifetime? A past lifetime? Both?

We often blame others, but we are the ones in control of ourselves, our choices, and our energy. Free will is a rule here on this Earth plane. It should be called the Law of Free Will since it seems no different than the Law of Gravity on Earth.

In this life, we may settle for someone, thinking they are the best we can do. We believe that the person who comes into our life is meant to bring doldrums and not excitement—like we need to live up to some sort of lame status quo. We do not believe someone can make our heart skip a beat or give us butterflies in our stomach. We lost hope on finding true love.

We simply gave up on some level.

If you are like most people, too many relationships in this life have ended in disappointment. Each one compounds the emotional pain of loss, causing you to feel extraordinarily numb or even dead inside. Eventually you start to feel unwanted and lonely. Each disappointment closes your heart even further. Each one adds another layer of protection around your heart. If you have done this, an intuitive psychic can see bars, boxes, cages, locks, metal, glass—nearly anything that will block and protect your heart (via the Heart chakra) from fully opening to true love. If you feel a pain in your heart as you read this, you might be feeling the blockage covering your heart.

Imagine, if you will, your heart, your beautiful beating heart—filled with life, pumping nourishing blood throughout your pulsating body. Visualize it. Put your hand on your chest. Go ahead. Do it. Feel it beating in your chest. Realize that you are not dead inside, just hurt. Which can feel quite the same.

So, how does one's heart get closed? It can often start in childhood, especially when one parent or both are not ready for a child. When a new baby comes into this world, they are very aware of all the thoughts and feelings of the parents and many of them around them. They hear all the words said. If the baby's spirit hovers around the parents or if the baby has chosen to integrate its spirit into the fetus while in-utero, then they know all that goes on in the family around them even before they are born.

Babies, having recently been in spirit form in Heaven, are absolutely born with intuitive abilities like telepathy and interdimensional seeing. In spirit, telepathy is the main mode of communication which is why some mothers get a knowing of what their baby needs when they cry. In spirit, we are skilled at instant manifestation, have psychic intuitive abilities, and experience no time. In spirit, we can see into other dimensions, this is why babies often are seen laughing at the wall, when in reality they are talking to or playing with passed over loved ones, angels, or even their spirit guides.

Oftentimes, a closed heart goes deeper than that. We have had thousands of lifetimes, and depending upon your experiences, you may have had many dearly loved ones die before you. During a past life regression, death of a loved one is harder to relive or remember than your own past life death. We may have not gotten time to resolve the grief or mourn for their loss. We may have made the decision to never feel such deep love for another because of the deep grief caused by their death. This decision becomes your soul's vow or contract that still might be in place today.

We may have chosen to turn off our feelings so that we never feel that type of pain again, not realizing that we chose to do this on a spirit level in this Earth plane—so we must now heal it in this Earth plane.

I challenge you to explore what is really happening on a deeper level. You could have very well shut off all your feelings and that includes love.

One way you can tell is that you feel numb in a relationship. It is like you settled with someone that sort of works for now. It may feel like you are just going through the motions in a relationship.

Some days it can feel meaningless. It becomes blatantly obvious when the relationship ends and there is no broken heart over the whole thing. You may never even shed a tear. Maybe you have not cried in an exceptionally long time.

Since you have not healed your heart, it is not open to a true love connection. Energetically, when you have trauma to your heart, you shield it. Grief will dampen it or loss of a loved one could close it off. There are many reasons, and they compound as more traumas happen. After experiencing one or even several bad relationships, you may feel hurt and place additional shields of protection around your heart each time. These layers prevent true love from being felt by you as well as prevent you from feeling the love you might have for another person too.

You cannot receive love if your heart is closed—therefore blocking the love from reaching your heart.

Whatever trauma we experience in this Earth plane (whether in this life or a past life), we need to heal in this Earth plane. We may not have realized it at the time. We may never have resolved it in that other lifetime.

If you are focusing on this chapter, you are now ready to heal and learn to open your heart again.

There are several emotions that can close your heart too. Anger is a big one. Resentment. Survivor's guilt is another. Depression. Grief. The more you hang onto, the more there is to heal.

Grief is the most common one. There are five stages of grief when someone dies. These can be experienced in any order and can take months or years to resolve. They include anger, bargaining, depression, denial, and finally acceptance.

Alternatively, many people who unwittingly closed their heart actually are not fully loving themselves. Loving yourself is the number one thing we all need to learn to do. If you cannot love yourself, how is someone else going to love you? Look in the mirror and tell yourself that you love you today. Like right now. No one can love you any more than you already love yourself. This basic tenet goes back to the law of attraction that says you can only bring unto you what you are.

Right now, you are surrounded and supported by your spirit guides, angels, and passed over loved ones. They cannot interfere in your life unless you ask. So, ask. Ask them to please help you understand what led you to close your heart off to love. Ask them to help you heal. Ask them to break any vows you may have made unknowingly. It is as though they are sitting around bored, unless you give them a job to do. They appreciate working to help you through this lifetime.

You are never truly alone. Those that have died before us are never really gone. We are spiritual beings having a human experience. Once we pass, we are aware of our true spiritual nature. If you think of someone on the other side, it is my experience that they are immediately nearby you. One of my spirit guides explained that loved ones get a notification in their Heart chakra when we think of them. It is of no effort for them to come visit us at that very moment.

So, prove it, you say? You can. Think of someone on the other side. This can be a passed over loved one, an angel, or one of your spirit guides. Ask them to show you a specific sign. Pick something that is meaningful to you. You can pick anything. Many choose a feather, flower, butterfly, insect, number, shape, smell—the list goes on and on. Once you see that sign or symbol, then acknowledge it by saying out loud or in your mind, "Hello Aunt Josie," for example.

~ CURRENT LIFE EXAMPLE: KAREN ~

After writing my first book, *Life Is Just Another Class—One Soul's Journey Through Past Life Regression*, I realized I had not experienced a genuinely loving, mutually supportive relationship in any of the sixteen past lifetimes written in this book or in my current life.

I delved into several past lives to find a root cause for this pattern. I found several very loving relationships ripped away from me, my heart broken, seemingly irreparably damaged, in past lifetimes. In this lifetime, I participated in two unhealthy, narcissistic, long-term relationships. I had no comparison for the feeling of deep love in this current lifetime, which made me recognize that I needed to focus on more self-healing work.

In the midst of working on my first book, I saw that I chose to do my duty in a relationship in several of my past lifetimes. This resonated with the relationship I was in at that time too. Upon that realization, I swore. A lot. What had I chosen on a soul level!?

My past life with Victor is one of the first loving lifetimes I remembered. I still smile thinking about him and the love we shared. It felt amazing to be respected, loved, and cherished by him. I found this past lifetime as a root cause as to why I had chosen unloving relationships in other past lifetimes and my current lifetime.

In this past life, two of my lovers died.

~ ROOT CAUSE EXPLORATION ~

"My curly, brown hair is long in the back with short cornrow braids across the front to keep my hair off my face. I am in my twenties, very independent, confident, and educated. I am tall and thin.

As I travel into the woods looking for mushrooms to cook, I surprisingly find a wooden baby doll wearing a gingham dress lying in the forest. Its jointed arms and legs make me think it is a real baby. I pick it up and look around the quiet woods.

I wear a long, heavy, leather-flapped skirt overtop my pants and knee-high boots for riding. It is not normal for upper-class women to dress this way in 1409 A.D., but it makes it easy to get back up on my horse.

I meander slowly through the Holland forest on my horse. I think I will find someone, hopefully the child who is missing the doll, in the woods.

I come across a cute, gingerbread-like house near a small creek. I walk up the cobblestone walkway to the door, knock, then wander around the exterior of the empty house. I gently set the doll down by the doorstep. I hope this is the right house for the doll. I try to peek in a window.

As soon as I turn around, I am surprised by a dark-haired man wearing an ornate vest standing there. He sternly demands to know why I am at this house but relaxes once I tell him the story of the doll.

Abruptly, for no apparent reason, he puts his arm around my waist, pulls me close, and kisses me. I am stunned, we did not know each other. It feels nice. His arm on my waist makes me feel very feminine. My knees go weak.

While I did like it, I push him away and slap his face. I put my hand on my heart-shaped necklace and said that I was betrothed to the man who gave me the necklace. I told him this even though that man had sadly died years ago.

He introduces himself as Victor. I tell him, "My name is Alexandra." After we talk more, he wants to hire me as a huntress and female woodsman. He is impressed with my skills to find things in the woods, like mushrooms, herbs, rocks, and other medicinal plants.

We rode our horses to his castle-like house. He offers me a drink of red wine as we sit at a long, thick wooden table in the great room. I look around to admire the tapestries covering the stone walls.

We soon become a couple. He respected me for my knowledge and confidence. He saw me as an equal and treated me as such. We flirt and have fun each time we are together. I love him.

While riding horses one day, out of nowhere, an arrow penetrated his back. This impact knocked him off his horse. I quickly stop and dismount from my horse. When he falls, it breaks off the back of the arrow. The arrow poked through his chest while severing his spine and paralyzing him. When I hugged him close to me, I could feel the arrow tip break my skin. He remained coherent for a few moments. Thieves shot him to steal from us.

I sob as he departs this life. I touch his face lovingly. He says, "In another time," as he dies. I wear a ring as a sign of our love. The thieves do not try to kill me, since I am female and not an obvious threat to them. As one approaches me to retrieve any spoils, I discreetly remove a dagger from my boot. I reluctantly hand him the ring. We had nothing more for them to take. He yells at me as though I am lying about any riches. As he steps closer to me to yell again, I stab him deep in the chest, and it kills him. I take back the ring.

The other wimpier man came at me. As he gets close, I defensively stand and kick him square in his neck with a roundhouse kick. He falls back, hits his head, and starts to bleed. They mistakenly thought I was a weak girl. I left both thieves in the middle of the woods to die.

My life lesson is to be strong.

I fashioned a travois carrier with ties from his horse's gear to carry Victor home. I hold the reigns of his horse while slowly riding mine carefully dragging his body on the travois. I felt numb the whole time. Constant tears with intermittent sobbing blocked easy navigation through the woods.

Weeks pass. I cannot even bring myself to remember the funeral. We had been living together at Victor's house. I lie in our lonely bed very distraught day after day just staring aimlessly around the room. I touch the small ornate box Victor gave me that sits on the bedside table and cry harder. My body wasted away because I refused to eat. My heart breaks. This is the second man I loved that died.

In this deep state of depression, I decide to end my life a month after his death.

Using my woodsman skills, I find poisonous herbs, grind them up and mix them in some red wine. I drink the small goblet of herbal poison, fall into a deep sleep, and die.

I stand in spirit next to our bed, in shock at what I had done to myself. Victor's spirit waited for me.

Disappointedly, he says, "Why did you poison yourself? You could have done more with your life!"

"I did not want to live without you," I reply.

I asked him to forgive me for taking the poison. He said, "I am disappointed, but I will always love you." After some time, we enter The Light together. I felt safe with him.

I hold his hand as many welcome us back—including the man who gave me the heart necklace, my parents, and several others.

Later, I go alone to spend time with the tall healing angels. Five of them put their hands on my head to heal me with love energy. I miss Victor. The healing takes longer because I remain emotionally distraught.

Victor tells me telepathically, "I will see you in another time."

Time happens so fast; it seems like it could be tomorrow. I spend a lot of time healing from that lifetime.

I continue to converse with him telepathically. He says, "I chose another life. I am going to be born again."

Reluctantly, I say, "I understand. Good luck." Then I feel him leave. I stayed with the five healing angels a long time.

As they heal my energy, I review my life by connecting with my Akashic Records in the Hall of Records. What would have happened if I had stayed? If I had chosen to be strong emotionally? I feel like I failed. I did not learn my lesson to be strong in many ways. Because I chose the suicide route, I lost a sense of self.

One of my spirit guide council members said, "You need to do your studies. What could you have done differently?"

I learn that the choices I make directly affect the future. I learn that I avoided true love relationships in future lifetimes to avoid emotional agony.

Had I overcome the emotional pain, I would have gotten remarried, had children, and been a grandmother.

Instead, I felt alone and distraught over loss of love. My children were never born because I committed suicide."

~ HEALING STEPS ~

In reviewing my lifetime with Victor, I work on forgiveness. I forgive myself for taking poison, committing suicide, the herbs, the wine, the thieves, and the trauma that the thieves caused. I forgive Victor for seemingly abandoning me.

I said, "The moment he took his last few breaths is permanently etched in my mind," so I worked to replace that final heartbreaking memory of him with the memory of our first kiss. I focus on remembering the feeling of love to bring it forward into this lifetime. I focus on the feeling of what it feels like to be loved, and to truly love.

I heard the quote, "Tis better to have loved and lost than to never have loved at all," by Alfred Lord Tennyson.

When I remembered this loving lifetime, I realized that I had also made a soul-level vow to never let my heart be broken again and to never feel the pain of the loss of a true love again. I recognized when I created my fear of heartbreak, I had established a few rules, "If I find true love in a relationship, then my heart will be broken," and, "It is easier if I do not care if or when they die." With that deep understanding, I break these rule-like vows. I asked for my spirit guides and angels to help me replace that soul vow with, "I am open to a beautiful, loving relationship."

I worked with the angels to release the emotional energy of grief and guilt from my Heart chakra. I cried deeply to release more of the trapped emotions from that past life. I saw layers of protection over my heart being removed.

~ CURRENT LIFE EXAMPLE: ANNIE ~

Annie came to me to work through her relationship issues. She said she could not fully connect with a man. She felt shut down and closed off emotionally. Over a few past life regression sessions, Annie remembered several lifetimes that closed her heart off from fully being open and available to love someone.

She remembered the root cause of shutting down her emotions in her past lifetime as Anthony.

As Annie begins to remember a past life memory, I ask her to see if a date comes to mind and to describe what is happening around her.

~ ROOT CAUSE EXPLORATION ~

"It is 404 B.C. in Rome. My name is Anthony. Our village prepares for an upcoming festival. Everyone looks forward to this event. I normally bake a lot of twisted bread for the festivities. I left my wife and 8-year-old daughter behind early that morning to travel for a few hours to purchase more nutty grain for the bread. Everyone looks forward to this exciting time of year.

When I get home, my daughter will play in the grain. She loves to run her fingers through it with me as we pull out impurities. We live above our bakery, so my daughter often stands at the opened window and gazes down the cobblestone street for my return.

I loved my beautiful wife and daughter deeply. I cherished our happy family life.

While I traveled to buy grain, our village was invaded. The invaders came on ships with horses and killed anyone in their way. They killed hundreds of people including my family. Later in the evening, as I walked into town, I noticed it was eerily quiet. I saw carnage strewn everywhere. I dropped the heavy sack of grain and ran towards my house.

When I arrived at my home, my wife and child were already dead. I do not want to contemplate what torturous things they did to my ladies. I never forgave myself for not being there to protect them. Through tears I scream, "I was only gone one day!" They took everything from me.

They took my ability to love. So much guilt and deep emotions from this lifetime affect me.

After this invasion, every able-bodied man was immediately required to join the military. I never received the chance to grieve.

I fought valiantly in the battles. It feels like I have been battling for years. My breastplate lost its shine long ago. I really miss the peaceful baking of bread, my wife, and my daughter. I think of them every day.

I never wanted to be a soldier. The military skirt is uncomfortable and even though my shoes have several layers of leather, they are well worn. I feel wearisome from so many battles.

On my last day, I rapidly ride my sturdy brown horse into a new battle. I admire the square braid in its mane. I notice the sun glistening off a large rock formation ahead in the distance. I am glad my helmet does not cover my face. My unruly beard waves in the wind; there is no time to shave. The army did not have funds to replace the worn battle gear.

Without warning, a mace hits me square in the stomach with its metal shards piercing me five times through my old breastplate. I fall off my horse onto another dead body. I cry out from the pain. I soon feel happy when I realize I will die shortly. As I die, I see groups of spirits leave their bodies. They vanish when they go into The Light. I walk towards The Light and enter too."

~ HEALING STEPS ~

In reviewing the lifetime as the baker, I have her work on forgiveness. I have her forgive herself for leaving her family behind, the flour, the festival, the fun she wanted, for not baking, for not being there to save them, for those who attacked them, for serving in the military, for the mace, and for their wife and child dying.

I have her release any pent-up emotions from throughout her energetic being. Annie and I worked on releasing any blocks to her heart. We asked for angelic healing for everything and especially of her heart. The angels suggested she wear green to help enhance the healing of her Heart chakra.

~ CURRENT LIFE EXAMPLE: ANDIE ~

Andie came to me about her current relationship with her on again, off again boyfriend, Ralph. We discussed many patterns regarding this relationship, but what stuck out the most is that neither of them wanted to commit to the relationship completely, but they kept coming back together.

One odd comment by Ralph was that he was afraid to have children with her. Andie wanted to understand why they were drawn together repeatedly and why did Ralph keep breaking it off without any solid reason, only to want to remain friends and then want to be more again. It kept Andie confused.

We started with a reading which led to into a guided meditation. During the angelic healing meditation, Andie began to remember a past lifetime with Ralph.

~ ROOT CAUSE EXPLORATION ~

"I am standing by the door of the nursery watching the baby sleep. My husband walks up the stairs in our Victorian-styled house and wraps his arms around my waist. We were so happy at that moment. We live in a peaceful neighborhood in the outskirts of London. This older wooden house used to belong to his parents. They died many years ago.

I cannot believe it is 1850 A.D. already. Time goes so fast. I am amazed that Abner turned three months old today.

My husband just returned home from work. He helped process taxes for the city. I told him that dinner was just about ready. We both walked back downstairs to do a few things before dinner. He walked out to our backyard to feed the chickens. I stood in the kitchen stirring the dinner I am cooking in the hearth over the fire. It has been a long day. Baby Abner cried a lot today. I wonder if he is teething. I hear my husband walk in the back door of the house as I walk into another room towards the front door to sweep and clean a bit while dinner finishes. I had not had a chance all day to get to this chore.

Out of nowhere, smoke pours throughout the house. I heard my husband yelling, "Fire, get out," and running towards the back door. I ran out the nearby front door.

He meets me around the front of the house as it engulfs in flames.

Neither of us had the baby. We stare at each other in astonishment and look back at the burning house, now impossible to reenter. Tears run down my face. The fire took hold of this house faster than we could blink. I scream and sob as the house collapses and black smoke fills the sky.

Each of us thought the other one had the baby. He was cremated in the house fire. We lost everything. Neighbors came to help put out the flames, but nothing could douse our pain of the loss of Abner. We tried for years to get pregnant before Abner. I suffered through three miscarriages. My husband never forgave me for the loss of this baby. He yelled at me as if I did not want children, I could not keep them growing inside me and the one time I do, I let it burn in a fire. I hurt inside too. He lost all empathy towards me.

I recognize my husband as Ralph in this lifetime. I see that he still has not forgiven me for the loss of our child in this past lifetime. Both of us suffered from depression after this tragedy. We were never the same again. We moved into a new house but stayed in separate bedrooms and rarely associated with one another. He got lost in his work. I sat in deep depression most of the time. We never tried to have children again."

~ HEALING STEPS ~

I immediately have Andie work on forgiving herself. She had so much guilt from this experience. This caused her to try to overcompensate in helping others in her current life. She currently works as a nurse and often goes above and beyond in her job too. We worked with the angels to help her remove all the pent-up emotions within and replace them with pure love and light. I asked the angels to work with returning any pieces of her soul she left behind.

I asked her angels and spirit guides to help her visit with her son from this past life to know he was okay. An angel carried a little baby in their arms over to Andie while she was still in the meditative state. She held him and asked for forgiveness. She could feel the baby's love and knew everything will be okay.

This experience brought a lot of catharsis to Andie. Her spirit guides explained to her that the reason she and Ralph came together in this lifetime is to complete the healing from that past lifetime. While Ralph and baby Abner were not active participants in the past life regression, they both were able to receive healing on a soul level.

Her spirit guides asked her to send love to her uterus in preparations for a future child in this lifetime.

~ LOSS OF A BABY ~

Loss of a baby through miscarriage or a planned miscarriage is always exceedingly difficult. When you lose a baby, it can break a relationship. All the grief, guilt, and the myriad of emotions you might feel from this loss can be stored within your physical body, cause a piece of soul to break away from you, and/or break your heart.

Let us take a moment to acknowledge a few things.

First, we are spiritual beings having a human existence. Having a human existence is a like taking a college level course—it is hard. Sometimes that little baby spirit decides that they want to drop the course they signed up for and try again later.

Second, little baby spirits are healers visiting from the other side. What I have seen through my readings is something that is never discussed. The little spirit comes to visit the mom's uterus for a short time to place a healing light within the mother. I see it as a spark of light. In one reading, I saw the little baby place a healing light towards the mother's back. I asked the mother if she had back issues before that pregnancy and if they went away after the miscarriage. She responded, astonished, yes, she did have back pain and it had gone away. This healing light was a gift from the baby spirit. Most of the time when I provide a reading for someone who has lost a baby, that little spirit comes for a short time, just to provide some type of healing, awakening, or inspiration to the mother via their womb.

Third, passed over loved ones do not seem to have to abide by the same rules that your spirit guides and angels do. Spirit guides and angels adhere to our free will rule—they cannot interfere in our lives unless we ask. However, it has been my experience that passed over family members can easily help you from the spiritual realm—with whatever. They have a special connection to you because they are family. Little baby spirits that chose to come for a short time in your cozy uterus, are family members. I have met quite a few who chose to have the special perks of being able to help and assist others from the other side this way. Think of them as spirit guides taken up a notch.

One of my siblings, that I never met in life, has spoken to me several times in spirit. He told me to call him Matthew. He provided me guidance before my birth, he was there during my near-death experience when my second child was being born, during a few meditations, and will always be part of my amazing team on the other side.

~ AFFIRMATIONS ~

I am love
I am made of pure unconditional love
I attract love into my life
It is safe to love
It is safe to love again
To be loved and give love is rewarding
Deep, mutual love is here for me
I am worthy of deep, long-lasting love
My heart is open to love
I only allow mutually supportive and loving connections
I have loving people in all aspects of my life
I open my heart to receive love

Chapter 6

Abuse Is Not Love

Everyone wants to be loved. That is the truth of it.

How do you define love? By genuinely feeling a deep connection with someone and them treating you with mutual support, respect, and more—that is love. But, if you grew up with parents or caregivers that emotionally, physically, or sexually abused you one moment and then in the next moment, showered you with love, you may have inadvertently associated or equated abuse with love.

In some instances, I have given readings to a few who—in this lifetime—only expected abuse from anyone who loved them as they have only received love from an abuser. It was as if they made the subconscious rule that in order to receive love, they must agree to receive abuse.

I have heard so many excuses to rationalize the abuse:

- "But he gave me flowers."
- "He is jealous because he loves me."
- "She had a bad day. I deserved it."
- "It was my fault. I will do better next time."
- "They bought me new clothes."
- "They said they were sorry with tears in their eyes."
- "They gave me a roof over my head."
- "They did not mean it. I should have had dinner on the table."

Abused and 'loved' people have heard it all, but since they were conditioned this way in relationships over the years, it feels normal to them. One could even say that this pattern of abuse feels comfortable. When an abused person receives authentic love and kindness without abuse, sometimes that person feels as though it is not real or that the person has ulterior motives. Receiving authentic love becomes downright uncomfortable for them. They do not feel worthy of authentic, true, deep, or even unconditional love. They may see tears or other emotions as pretend or fake emotions.

Some people who have been abused in the name of love have a hard time with the word love since they equate it with abuse. Children who have abusive parents equate love with abuse on some level. I am going to call this the abuse-love cycle.

All of this goes back to memories of a psychology class I had in college. In the textbook, they spoke about four types of addiction. The worst type was random reward addiction. One easy example is gambling.

B.F. Skinner, an American psychologist and behaviorist in the 1950s, called it a variable schedule of rewards (or variable ratio reinforcement schedule). Skinner observed that lab animals responded best to random rewards. (See Skinner's book, *Schedules of Reinforcement*, for more information.)

A clear example of abuse was found in lab experiments where mice were shocked repeatedly when pressing a lever while randomly provided a treat or drug as a reward. This poor little guy would die trying to get that next treat.

I think of these mice when I hear of this abuse-love cycle. The abused person will withstand abuse to near death for that random speck of love. Have you met someone who was severely abused and willingly stayed in the relationship?

Someone who is repeatedly abused begins to believe that when they are being treated lovingly on a random basis, it makes the relationship worth it. Sometimes love can be confused with attention provided through abuse. If you have lived only knowing abuse in a relationship, you might equate any attention given through abuse with love.

There are several different kinds of abuse including sexual, physical, emotional, financial, and electronic. The bottom line is that they are all about control—controlling YOU. There are varying degrees of each type of abuse. If you are constantly compromising yourself by denying who you are and what you enjoy in order to maintain a (i.e., keep them from getting angry) relationship, that is a red flag or warning sign it is abusive.

Please take a moment and read through all the items contained in "Chapter 18: Warning! Danger! Signs of Abusive Relationships." I have included lists that will help you identify abusive traits in someone. If you answer, "Yes," to any of the items listed or resonate with several of them, please get help. Most of these lists were provided to me when I stayed in a women's shelter a long time ago. I hope they help you as much as they helped me.

Abuse is still attention—especially when all sense of self and confidence has been eroded away. Love can be confused with the attention received via abuse.

Please be aware, those who are in an abusive relationship may get stuck in victim mode. They may talk about how awful their abuser is and different aspects of the relationship with the subconscious hope of receiving love, support, and vital energy from their friends and family. However, no action to change is taken by the abused person. Months or years later, a similar story is being told.

How can you jump off this hamster wheel of abuse? Awareness of the problem is always the first step to healing. Then, accepting you are abused and need help by taking active responsibility for your life is the second step. If you do not heal the pattern of abuse, it will not matter if you move to the other side of the world, abusive people will find you. If you are stuck in the pattern of abuse, then one of your life lessons may be to learn how to overcome the abuse.

What is a life lesson? You chose this life and the challenges you have encountered. You chose your parents, major events, the people, and more. A life lesson is one of many things you came here in this life to learn more about or to experience.

Our life as a spiritual being is filled with unconditional love. We came here to this Earth plane to experience more than we could ever understand in spirit. As an analogy, we could read volumes about how to ride a bike or drive a car, but we do not really 'get it' until we start to pedal or press the gas.

Sometimes when you choose to have an experience that is abusive, it is normally about how you can: overcome that challenge (you become aware of the abuse, take steps to prevent it, and start to feel selflove) or learn to be courageous and feel empowered (you leave an abusive situation and heal your Solar Plexus).

If you find yourself in an abusive situation, please seek out professional counseling help. When you take the step to get help, you are in fact, showing love to yourself.

Get legal help. Being in a relationship with an abusive person may require you to utilize the court system to acquire a PFA (Protection From Abuse) which can legally prevent an abuser who caused physical injury or the threat of physical injury from coming near you. A PFA is something available in the US. I would hope other countries have their own version of this legal help.

Call and go to the nearest women's shelter. Some cities have men's shelters. They offer emergency shelter and housing for victims of domestic violence and their children. The confidential location is provided when services are needed.

Leaving an abusive situation can cause PTSD (post-traumatic stress disorder). You will have to become hyper-aware of each and every trigger that is associated with your past abusive relationship and heal each one individually to release the PTSD. This is in addition to healing yourself and releasing the trauma with the person who abused you. It may take years and that is okay. Time can heal all wounds, even if it takes many lifetimes. Stay strong, you will get through this.

How can you break this pattern of abuse? First, I want to applaud you in reading this chapter of this book, you have acknowledged there is a problem and taken your first step to finding help. I ask the angels to send love and courage to you as you read these words. There are several different ways and many different techniques to help you heal. You will find the right way for you, and you can start here.

Let us first understand some of the causes that brought you into this lifetime of abuse.

Not feeling worthy of meaningful, long-lasting, unconditional love is normally the root of abuse. Possibly you had abusive parents and you grew up thinking abuse was normal. This goes way deeper than this lifetime. Every time I have given a reading to help someone release from a pattern of abuse, it always goes way deeper than this lifetime.

Somewhere, sometime, you decided on a spirit level that you wanted to learn how to overcome extreme hardship to learn that you were worthy of love. What were you thinking, right? Loving and respecting yourself is a key factor in overcoming this challenge. Remembering how to love yourself is extremely important.

Many times, the root cause lifetime has to do with being abandoned by parents. The parents sell you or you are born into slavery of some kind. Or worse, a parent beats a child to death. This brings on deep feelings of being unworthy of love. The slave life is not enjoyable and often torturous. You start to equate the abuse with someone who loves you because they must if they keep you. The problem is that the person or people that abuse you are associated with having a place to call home and feeling wanted there. This is clearly the wrong feelings to have, but many are not aware of this connection.

~ CURRENT LIFE EXAMPLE: LISA ~

When Lisa walked in my door, she looked apprehensive and clearly worried. At first, it appeared to be first time jitters. After chatting, as I do to help others feel more at ease and to answer any questions on the process, I found she was concerned about getting caught at my house. Lisa's husband was very controlling, and she feared for her life. I immediately gave her a packet of helpful abuser characteristics and personal rights lists (now found in the back of this book) to keep and hopefully read.

We began to discuss why she came for the past life regression. Her father was possessive and would abuse her as a child. She left home as soon as she turned eighteen to get away from the abuse. Her current relationship was abusive and now with a one-year-old, she feared her son would be abused next. In order to protect her son,

Lisa was now taking action to find out why she repeatedly found abusive men in her life. She felt she was a magnet for them. I talked to her about relationship patterns, and she agreed to set the intent for this past life regression to find the root cause of her abusive relationships.

~ ROOT CAUSE EXPLORATION ~

"Sweat drips off my forehead as I run away from home. My name is Sheila, and I cannot believe I am only 12 years old. I put my hands through my matted, messy hair and look down at myself. I see that my clothes and body are filthy. I wear an apron over my plain brown dress that hangs on my thin body. My worn shoes barely fit.

My family spun and dyed yarn for a living in Ireland. My fingers seemed permanently dyed with color.

My dad spent all the money on himself and his drinking, yet blamed me, my mother, and older brother for staying poor. My mom hid when he would get in a rage. Any food we did have went to my father first, then my brother. If there were scraps, my mother would eat some and give the rest to me if I was lucky. I tried to forage the woods for food while collecting plants for the dye.

My brother received food and some education from a friendly neighbor. I was never invited to go there. My brother could now read and never worried about food. The elderly neighbor helped my brother so he could leave on his own once grown. The neighbor did not feel it would help me since I was a girl. My brother hid this friendship from my parents. I knew something good was happening to him, only because he snuck out often, seemed happy upon return, and never complained of hunger. I was jealous and happy for him at the same time. My parents rarely let me out of their sight.

The day I left; I had inadvertently spilled hot dye on my father's foot. He beat me severely with a darning board. He repeatedly kicked my stomach and hit my face. I was furious that no one tried to help protect me from his fury. I could not comprehend the unnecessary violence for an accident.

The anger I felt empowered me to leave our small, decrepit wooden house. The constant smell of boiling animal wool could make you gag. The old, thatched roof leaked, a constant cold draft chilled us in the winter, and I never had much of a bed, let alone clothes or shoes that fit. I ran away because I could not stand being beaten any longer.

That day I chose me first.

I am hungry but I have always been underfed, so this feeling was not new. I emerged from the woods near a path and stopped to rest. I had run for hours and had no idea where I stopped.

Days passed. I felt guilty asking for food, but I was desperate. People would pass by, and I would ask for food or a drink. One nice lady gave me salted fish and cheese. Even though my feet and body ached, I walked with her for a few hours, but she could not care for me. I felt love from her. Strangers seemed nicer to me than my own family. My undernourished body would not survive the trek into town.

Now, a few weeks after I left home, a man riding past on a horse shouted, "Insolent child!" Then he kicked me hard enough to rupture something in my stomach, while mumbling under his breath, "I am so sick of beggars."

I wandered into the woods to hide and rest. Blood poured down my legs from the blunt force trauma. It smells horrible. I could not find water and wished it would rain. I lie down, fall asleep, and die of blood loss.

Archangel Ariel shines a beautiful light on my face and said, "I have come to gather your soul." I felt so warm and loved. I walked into The Light. The greeting room is filled with food and other children. I felt so happy, so clean, and finally not hungry."

~ HEALING STEPS ~

Lisa, as Sheila, died believing she was not worthy of love, but only worthy of abuse. On some level, love was equated with abuse. I asked the angels to overwrite this programming with a mantra of, "I am worthy of love."

Sheila was born into a family that basically became a jail sentence of servitude and starvation. Why did Lisa choose to experience this lifetime? It boiled down to two things. One, on a soul level she was learning to appreciate the feelings of being loved and two, how to stand up for herself.

I asked to break any conscious or subconscious vows or contracts that she may have made in any lifetime that would inhibit her from experiencing a loving, supportive relationship in this life and in future lifetimes.

I focused on helping her release any pent-up emotional trauma from her energy and asked the angels to fill her energetic being with healing unconditional love. I asked the angels to bring back to any pieces of her soul that she left behind due to trauma and to reintegrate it within her.

I worked with her to forgive everyone involved in that past life. Forgiveness of her mother for not protecting her, forgiveness of herself for not leaving sooner, forgiveness of the wool and the dye, forgiveness of her brother and releasing any jealousy of the care he received from the neighbor, forgiveness to her father, forgiveness to the nice lady who showed her love but could not care for her, and forgiveness of the man who kicked her and caused her death.

I spoke to Lisa a few months later during a follow up reading. She had left with her son and moved in with her mother until she could find a new place to live. Her life was beginning to shift in a positive direction.

~ CURRENT LIFE EXAMPLE: MONICA ~

Monica came to me for a past life regression. She had already had a reading with me that uncovered some abusive patterns in her current lifetime as well as in past lifetimes. With that knowledge, she totally cut off a relationship she had with a controlling man and had started attending counseling sessions. She had made great strides in healing so far. Her spirit guides told her to take a break from relationships in order to heal herself for a period of about 18 months. Monica began to trust her intuition more and had recently been attuned in Reiki.

She said she was ready to experience a past life to continue to heal.

We asked Monica's spirit guides and angels to help her locate a root cause of abuse in a past life. I guided her along the path to one of her spirit guide council members who held out her Akashic Records' book for a review.

They spoke for a bit. He told her how proud he was of her progress in this lifetime. He also mentioned she might encounter a few more men who will test her strength and will help her confirm that she has overcome this abuse pattern. She touched her Akashic Records' book and immediately entered a past life.

~ ROOT CAUSE EXPLORATION ~

"I am walking in a very sunny, brightly lit field. The grass is so dry it crunches under my feet. Dust flies up into the air as I walk down the hill. This drought has lasted too long and has caused tremendous damage. It has been a couple of years since we have had a good rain. I live near modern day Cushendall, Northern Ireland in the 1400s.

The wind blows off the nearby ocean shore causing my two long brown braids to flitter about my face. As I walk along this familiar steep path towards the nearby beach, I glance at the ocean to check the waves to make sure they are not too wild. The view of the ocean feels like home, but I do not take time to appreciate it.

I look down at my feet to watch where I walk. I groan at my well-worn leather shoes barely covering my feet. The drawstring has been mended to an irreparable point, so they are loose. My gingham dress is in no better shape. I make do with what I have and try not to complain. My only other dress is in far worse shape.

I walk down to the beach often—nearly daily to fish, so we have food to eat. Sometimes I collect the seawater to make salt.

Each time, I gather a few shells to add to my collection. This always makes me smile. When I get home, I add the shells to long strings that hang on my porch. It is comforting to hear them clink like chimes in the wind. This sound reminds me of my mother. I really miss her. She passed away when I was 16 years old. Mom died 14 years ago; I cannot believe I am thirty. The sound of the shells clinking together, and my little silver pinkie ring are all that I have left of her. I think the world of her tarnished ring as I touch it to admire the etched markings that my mother always said meant peace and love.

After my mother died, I inherited the house. It is nothing special. The wood is greyed from age. It has a porch, four rooms, and a small cold cellar. It is the only house I have ever known.

I do not have any other family. My father died when I was young, which never gave my parents the opportunity to give me a sibling. After my mother died, my sweet neighbor lady, Roisin, watched after me. She gave me this gingham dress and introduced me to my husband, Seoirse. She was like my surrogate mother who taught me to sew and bake bread. She always said, "I admire those big brown eyes, Caitrin."

The marriage feels like an abusive situation. I realize my husband is much older and an alcoholic. His serious personality turns abusive when he drinks.

We have been married for about ten years. He tells me that I must be barren since we never had children. He makes me feel bad inside, but I feel like I must put up with it all to stay with him otherwise he might abandon me too.

We have been eating more fish than usual these past few years. I am grateful we live so close to the shoreline. We are either eating fresh fish or salted fish it seems. When I am not at the ocean fishing, I spend my day cooking over the fire, cleaning the house, or tending to him.

As I stand here cooking fish over the fire; I dread the long walk ahead to deliver his dinner. I bake bread at least once a week because he likes it with his meat. I package up the food for him and begin walking towards the tavern.

He manages and owns a tavern that is a few hours walk. We own a mule, but he normally uses that for transportation to the tavern. His father owned the tavern before him.

We seem to live in the middle of nowhere and the tavern is definitely off the beaten path. It used to be quite popular, but we have lost a lot of people to this drought. Times are exceedingly difficult. He used to receive payment in coins, but lately it is only in trade. Money only comes into town when people travel through.

The tavern is not that large. As I walk in the door, I see him doing paperwork. He looks disgruntled and seeing his stein-like mug of alcohol nearby makes me cringe.

He regularly stumbles home drunk a few hours after sunset. If I do not see him by midnight, I know he is passed out unconscious, so I walk back to the tavern to drag him home with the help of the mule. I hope that does not happen tonight.

I walk past the few tables and chairs to give Seoirse his dinner.

I glance in the small, polished tin-like mirror behind the bar to see in the reflection just how many barrels of mead and rye are left. I sigh as I do not see too many amongst the bottles and glasses stored under bar. The mirror is there so you can see customers when your back is turned but I use it to gauge his drinking.

I look around to see a few regular customers. One is the local pig farmer. The pig farmers were doing well, as they could feed the pigs the ruined crops. The farmer traded a pig for regular drinks. I salted it to make it last. Years ago, this tavern was a crowded, happy place to visit. The drought has changed so many things.

When Seoirse received food and other goods in exchange for drinks, he made sure he took care of himself first. Sometimes he only shared a small part with me, like cheese or biscuits. He made me feel as though I should be grateful for any morsel or crumb.

I set the ham and bread dinner next to him and start cleaning the tavern as usual. He barely says a word but makes a snarky face at his meal. I get frustrated and think, "Nothing is ever good enough for him. I slave away all day making him food like this homemade bread and ham spread." If I say a word out loud, he will complain and hit me.

I sweep and wipe off the bar and tables. I carry the collected dust and dirt out to the back. There I am met with the stench of ingenuity. The tavern has an outhouse on the left with a long pig trough tilted to flow down into the right side of it. For convenience, the men stand at the trough to urinate and continue to chat while watching it flow into the outhouse.

Seoirse drinks more as the tavern business gets worse. I do not understand why he thinks this helps since it just covers up his sad, frustrated emotions. He becomes so angry when he drinks.

As his tavern business starts to fail, he takes his anger out on me more often. He complains he will lose the tavern.

The day he lost the tavern he came home extremely drunk, screaming that, "It was maliciously taken over by the evil local officials." I should have left as soon as I heard him coming down the path. He was yelling and shouting profanities as the mule slowly carried him home.

He is upset and starts taking it out on me physically. I try to run away from him. As he holds my wrists, he grabs at the chains that hold the pots hanging on the wall. He throws the pots across the room. He chains me to the wall instead. He beats me relentlessly, hitting me repeatedly across the face and head until I bleed.

I felt like I deserved it. Abuse is all I have ever seen and seriously thought it was normal. I remember seeing my mom be abused by my dad and other men. She always told me that she deserved it. I never received schooling or anyone to tell me otherwise.

Finally, he stops. He slumps onto the floor and passes out. I breathe a sigh of relief.

I cannot take it anymore. I immediately wiggle myself out of the chains that bind me. I run down the hill to the ocean and wash off the blood from my face. I feel confused, lost, and depressed. I do not know where to go or who to turn to—I feel I must run away from here. I had no one to turn to—I spent my whole life cleaning, cooking, and caring for him, the house, and the tavern. Roisin died years ago, and I never took the time to make any other friends.

My crying dripped blood down the front of my best dress. Ugly brown streaks stain it. I try to wash it off, so I look presentable. It is futile.

It was not long before he woke up and followed the path down the hill. He found me and pulled me back to house by my long hair. After a final beating, I die. Once he realized he killed me, he brought my body back down to the ocean to throw it out into the waves.

He knows his life is ruined. He sits and stares into the darkness. The moon's reflection moves in the waves.

In spirit, I sit nearby in the grass watching him watch my body float in the ocean waves. He sits there for a long while.

My guide sits next to me. She says, "It will be okay. Watching this is helping you love your body." This makes me cry. She continued, "You never learned to speak up for yourself and love yourself until your last day, but it was too late. You can learn this in your life now." I never spoke back to Seoirse. This last act of leaving him was my attempt at learning confidence.

In my spirit state, I recognize that I always felt like a burden so I tried to act as though I could take care myself and did not need help. This meant suffering through any abuse.

After I enter The Light, I am greeted by my mother. She apologizes to me for teaching me the abusive relationship pattern. I forgive her and hug her. My mother tells me she was beaten more than I realize, and she had learned that pattern from her mother. As she says this, my grandmother comes to greet me. We all hug. Then my sweet neighbor lady, Roisin, greets me. Roisin apologizes for introducing me to Seoirse. Of course, I forgive her, and we hug."

~ HEALING STEPS ~

I ask her spirit guide to show her the way to the healing angels' room. There, she is met by six healing angels who surrounded her spiritual being and provided her with pure unconditional love healing energy. I see it as bright light moving down through her energetic body.

In this lifetime, she was given another chance to learn to love her body and herself. The angels concentrated their healing energy on her Throat chakra to help her speak up for herself. They focused on boosting her Solar Plexus chakra to help her learn self-confidence.

We worked on forgiving all who abused her, not saying what they did was okay but just to release that trauma energy connection. We also cut cords with anyone in any lifetime who abused her and set down the new rule, "I only allow mutually supportive and loving connections from this point forward."

She healed any patterns of acceptance of abuse from this life and other past lives and replaced them with selflove.

~ AFFIRMATIONS ~

I only allow a healthy, loving relationship
I only allow mutually supportive and loving connections
I am worthy of amazing love
I always feel safe in a relationship
I can express my thoughts and feelings with ease to anyone
I am valued
I am treated with respect every day
I am safe
I am a confident, powerful, loving being
My body is my own. I love my body

Chapter 7

Doing Your Duty

"Fuck me." I groaned those words the day I realized that I chose doing my duty several times as a life lesson in my past lifetimes.

The realization came after writing my first book, *Life Is Just Another Class—One Soul's Journey Through Past Life Regression*. In those lifetimes, I did my duty to my parents or caregivers, I did my duty to my spouse, I did my duty to my children, I did my duty to my lover, etc. All the while, giving up doing what made me happy and ending up feeling like more of a maid, a servant, or a sex slave. It was eye-opening.

I gave up myself for others.

Doing your duty is a lesson in learning self-confidence. It is vitally important to empower your Solar Plexus and Throat chakra to express how you really feel and do what you really want.

When you take doing your duty in a relationship to the extreme by compromising or giving up everything about yourself, it might as well be called slavery to a relationship. It is not healthy. It is not mutually supportive. It is not mutually loving.

How many times have you said:

- "I cannot do this because my spouse, parent, or child comes first."
- "I should stay with them, even though they beat me down, because I made a vow to them."
- "I cannot leave them, they need me. Someone needs to take care of them."
- "I am financially dependent upon them."

- "I will marry that person because my parents arranged it or approved of them."
- "I cannot do that; I do not have the time, or they will get mad if I do."

When are you going to take care of you, do what makes you happy, do what makes you feel safe, or do what makes you feel supported and loved? When? When you die? Next lifetime?

When I realized I was doing my duty to the extreme again in my current lifetime, I got an icky taste in my mouth and became acutely aware that I had always felt like a slave in that relationship. I died in those other lifetimes with a feeling of relief, as if death seemed like my only escape from the servitude. I never realized that the cage I had put myself in had the door swung wide open.

So, how does this happen? As a female in our modern society, we are pressured by family expectations, social rules, religious doctrines, peers, to always take care of others and to help others. We are rewarded for it, shown how to put ourselves last and everyone else first repeatedly in television shows, movies, and even romance novels. We are frequently taught to put ourselves last, suck it up, and do for others first. God forbid if we do something for ourselves; according to religious tenets, it would be selfish.

Yet … is it?

It is selfcare when we take a relaxing bath, read a book, walk in nature, paint on canvas, write a book, or say no to too many tasks. Saying, "No," sets boundaries to help us avoid giving away too much of ourselves through time or energy.

This unbalance causes a lopsided pattern of giving away most of our energy. It will take some time and rewiring of our brains to see that when we take time for ourselves, we grow exponentially.

Which brings me to those who do their duty to their workplace and job. If you find yourself working several hours outside of your normal workday without extra compensation—this is a red flag that you have a problem. If you feel you are doing a two-person job, you probably are, and your employer will take advantage.

This can be compounded by having a boss who expects way more from you than you can physically do in a week, then they make you feel guilty or act passive aggressively towards you and your work. Plus, your work is often accomplished without any appreciation.

You could quit your job and find a new one, but until you break the pattern of doing your duty, you will continue to feel like you owe so much extra time to your employer. No matter where you work, you will eventually fall into the same pattern.

It is time for you.

~ CURRENT LIFE EXAMPLE: DONNA ~

Donna came to me frustrated with her relationship and her job. She felt like she gave all her energy to everyone and everything else. It had been years since she felt like she could sit and relax. She never took a vacation. She worked non-stop. She just found out that she had high blood pressure and her doctor told her she needed to learn how to relax to protect her heart. She laughed at the thought, but her concern about her heart brought them here. She had read several books on the healing and higher perspective on life that you can receive during a past life regression.

Donna wanted to try past life regression to see if it would help bring some clarity to explain why she did not relax.

She remembered a root cause for this issue when she experienced a lifetime as Gustav who worked himself to death. Gustav gave up his whole life to work for the queen.

~ ROOT CAUSE EXPLORATION ~

"I fell into a deep depression after my wife passed away. The day my wife died, I died emotionally. We never even had the chance to have a family. I soon realized that I needed to get away to find something else to focus upon, like a job somewhere new. I am an artist in my late 20s. I put word out that I am searching for work.

They move forward in time in that lifetime.

I see myself standing in a long line. It is hot outside, I sweat from fear compounded by the heat of the sun. I notice I am much shorter compared to most of the men in line. I straighten my vest, stand tall, clear my throat, and clutch my painting tighter to my side. I know I am a great artist. I feel confident.

The castle is looking for a small group of new artists. One by one we walk inside the front door. She sat there reviewing each piece. As I move nearer, I see her throw every rejected artist's painting into a large pile for garbage. She would yell, "Garbage," or sneer, "Novice," as she looked critically at each painting sample. Many men left crying. She was downright mean. I gulped. I had been summoned to come to this event therefore my only choice was to attend this harsh interview process. Several unsympathetic palace workers moved the artists along during the interview process.

I brought one of my best paintings to present to her. Clearly, she ultimately picked who would work for her. One of my artist friends told me what she desired in a painting. It was exceedingly difficult to be hired by the queen.

I had conflicting feelings as she picked me to be part of the painters' group. It was one of the few times I saw her smile. I am not acclaimed but my paintings were flawless, plus I had all the right the credentials. Once chosen, I reluctantly accepted the job. No one denied Queen Elizabeth anything.

They forced me to agree to castration, a requirement to work closely with her. I cannot believe I let that happen! They gave me alcohol to drink and a rag to bite. Two men roughly wound my balls up tight and simply whacked them off. They said in a week I would be alright. It took a solid month. I still cannot believe I agreed to be castrated!

I joined a roomful of painters. There were about ten of us when I started. As I walked into the room for the first time, they all looked up, nodded, and simply went back to work. That should have been a red flag to run.

We were forbidden to sign our names on any of the paintings. We all took turns in different roles during our time there. One man blended the paints. Another man would deliver the horsehair brushes—some of which looked like little baby brooms. I dreaded the task of gilding.

It became clear all of this was just for show. I hear the words, 'pomp and circumstance.'

I did not get paid much. Money did not matter though, I never had time to spend it. My fingers were permanently stained from the paint and ink.

Some of the paintings were tall, which caused me to continually walk up and down a ladder.

She expected perfection—everything had to be just so. It was ingrained in me that if I did not always seek perfection, I would die. The threat of death for imperfection gave me motivation to work harder every day.

A handful of paintings finished and approved sat in the midst of hundreds of unfinished or rejected work. New paintings would rarely come. We painted family portraits, large pictures, tiny pictures, portraits of the queen and more. Once she approved it, then we reproduced it again and again. There was always so much to do.

Every day I would paint from 6am until midnight since it had to be 'just so'. I often thought ahead to anticipate what she desired in a painting before she asked for it. This saved repainting it.

Some of the paintings were rejected. I had worked countless hours and a few years on one painting that I considered a masterpiece. After she visited for five minutes, she said it would have to be completely redone. I used to cry after she left but soon became numb to rejection. She was never satisfied. She would pick out things that no one would notice. She would point and say, "See, we do not want that to happen again." All because she missed a mistake in one of the paintings, once. She was mean.

I admire one of my works. It is a portrait of Queen Elizabeth I. Her dress has exceptionally large shoulder pads with lots of material ballooned around the shoulders. Then the dress puffed out excessively at each side at the hips but not in the back or front. The large decorative collar was very ornate. I made her look young and vibrant. She accepted this painting. I sigh in relief.

I gave up my whole life for that job. Painting never felt fun or enjoyable at the palace. I never again painted for myself. I never received fame or glory from all my hard labor. I succumbed to a miserable existence. I barely remember ever smiling. I worked nonstop for the last 20 years of my life.

I completely neglected myself. I continuously felt tired but tried my best to perk up if she stopped to see the progress of a painting. I stayed too thin for my short stature—I hardly took time to eat. I lost most of my hair years ago.

She would yell my name, "Gustav!" I would promptly rush to get done whatever she needed—even if it took all night. I became obsessed with pleasing her, I had no other reason to live.

Most nights, I would lie down with my paint brushes still inside my pockets, sleep, then return to work. Often, I had to be reminded to change my clothes and bathe, I worked so much.

My home was a 15-minute walk from the painting room in the palace. On my return, I trudged past some of my artwork in the hallway of the palace as I made my way to the artist's room. I glanced at them with less of a sense of pride and more of a feeling of disdain. My work was not openly appreciated, but she knew I was good at my job.

For the last five years of my life, I oversaw framing. During this time in my life, I felt sickly, so they gave me this easier task. I still painted too. My last day, I fainted, fell off the ladder, and cracked my neck. That fall caused my death in 1601 A.D.

Death brought me peace. My wife stood there, waiting for me in The Light. That brought an eternal smile to my face."

~ HEALING STEPS ~

Donna had equated rest and relaxation with death in this past life. We worked to replace that rule with a new one, "Rest and relaxation is beneficial to my health." Allowing yourself time to relax heals the Solar Plexus chakra plus is a great example of learning to set boundaries.

Several things were going on here. She gave up her sense of self. She put everyone else's needs first over hers. She worked endlessly trying to please everyone. Donna became acutely aware of the similarities in this past life as Gustav and herself now. She did not want to work herself to death again.

Gustav drowned his grief in his work. He never fully dealt emotionally with the death of his wife. I had Donna work with the angels to release the grief stored in her heart from this past life and replace it with healing love and light. Donna made the realization that she started this pattern in her current life after her mother died. We worked to release the grief from her mother passing too.

~ CURRENT LIFE EXAMPLE: KAREN ~

Here is an excerpt from my book *Life Is Just Another Class—One Soul's Journey Through Past Life Regression*. What I do not express in this book, in addition to all the healing that past life work has given directly to me, is the knowledge that I was repeating the duty pattern again in my current life. Healing my Throat and Solar Plexus chakra through remembering past lives provided me with the courage to end that relationship.

Remembering my past life as Rosalina Ornithadopoulos in 1449 A.D. became a catalyst to a major relationship change in my current lifetime.

Making the decision to leave a relationship is never an easy one, especially if children are involved. However, after clearly remembering that I coexisted with the same person again in this life and still felt the exact same feeling of being trapped and unloved, I became alarmed. I realized I repeated the lesson of doing my duty to a marriage certificate. The life lesson of healing my Solar Plexus and choosing to stand up for myself was incomplete from 1449 A.D.

After I left that relationship, several of my psychic friends commented on how they could hear that my spirit guides were so proud and happy that I chose me, I chose my healing, and my happiness. Leaving was hard, but I learned a deep soul growth lesson that was long overdue.

As Rosalina, I complete my duty towards my parents by honoring their wishes for an arranged marriage. The hardest memory was the realization that I willingly joined a loveless marriage. I do my duty to a relationship without love. I feel like a servant since my husband expects me to fulfill my obligations: to cook, clean, sexually serve, and then work to process all the olives we have picked. I feel such relief when I die. I did not have the inner courage to leave otherwise.

~ ROOT CAUSE EXPLORATION ~

"*The smell of baking bread fills the house. I take in a deep breath to absorb its essence.* "*Yum,*" *I exclaim. The olive bread smells marvelous as usual. I worked all morning preparing to bake it.*

I do not think I could ever get tired of olives—I grew up on an olive farm in Greece. Olive oil runs in my blood. I walk over to the stone cut fireplace in the main room and check on it.

The bread bakes on a large round rack situated above the stewpot in the fireplace. I move the stewpot over a bit on the metal bar to take it off the main heat of the fire. The stew tastes finished, so it just needs to stay warm while the bread finishes. The bread looks nearly done. I smile. I like cooking.

With the well up to the left of the house on the hill, cooking is far easier here than at my parent's home. A spring up on the hill delivers water to the well. The water tastes good, and I enjoy its convenience.

Later, my kitchen will turn into my bedroom. Sometimes I sleep next to the fireplace. I avoid going into Marcus' bedroom.

I grab the broom from the corner near the fireplace and sweep out some of the embers. I try to be careful not to get the embers near the wood flooring. Years of use has weathered the hardwood floors to a nice shade between dark brown and grey.

I stir the meat in my big black stewpot over the fireplace and take the bread off the rack. I decide it is time to eat dinner. I only need to tell Marcus it is ready.

I remove two dinner plates from the wall. I set the plates on the wooden table, straighten the chairs and head towards the door.

As I walk up the stairs to go outside, I reminisce about my life back home with my parents on the olive farm. I still miss living with them, even after all these years.

I go back in time several years to when I still lived with my parents.

I honored my parent's wishes and agreed to an arranged marriage with Marcus. He is at least twenty years older than I am. There is no love between us (not then and not now). I believe he jumped at the chance to marry me, not for love, but for the help. I think he just needs someone to cook, clean, and work with the olives. I can cook and clean—I never met a woman that could not. I already knew the olive business. Besides, I held a dowry of several olive trees and olive processing equipment.

My parents do not want me to be an unmarried woman; they thought the arrangement with Marcus would be best for me. My brother inherits the family farm and home since he is the only son. I have no place there once he marries. They gave me no choice in the whole situation. I agree because I feel like I must, for my parent's sake, not because I want to be a wife. I feel like my parents sold me into slavery. I cook, clean, and occasionally have sex.

None of it is fun when you have no connection with the other person. My work with the olives is the only thing that brings me joy.

I place my hand on my neck; I held all this bitterness in my throat since I had no voice in the matter. Where did the girl I knew go? Where did the real Rosalina Ornithadopoulos go? She was lost forever the day she married Marcus. I gave up on me, all in the name of duty.

Marcus beat me at first. He hit me repeatedly. He yells in my face. He wanted to make sure I knew my place in his house. I became complacent.

Marcus and I never have any children.

I always thought of myself as a good catch. I am a hard worker and a fast learner. I still feel young and pretty at forty-three.

I sigh, "There is nothing I can do now."

I peek out the door and look up the hill to see Marcus checking and picking a few olives off a tree. Up on the hill we cultivate a variety of olives. I smile as I gaze at the olive grove. We spend time each year pruning the trees to around ten feet high. It certainly makes our lives easier when it comes time to pick the olives.

All through the picking season, we harvest barrels and barrels of olives. Nearly every day is the same. I get up, make breakfast, put on my white apron (the one with the large pocket-like pouch), grab my short ladder and head outside to pick olives. It becomes repetitive going up and down the ladder all day to empty my apron's pouch and move to a new side of the tree. Sometimes I make a game of it. I have to, or else I think I would go crazy from the monotony. In the end, it is worth it. I love the olives so much.

I hold my hand up to block the sunshine from my eyes as I step outside the door. I walk up a few steps and yell up the hill, "Marcus, dinner is ready." He motions in acknowledgment. I can tell from his response that he will be a little while.

I sigh and pick up a freshly picked barrel of olives and bring it into the house for storage. I cannot believe it is time to process the olives again.

We store the barrels of olives in a room off to the left of the main room. We use this original part of the house for olive processing and storage.

The room at the end of the hallway is my favorite place to be. I walk down a few steps into the area and smell the delicious aroma. This room holds wooden workbenches that contain several wooden tools for processing the olives.

I walk back into the main room, only to be greeted with smoke. I panic. Marcus will be furious if the house catches on fire. I do not know what to do.

We keep a container of fresh-boiled water near the fireplace. We leave the container sitting nearby for drinks, so it does not stay full. I keep the prepared water in an old olive barrel that we have cut in half. I grab it and throw the little bit of water on the fire.

It does no good whatsoever. I look at the shelf of pillar candles on the left. None fell.

I shout, "What started this fire?"

I remember. I just swept out the ashes. Some must have been too hot. A smoldering ember reached the hardwood floor and started the fire; I can see the place it started, not far from the hearth. I think, "I should have been more careful."

I keep a second halved olive barrel container near the fire. I grab it, thinking it was more water and throw it on the fire. This had been a container of olive oil. The oil popped, sizzled, and spread fire all over the room. I scream, "Oh my God! No!"

I get down on my hands and knees to try to put out the fire. The smoke became thick the moment I splashed the oil on the fire. I cannot see where the fire spread. It is hot. I burn my hands, desperate to put it out. I cannot stop coughing from smoke inhalation. I try my best to extinguish the fire.

It is futile. I cannot breathe. I pass out, fall facedown, and die.

Everything happens so fast. The house succumbs to the fire.

I feel relief from the stress of the events only after I die. Still within in my body, I look up and feel no sorrow. I think Marcus will be miserable now that he must do all the work. He might be a little sad that I am gone, but not much more than that. He will miss my cooking.

Death becomes the only socially responsible, honorable way out of the binding contract with Marcus. I recognize Marcus as a man I had a similar relationship within my current lifetime.

I separate completely from my slumped over body and in spirit watch the main room burn. I see The Light and meet with a few of my loving spirit guides."

~ HEALING STEPS ~

I see my parents waiting for me. My parents apologize for arranging my marriage; they knew of my sadness. I forgive my parents for the marriage. I reply to them, "I know the relationship was meant for life lessons, not malice."

After visiting with everyone, I walk into the healing room where two angels work to heal me.

They stack several blankets on me afterwards, one for each color of the rainbow. Each color synchronizes with each of the main chakras.

As Rosalina, I always felt so bitter married to Marcus. I stored my frustration in my throat and especially in my voice, literally, since I had no say in the entire arranged marriage.

I pardon my brother for being the reason my mother decided to find me a husband. I forgive Marcus for his part in this arrangement. I forgive myself for giving up on me and becoming complacent. I release the pent-up emotions from my lungs and throat so I can now heal.

I thought that only through death could the duty contract be broken.

This is apparently not the case. While reviewing my Akashic Records, Daniel my spirit guide, showed me that had I summoned up the courage to tell my parents that I did not want to be part of an arranged marriage in the first place, my life would have been very different. Daniel showed me that, alternatively in that past life, I could have married for love.

This one alternative decision would not only have affected my lifetime as Rosalina but subsequent lifetimes too. Each decision we make affects what happens next in our current life and can reverberate throughout our next lifetimes. My advice: choose wisely.

While re-experiencing this past life, I was not aware that I was doing my duty to my parents. I actually thought that I was being taken care of and loved by my parents because they set up this arranged marriage. Meanwhile, had I said no, I would have enhanced my self-confidence, healed my Solar Plexus chakra, as well as found love.

It is our own free will to choose what direction we take in each life. Sometimes we make bad decisions. We can still learn from them, even if we do the learning five hundred years later.

~ AFFIRMATIONS ~

I am free
I am happy
I am confident
I say what I feel
I speak clearly
Others hear what I am saying
I can do anything
I can go anywhere
I can be with anyone
I am my own person
I am free to love anyone
I am empowered
Rest and relaxation are beneficial to my health

CHAPTER 8

THE NEED TO FEEL WANTED

Do you feel as though you are a puppet or marionette being pulled in all directions by others; often waiting for them to tell you your next move? When someone else is directing your life, it is unfulfilling. Sure, it may feel as though you are needed by them, and they are appreciative, but, in extreme cases, your life revolves around helping others. Do not get me wrong here; it can be very rewarding when someone is truly deserving of help, and they do not take advantage of you or are not enabled by your constant help.

There are some of us who live for others and live to help or take care of others. It is a red flag that you have gone too far when you realize that you repeatedly plan your life around how you can help someone and rarely take time for yourself. Now, that is when you know you have a problem.

Giving yourself away is similar to doing your duty to your spouse or family, except that in this pattern, you are freely giving your time and energy away to everyone and anyone else in your life.

Giving away endless emotional support, energy, time, money, and more is exhausting. Giving away money, gifts, and buying lots of things for others can have a negative effect on your own financial security.

Some help because they want to feel needed in a relationship. This may be conscious or subconscious.

We may have been taught to mother over people, to be givers, and most alarmingly, to not receive.

We perceive that this mothering we do makes us happy. It may seem that way but what happens in reality is that those who continuously do this pattern of taking care of others are physically, mentally, and emotionally exhausted at the end of each day.

Social rules are impressed upon us via television shows, advertising, and movies. Religious rules oftentimes push the tenets of giving selflessly and reward it; family pressure and family dynamics reinforces this teaching. The truth of it is, we must receive as much as we give in some form or fashion. It is the yin yang of life. It is not selfish to receive, it is selfcare.

We are energetic beings constantly striving to maintain and raise our vital energy so we can take care of others.

Energetic and emotional giving becomes hard to quantify because your own personal vital energy is the currency. Please cherish your vital energy as if it is equaled to any expensive, high-priced asset.

It is so important for us all to become more aware of our vital energy levels. Some of us give so much, so often, that we are constantly striving to maintain our vital energy. When our energy levels get too low, we become sick or depressed. You might often refer to yourself as burnt out.

An example of giving yourself away and not tending to your own needs may be something as simple as allowing yourself to sit and read a magazine with a nice hot cup of tea. It never fails, as soon as you get comfortable, someone calls you to help them. Maybe you need to drive them somewhere? You put your magazine down, let your tea get cold and run out the door. You get so involved in helping others that you no longer tend to your own simple needs and sometimes, your family's needs. Someone might support a needy child, friend, or sibling monetarily to the point of putting themselves in debt. You may make sure everyone in the family has a lunch packed each morning but do not pack one for yourself because you ran out of time.

Years later, you realize that you compromised your own hopes and dreams. You might say, "Well, I do not have any hopes and dreams," or "Helping others feels very fulfilling," as a way to rationalize it all.

Really, it is about balance. It is so important to maintain the balance within your group of mutually supportive and loving friends and family. When you support someone there should be support returned in some way. On a metaphysical level, this is called an energetic exchange. If you are always pouring your energy into someone else, and receiving nothing in return, who will be there when you grow depleted?

Sometimes we do too much because, deep down, we want to feel wanted or needed. We want for: undying love, affection, attention, sex, company—the list goes on and on.

We all want to feel wanted and loved. There is a point where some will search for any smidgeon of attention to feel wanted. This is especially obvious when the person you are with is narcissistic or selfish or is not good at expressing attention towards another.

Some will go to extremes to receive affection or to be noticed in a relationship. It is like going gambling. The win is when you get the reward of attention which can feel a lot like love.

When you feel unwanted by someone, let us say in this example, you are in a marriage that has fizzled out. You are trying to get his attention—you cook, you clean, you buy sexy lingerie, you learn new sex techniques, etc. You are hoping, maybe, any of that will bring you the reward of feeling close to your spouse.

It could work, but you are exhausted trying and clearly there is no effort on their part to go out of their way to respond with any of the following:

- "Yum. That was a really good dinner!"
- "The house looks fantastic!"
- "You look beautiful."
- "Make love to me."
- "Thank you."
- "I love you."

This is the type of person that spends barely a moment cuddling with you after they orgasm, never noticing that you have not had that same opportunity to cum. In this relationship, they do not ever notice, they assume this is what they deserve, and fall asleep right after they have orgasmed without noticing you did not even get off. It feels bad. You feel used.

You definitely feel completely unappreciated for the money and hours you spent on yourself to please them. There is no difference whether we are talking about sex, dinner, remodeling a room, landscaping, or anything else you try.

Where does the desperate need to feel wanted and loved stem from in your current life? Maybe your parents conceived you when they were not ready. Maybe your mother thought seriously about a planned miscarriage and was guilted into keeping you.

Maybe one or both of your parents expressed how they did not want kids and that you were a burden to them. Maybe you were killed by a parent in a past life and you are subconsciously picking up the feelings of unwantedness again in this life. It could even be brought to you by friends who drop you as a friend or being excluded from child groups and playdates.

Awareness is the first step to healing. When you make the choice to start taking your energy back and not continuously give it away, you will start to feel better emotionally and physically.

Think about your last three weeks. Take a notepad and write down all the things you remember doing for yourself in one list and then on a second list write what you did for others. Once you have that spelled out, put a guesstimate on your time involved doing things for others and then for yourself. Sleep does not count. Showering does not count. Taking a leisurely bath does count, but when you take work home and go beyond your normal hours without compensation that counts as doing for others.

There are only 168 hours available in a week. If you minus a 40-hour workweek, it leaves you with 128 hours. Remove the over 56 hours of average sleep and another 11 for showering and getting dressed and we are left with 61 hours. Deduct commuting to work for about 5 or more hours per week plus the 21 hours of eating and grocery shopping (more if you go out to eat) and we are down to 35 hours of free time. Do not forget housekeeping and a few miscellaneous tasks including pet care, lawn mowing, and more. What do you choose to do with the 21 hours you have left in one week? This works out to only 3 hours a day or way less if you spend time on social media.

Now go back to your list. If you are spending an average of 20-30 hours doing things for others without compensation (monetarily or energetically), that is a red flag screaming that it is time for a change.

~ CURRENT LIFE EXAMPLE: ALLISON ~

Allison came to see me for a reading. It took several tries to schedule something that would work into her calendar. When she arrived, she looked exhausted and mentioned all the endless errands she had just finished. It took a while for her to relax since she worried about a second list of items to do after she left the reading.

I tuned into her spirit guide, Cayden. He wore a tunic of yellow which is symbolism for his focus to help Allison with healing her Solar Plexus chakra. He showed me several of her lifetimes related to excessive giving. She had fifteen major lifetimes that were related to this issue. I asked Cayden to show me the root cause of this pattern of giving too much. He said that two lifetime reviews would help Allison understand this pattern.

~ ROOT CAUSE EXPLORATION ~

It was no surprise that her spirit guide led me to the root cause lifetime as a young female, Kiyah, forced into slavery. By the time Kiyah was only five years old, both her parents had passed. Her father died a few years ago from an accident. Her mother died from a blood infection caused by a deep cut from a broken vase. Neighbors found Kiyah lying over her mother's dead body, sleeping.

Orphaned, as a low-class ancient Egyptian, life would be difficult. Her neighbors took her to a government building where she could get food and a place to sleep in exchange for work. They immediately placed Kiyah into worker training to prepare for a life of work as a slave. By the time she turned seven, they considered her a trained slave. She worked long hours inside a large building on the outskirts of Cairo, Egypt.

She worked endlessly. She completely forgot how to have fun as a child, she only worked and slept. Her hair was long, black, and matted down from being unkept. One day they shaved her head so the bugs would not make a home there.

No one gave her the love and attention she deserved as a child. Instead, she was thrown in with a group of teen orphans turned slaves. They stayed in a large room filled with bedding on a cold floor.

Frequent beatings convinced her that she needed to serve others to avoid death. If caught taking a break of any kind, she received a beating. If late, she received a beating. She lived in constant fear of rest and often had nightmares about forgetting work. Resting and caring for herself remained forbidden. There was never time to bond with the other, older kids. They were in the same situation as her. The food provided once a day was reminiscent of mush. Sometimes they got lucky and had something green or a bit of meat.

Kiyah died at the age of twelve from internal hemorrhaging from a ruptured spleen related to a beating. She died believing she did not do enough for others. It felt like brainwashing."

Her guide, Cayden, showed me the second lifetime through more visions.

Allison lived the second example lifetime as a male during warring times in 535 A.D.

"Fire erupted in areas all around their town as many fought against the attacks by Huns. It appears the Huns were just looking for food supplies and clothing to prepare for winter. They wrecked deadly havoc for days as they collected supplies. One day, as the cover of the night sky came, the Huns retreated.

Fear prevailed. Many prominent men gathered late that night to discuss protection of the local towns. Soon, several local towns banded together to figure out how to fend off the Huns. These heated discussions lasted all night. Out of terror amongst the town leaders, they decreed that every male should serve in the war effort to protect their land by volunteering to serve in the military. They did not care whether they were boys or elderly men.

Nearly everyone knew battle against the Huns meant torture to the death. Volunteers remained scarce. Leaders made a law that forced joining their army mandatory and without complaint. As a young, male teen, Sergius joined. This new group of military leaders punished those who did not conform to the rules within the military. A position of control through fear forced them to keep incredibly strict rules. They often withheld food, severely scolded, or publicly scorned the men for not doing exactly what they were told. There was no rest for the weary. This meant that the abuse had to be accepted or death would occur, either through military leaders or the Huns.

Sergius sharpened knives and swords as his job in this new army. He worked from sunup until late into the night. His orders were to sharpen any weapon by the next day. Rest and food remained scarce as they prepared for the pending battle. He fell sick after obtaining tetanus through one of the frequent cuts on his hands. When a battle ensued, he participated as per the rules. Weakened from the illness and starvation, he had no strength to fight back. A Hun killed him within an hour of his first battle. He died believing he failed to work hard enough for his country and vowed to work even harder in his next life."

~ HEALING STEPS ~

See the pattern? Her past lifetimes revolved around extreme care for others. She endlessly worked taking care of others to prevent being killed, ostracized, or starved. She continues to repeat the pattern of only taking care of others in this life and avoids caring for herself.

I worked with Allison to forgive every aspect of her traumatic lifetimes to help heal her current life. We offered forgiveness to herself, all those involved in her past lives, the tetanus germs, the Huns, the swords that cut her and more to begin her healing journey.

The angels guided me to work with Allison to heal through soul retrieval.

Soul retrieval is extremely healing. When you experience a trauma, whether it is this lifetime or a past lifetime, you subconsciously set aside a small part of your energetic self. Remember, you are a large, beautiful, energetic being having a human experience. I see this small energetic part of you left behind for safe keeping wherever in time you left it.

When a trauma occurs, highly charged emotions can be so overwhelming that your subconscious reacts by preserving a piece of you for later healing. This separation of a piece of your soul happens because there is so much energy to the event that it is impossible to store it within your body, so it sort of explodes off you to be stuck in time and space. Sometimes these pieces include a talent, part of your chakra health, a creative aspect, or more. For Allison, she set aside her personal power to stand her ground for her rights as part of her Solar Plexus chakra. She also set aside her ability to enjoy life.

Allison had mentioned her concern that she had not had fun or genuinely laughed in an extremely long time.

We worked with the angels to help these lost parts of her energetic being to be reconnected and reintegrated into her. She could feel the energy pouring down in through her Crown chakra and integrating throughout her body.

In this life, she subconsciously tried to fulfill the duty to endlessly care for others, so people would stay in her life. She felt forced into caring for someone else endlessly. It exhausted her physically, emotionally, and spiritually.

First, forgive yourself. Taking care of yourself is part of loving yourself.

~ CURRENT LIFE EXAMPLE: SAMI ~

The feeling of being unwanted can stem from a past life in which you were blatantly unwanted.

Sami remembered a lifetime as a young child unwanted by her parents. In this lifetime, she had an unfounded fear that her parents were going to disown her. She did many things above and beyond necessary for her parents to prevent that from happening. Her parents would describe her as the perfect daughter.

Sami came to me for a regression to see if she could find the root cause of this fear. Even though she was 18 years old, she still felt like she had to prove she was worthy to be at their home. She was exhausted from working a full-time job, going to college, and then coming home to prepare meals and clean the house.

It took a little longer than usual for Sami to relax and allow herself to remember a past life. As always, I asked for her spirit guides and angels to help her. During the induction, I asked her to hand all her worries and concerns to the angels and to let them hold them while she allowed herself to have this experience. It was only then, that she found her first memory of a past life in an upper-class home.

~ ROOT CAUSE EXPLORATION ~

"I am four. I have on fancy clothes and feel very upper class. My parents kept a very busy social life here in London and did not have time to tend to me and my brother. Mother hired a wet nurse and a governess to take care of us day and night. The governess lived next to my room in our large house. My parents lived in a separate wing of the house, so they did not have to deal with the distraction of children. They had my brother and I because it was popular to do so, not because they wanted us. We were taught to be barely seen and never heard. The governess was mean to us behind closed doors. In reality she did not like children. She only took this job because she needed a place to live.

I remember a day she took me to church with her. I am hurrying to buckle my boots with a shoe tool. It was so hard to use. I got no help or sympathy from the governess, so I buckle enough of them to go. We walk very fast down a snowy street to the church. She warned me I would get the switch if I misbehaved.

The only time I saw the governess' loving side was when my parents requested us to visit with them. Normally, this occurred when company visited. The governess would be so nice to us during this short time. I pretended to feel loved even though I knew it was fake from my parents and fake from the governess.

When I was 8 years old, I contracted dengue fever. My brother caught the sickness when he played with a few children who were visiting from afar. My brother felt better after his fever broke. The governess showed anger towards me even when sick because it caused her more work. At this point in my life, I felt dead inside since I felt no compassion from any adult in my life. I died three weeks later feeling as though I was and would never be wanted.

After death, I was shown that the governess had once loved a child. This child died and broke her heart. It hardened her from loving any other child. I could feel her sadness and forgave her for what she did to me."

~ HEALING STEPS ~

To start, I had Sami focus on forgiveness. Forgiving herself, the dengue fever, her parents in the past lifetime, her brother, the governess and her body for not overcoming the sickness.

I asked her to find and locate anywhere she stored the feelings of being unwanted, abandoned, unloved, uncherished, abused emotionally and physically, feeling used, being a burden, anger, and any other emotions and trauma stored within her energy, to gather them up and pour or stream them out of her, out the window to the ground outside so they can be transmuted back into positive.

I asked the healing angels to pour pure unconditional love down through her whole body to help her heal and to raise her vital energy.

I brought to Sami's attention the connection between this past lifetime and her current lifetime. This brought catharsis and the realization that she did not need to work herself to death to prove that she was loved or wanted by her parents.

I took it one step further by having her spirit guides show her a few times in this lifetime where her parents showed her love and acceptance. I also helped her become aware of the loving energy her spirit guides and angels were showing her at this moment, so she could fully feel the amazing feeling of love.

~ AFFIRMATIONS ~

I only allow mutually supportive and loving relationships in my life
I only allow mutually supportive and loving experiences in my life
I love myself
I value my energy
I am worthy of receiving
I am open to receive
The energy I give is valuable
I appreciate a positive energetic exchange
I raise my vital energy more every day
I am more aware of my energy expenditure every day
I take care of myself in every way
I am wanted and loved

Chapter 9

Perfectionism and Being Type A

Let's make everything perfect.

Iron clothes, shower, and double check your clothes and hair before serving breakfast to your family. Review the day's schedule with everyone. Make the beds. Bake cookies for the kids. Have some quick sex to satisfy your partner. Clean up after everyone and verify that everything is in its place while making sure everyone is happy. All before heading to work for 8am. You are exhausted and the day has barely begun.

The problem is that perfection remains impossible. Something more can always be improved. While there may be others, I have seen one main root cause of perfectionism, which can be related to a Type A personality, having OCD (Obsessive Compulsive Disorder), being an overachiever, etc.

All this extreme effort to please others by exhaustive, meticulous work is to allow the perfectionist to receive some sort of glimmer of adoration, love or attention from their spouse, boss, friend, parent, child, and more. That attention keeps the fuel on the fire to keep moving and doing until you fall asleep, worn out from the day.

I found it goes deeper than that; way beyond the speck of love felt from doing so much endless work trying to make things perfect.

The root cause for perfectionism and Type A personalities seems to be rooted in feeling like a burden. What makes someone feel like a burden to your partner, boss, parents, etc. lies somewhere in your subconscious mind. If you clean, write reports, mow the grass, and bake cookies for the bake sale you can keep your job, be wanted in the relationship, stay in your family, or feel accepted by the other PTO (parent-teacher organization) parents.

Some of you are saying, "This is bullshit. I don't believe that." Yeah, I was there. I would have skipped to the next chapter already, but you are still reading because you want to heal too.

Maybe as a child, your parents worried endlessly about money and made you feel like you cost them a lot. Or your parents talked about you as a burden or frequently mentioned the monetary burden of a child and how expensive kids are. As a child, you take this personally and literally. All this talk of you costing them money became engrained into your psyche. Somehow, this burden feeling reconnected with a past life memory that reignited the pattern to overachieve to be accepted and loved. Now, on some subconscious level you must provide the endless service to pay for your cost.

Perfection is an impossible goal to reach. There is always something more you could have done or still do to make something better. Striving to be perfect all the time in all aspects of your life can become an unfulfilling obsession. It is mentally and physically exhausting to strive for constant approval by parents, approval by a spouse, or even approval by your boss. Perfectionism can turn into an addiction to achieve an unrealistic, unattainable goal.

Some ways to help tame the 'I can do it all,' perfectionist, Type A attitude is to prioritize selfcare and invest time in yourself. Practice saying 'no' more often as well as saying 'yes' to asking or receiving help. Create realistic personal goals and expectations and acknowledging that your to do list does not have to be completed all in one day. Learn to meditate and recognize that taking a break is time well spent on your own selflove.

In 2016, when I had my car wreck—and second near death experience—I seriously hurt my brain. Post-concussion syndrome is no joke. This whole experience could be a book. Talking to angels, seeing my future, and choosing to come back for more fun on Earth became the easy part. Relearning how to balance, focus, use depth perception, and not get nauseated with every flashing light, movement of any kind, or loud sound became quite the inconvenience.

I am a confirmed Type A personality. If you would have met me ten years ago, you would have become tired just hearing about my day. After this wreck, I had no choice but to learn to slow down, take it easy, learn to relax, and really understand that I do not have to do it all. Not the preferred way to learn for sure. I did not realize how much of a Type A personality I truly was until this experience. The time it took for me to heal from my head injury gave me the opportunity to do a lot of inner, personal healing. Do I still keep busy? Sure, but I definitely do not go at the crazy rate of speed I had worked (in all aspects of my life) before the wreck. Now, I get help to do a lot of things that I normally would have tried to do all on my own.

~ CURRENT LIFE EXAMPLE: KRISSY ~

Krissy came to me for a past life regression. Her hair was perfectly in place. Her purse and the color of her nail polish matched her outfit perfectly. She had everything planned out for the experience. She pulled out her notepad, pen, water bottle, and recorder. She did not want to impose on me at all, even though I write notes during the whole process for each person to keep. I was exhausted just looking at her, knowing the effort she went through to come to this session at 9:00 a.m. in the morning.

Note that most people come dressed in sweats and t-shirts to help them relax for a past life regression experience.

Krissy wanted to figure out what her passion should be since she felt pulled in so many directions every day. She felt she helped a lot of people in a lot of ways, but it all still felt unfulfilling internally.

Her spirit guides had other plans for her that day. They know where the deepest healing can be found. She remembered a past life as a burden.

~ ROOT CAUSE EXPLORATION ~

"I am crying. I am a baby who has just been born. They set me to the side of the room on a blanket on the floor. Everyone is around my mother. They try to save her to no avail. My birth took my mother's life.

It is medieval times in Ireland. I hear bagpipes playing in the background. My father traveled by boat for months at a time for his job. He returned two weeks after my birth to find his wife passed. He stayed home to care for me for nearly a month until the money practically ran out. Our nearest family was a distant aunt and uncle who were without children. We traveled several days to visit with them. My father gave them coins and other items so they would care for me until he was able to find a new wife. These relatives were not thrilled to be taking in a baby, but the aunt took pity on me. She convinced my uncle that the coins and other things would outweigh the cost of caring for me. They genuinely believed raising me would only last a short time.

My father tried to visit me frequently. He changed his job so he could visit more often. He always brought coins and such. My aunt and uncle enjoyed that dose of wealth.

I always enjoyed the loving visits with my father. He would care for me for a few days and then return to traveling on the boat. My aunt and uncle continued to agree to watch me while he worked.

I do not think my uncle worked much because of rickets; his bowed legs made it hard for him to walk. He seemed to be in pain a lot. My aunt worked in the fields nearby. My uncle sometimes sat and thatched wheat. The extra money from my father made their life easier. They sheepishly hid it from the tax collector.

My father came back every few weeks from his job as a trade route runner. He gave most of his earnings to my aunt and uncle in gratitude for their help. It was more money than they had ever seen before.

My aunt and uncle continued to agree to watch me.

My father visited for a few days when I was 6 months old. He brought gifts and a large stash of money. The aunt and uncle enjoyed the extra money and thus did not mind the chore of continuing to care for me. He told them he would be gone longer this time, but sadly he never returned. Unbeknownst to us, he died at sea. We never knew what happened to him and everyone assumed he abandoned me for a new wife.

The extra money ran out by the time I turned two. As I grew up, they despised me for this. They did not put me out on the streets to prevent gossip, plus they decided to use me as a slave for repayment of their care.

I do not remember my name since they only called me 'The Burden.'

By the time I was eight years old, I worked endlessly from sunup to sundown to cook, clean, garden, shop, sell, etc. to prove my worthiness and to feel some affection from them—which barely occurred.

I felt like a constant thorn in their side. I tried extremely hard to keep an uplifting attitude to get through each tiresome day. I felt I owed them for allowing me to live here. Of course, I was constantly reminded that I owed them.

It has been 16 years since my father abandoned me here. I only have a simple woven necklace with one small blue stone bead to remember my parents. When I touch my hand to the bead, it gives me strength.

That winter, in the midst of my two-hour walk down the hill into town, I slipped and fell on ice just as a carriage barreled down past me. It was carrying very heavy cargo and the thin spoked wheels ran over my legs cutting them off just below the knees.

A kind woman found me and immediately had the butcher sew up my legs into stumps. I screamed in excruciating pain. Word was taken to my aunt and uncle, but they wanted no part of an invalid and never came to fetch me.

The kind woman cared for me for several weeks while I healed. I felt deeply in debt to her and had no perceived way to repay her. She showered me with so much kindness, it became uncomfortable. I worried I would become a burden to her too, so I asked her to set me in the street. I told her, "It might be the only way for my aunt and uncle to find me," even though I knew they would not come for me. I lived on the street for about a year by crawling with my stumpy legs. With my tattered clothes and gaunt face, I became unrecognizable.

My stomach always growled of hunger even though I begged for food or work daily.

Starving one day, I stole a piece of bread. An upper-class man saw me. He called me, "A burden to society," as he hit me shockingly hard on my left temple. I slumped over, fell into a coma, and died."

~ HEALING STEPS ~

To assist Krissy's healing, I helped her focus on doing forgiveness work to release her from that traumatic connection. She forgave the aunt and uncle for their abuse. She forgave her mother and father. She forgave the driver of the carriage, the carriage, the wheels, and her legs for not being stronger. She forgave the man who hit her in the end. She forgave herself for not being self-confident enough to agree to stay with the kind woman who would have continued to care for her.

I guided her to gather and release all the pent-up emotions from this traumatic lifetime and asked for angelic healing. These feelings and trauma energy included feeling unwanted, abandoned by mother via death, abandoned by father via death, abandoned emotionally and physically by aunt and uncle, abuse, unworthiness, and the stored energy of pain in both of her legs. I had her ask the angels to replace these areas with pure love and light energy.

I helped her release the energy of the pattern of, "I am a burden and must prove myself, so I do not die," and replaced it with, "I am loved and accepted for who I am, and I am worthy of love." We worked with the angels to infuse self-confidence within her.

~ CURRENT LIFE EXAMPLE: RYLEE ~

Rylee came to me to explore why she was afraid of the water. A young mother of two, she was happy to get away from the house for a few hours to try a past life regression. Her husband encouraged her to come since her fear of water affected her ability to comfortably drive over the many bridges in Pittsburgh, Pennsylvania.

As she talked to me about her family, I became aware that she did the lion's share of work, tending to the house and children and more. She acted as though her husband would not normally have watched the kids, and this was a big deal for her to get out of the house alone.

Rylee entered the meditation walking down an illuminated path. There, she had the delight to meet with her grandmother who had passed over recently. This allowed for Rylee to heal some grief of her recent loss. They hugged and visited a bit. She told me that her grandmother said to her, "Everything doesn't have to be perfect, honey."

Rylee said she knew she was considered a Type A, but never thought about it as perfection. I asked her to ask her grandmother and her spirit guides to help her understand the message. As she continued down the path, memories came to her about a lifetime as a young girl in a seaport marketplace.

~ ROOT CAUSE EXPLORATION ~

"As I start to remember this past lifetime, the first thing I see is my body underwater, floating around near a school of fish and then two of my spirit guides coming towards me. I am drowning.

She is guided to go back to an earlier life-changing moment.

I see myself happy and living at home with my family. I am the middle child of five children. I just celebrated my tenth birthday, so I do not have a lot of worries in life yet.

Today, I am shopping with my mother in the big marketplace right alongside a port by the Mediterranean Sea. I liked coming along to help. My mother says I dawdle too much, but it is because I enjoy looking around at everything. There are so many smells and interesting things. My father bought the dress I am wearing at this market. I love the little blue flowers embroidered on it. Being here makes me smile.

The marketplace is very noisy, busy, and crowded today. People are so crammed in the walkway, that it is hard to move in some places. I see my mother getting further away from me, so I start walking towards her. It is my last memory of her.

Unbeknownst to me, a few men are standing nearby, scanning the crowd of people in the market. The older man is watching me. He was trying to find someone younger so they would not be sensual or feminine yet.

I was not aware they were stalking me.

Just as I walk into the crowd of people to find my mother, one guy puts his hand over my mouth. No one noticed I was trying to make a fuss, if they did, they probably thought I was being unruly. I am just a little kid in 1410 A.D.

They carry me like a satchel to their wooden boat. I kick and try to scream. The man carrying me says, "Shut up waif!"

Once onboard their boat, I never saw that market near those docks again. I suspect it was on purpose. I do not remember the name of my city, but I have fond memories of watching the Mediterranean Sea from the shore with my family. I miss them terribly. I was not allowed to talk about my family or where I came from. The owner enforced this boat-wide rule on everyone.

For 15 weeks, they only feed me a weird broth. It is not enough nourishment, so it weakens me and my spirit. They starve and beat me if I whine. They picked me up off the street to be put to work on this boat.

Ricardo is the owner and captain of the 75-foot-long boat. It was not an exceptionally large boat, but it was not small either. No one calls him captain; we all call him, "Sir." He expected to be respected or you get thrown overboard.

Normally between 12-15 people live and work on this boat. Workers come and go at each dock.

They never left me off the boat. For the first few years, they tied my wrist to a pole when we docked so I would not run away. Watching two feet from the side of the boat is the closest I would ever be allowed near land, otherwise I only saw glimpses of distant shorelines when out at sea.

I succumbed to doing my duty on the boat. I learned that continuous hard work avoids beatings.

I gave up on the idea of leaving. When I began to take initiative in helping, I became slightly more appreciated and did not receive beatings quite as often. We all worked day and night it seemed.

I always felt I had to constantly prove my worth so I would not get thrown overboard even though Ricardo said he appreciated my help.

Ricardo was strict with everyone regarding me—he told the crewmen to never touch me, even threatening castration. He was kind of a father figure, but extremely strict. He had me dress in the same kinds of clothes the men wore—complete with drawstring pants to make me appear less feminine.

I often tied my black, matted, straight hair in large knots to keep it out of my face and from being windblown all the time. It seemed futile to try to take care of it.

After a few years, it starts to feel like family. We all take care of each other.

They considered me the low 'man' on the totem pole, so I had many menial jobs. I cook, clean, do laundry, scrubbing and more. I clean so many fish that I am used to having several cuts on my fingers.

I remember a day I am making soup—I prepare it all, including the prep, serving, and all the cleaning up afterwards. I am constantly moving. I endlessly walk back and forth when serving and cleaning up. I try to make everything perfect.

On board the boat, they only kept a few awful tasting beverages because you cannot drink the seawater.

I realized one day that if I secretly collected rainwater to drink, I then had an alternative to the awful tasting drink. Water was normally reserved for cooking.

Around the age of fifteen, I learned that Ricardo had been married when he was younger. He and his wife had two children who both died as infants. His wife blamed him for the death of his children. Not long after the second child died, his wife found another man while he was at sea. When he returned home, his wife was pregnant with someone else's baby—he had been traveling too long for it to be his. She decided to have children with someone else.

He had serious trust issues. He is still bitter because of her infidelity and sad at the loss of their children. That day he found me; he was looking for someone who would have been around the same age as one of his kids, had they lived. He tried being fatherly towards me but always became abusive and awfully hard to please. I would pretend Ricardo saw me as his daughter. One time he bought me nice smelling soap, but it was probably in recompense for a beating.

Sometimes I relaxed by lying on the deck and watching the stars. I often ended up falling asleep listening to the peaceful splash of the waves at night.

I am now 17 years old. I do not feel I stay on this boat much longer. I started wearing dresses again as I became a woman—it was easier during menstruation.

An important job is the watchman. They always watched the weather and for other things out at sea from the highest point on the boat.

Saul, a young man in his 20s or early 30s, joined the crew on the boat. He became the night watchman.

He would do his turn on the watch and afterwards he and I would talk. It was nice to talk to someone around my age. Everyone was normally much older than me.

Romantic feelings started to happen between Saul and me.

One night, Ricardo saw Saul not doing the watchman job but instead kissing the top of my head. At first, he yelled at Saul because he was not watching, but once he realized that he was kissing me, he freaked out. Ricardo nearly beat Saul to death. By morning they had removed Saul off the boat. Since he was a newcomer, they left him for dead at the next port.

Several weeks went past. I became depressed that Saul had left. My work suffered. I cared about him more than I realized.

There were whispers the crew thought I was pregnant. I am quite sure I did not know how it happened. I was oblivious to my pregnancy. I started showing, which was completely unacceptable. Ricardo looked at me, pointed, and yelled, "This young girl has been soiled!"

Once the boat sailed far enough away from the port and the land—Ricardo confronted me about Saul and my ever-growing soiled condition. I did not understand his accusations because no one ever explained it to me, I have not spoken to another female in seven years.

There was no privacy on the boat. Nowhere to have private sex, even if I knew fully what that entailed. It does not feel like it happened. Ricardo was already furious and became more enraged when I did not understand this accusation. As he began to beat me and yell about how I avoided doing my duty to the ship lately, he knocked me overboard into the sea. I drowned as soon as I hit the water. I fell in such a way that I was overcome with water in my mouth and in my lungs.

I knew I had died once I noticed the bubbles floating up gently in the water and saw the movements of a nearby school of fish. I watched the fish peck at my body as it floated down into the depths of the sea. I felt this was unjust punishment for being pregnant.

Two of my spirit guides are nearby ready to help me into The Light.

I have been working on the boat nonstop since I was 10 years old. I learned that if I stopped working, I would die. This was reinforced when I was knocked overboard when my work slowed down."

~ HEALING STEPS ~

We do forgiveness work. I have her forgive herself, Saul, Ricardo, her mother. She forgives the water and the fish. She forgives the baby.

I have Rylee ask her spirit guides to help her break any rules, vows, or contracts of working to prevent death and to replace them with affirmations that she is worthy of love, she is wanted, it is safe to work and to play.

I have her release any pent-up emotions within her energy and allow the angels to fill her energy with healing pure love and light.

~ AFFIRMATIONS ~

I am worthy
I am loveable
I only allow mutually supportive people in my life
I am strong
I am capable
I am open to receive in all ways
I am open to receive help
The angels support me in all I do
I am allowed to relax
Relaxing is fun
I am loved
I am good enough

Chapter 10

Silent Partner. No Voice. Not Being Heard. Be Quiet!

SShhhh. Be quiet. Do not make a sound.

Internally, your mind has a million conversations and thoughts happening, but none are expressed.

It often feels like you are somehow not allowed to speak. Even if you do speak, then it feels like you are not heard.

Is it that you are introverted, or does it go deeper than that?

Your voice, itself, is often described as soft-spoken or as having a sweet little voice. Someone might have called you mousey.

Some people I have met have been born into families where they were not allowed to express. One or both of their parents yelled a lot, expected them to be quiet, or hit them when speaking out of turn. Worse yet, I have met some people who were beaten if they tried to express anything.

Some were not allowed to express any emotions outside of a stoic range. No loud laughter, no crying, no screaming, etc. allowed. They were told to be quiet, sit still, and do as they were told. It is the old adage that children should be seen and not heard.

As a child, things that are said to you are programmed into your psyche.

As we develop and grow from a baby into a teen, our brain goes through different stages of growth too. From birth until around the age of eight, our brains are mostly in a theta state. In this state, things that are said stick in our minds like computer programming code.

Keep in mind that we normally, as adults, go in and out of the theta state all day. Our brains are in the theta state as we fall asleep, read a book, watch a movie, drive a car, etc.—anytime we get so engrossed we forget we drove home or are surprised when someone walks into the room—that is the theta state.

The theta state also occurs when we meditate or are hypnotized to remember a past life. It allows for focused concentration of the task at hand. The theta state is the same brainwave state where a person can accept a post-hypnotic suggestion.

As a child's brain grows, it stays in the theta state. According to Bruce Lipton, as written in his book, Biology of Belief, nearly everything that is said to a child is programmed into them as fact, up until around the age of eight. It is similar to writing a computer program into a child's psyche.

Be very mindful of what you say to any child. Many words could negatively affect a child as they grow into an adult. This warning should be written in the thick handbook that ought to come with all babies.

The programming to 'be quiet' affects how we effectively communicate and express ourselves throughout our life.

Some believe that the purpose of adulthood is to undo all the programming that happened as a child.

Not feeling like you can speak or be heard is directly related to Throat chakra damage. It could be very specific on what you speak about or to whom. Some people with Throat chakra issues wear a lot of scarves to cover that chakra—like protection. Some lose their voice a lot, have jaw pain, stutter, or often have neck pain. Issues with any chakra can express in the physical.

Think back through your life. What comes to mind as you read through this chapter? Are you able to speak how you feel to your partner, child, or parent? Are you having a hard time speaking to just men? Just women? Have you told everyone else, even strangers, that you want a divorce, except for your partner? Do you spend hours going over in your mind what you should have said, or wished you had said, in response to someone's remarks?

Where did the pattern of not feeling as if you can speak begin? I believe it could originate in a previous lifetime and can be compounded in this current life.

Practice strengthening your Throat chakra by wearing blue, eating blue things, singing, saying how you feel, writing how you feel, etc. Expression helps to heal your communication ability.

~ CURRENT LIFE EXAMPLE: JOLENE ~

Jolene came to see me for a past life regression. She was very shy and hard to hear. I had to strain to listen to her talk as we discussed her intent for the session. It was as if she was afraid to be heard. She wanted to strengthen her Throat chakra to communicate better with her girlfriend. She remembered a lifetime related her intent for healing.

~ ROOT CAUSE EXPLORATION ~

"I am a male back in the Middle Ages. The year is 1310 A.D. I am 35 years old and somehow, I am involved with the ruling power in the area. A new king took the throne recently. Many loved him, but I saw him in action as his true self and not how he presented the façade of himself when in the public eye.

The king would give inspirational speeches. The common theme was clearly inspiration to pay more taxes to the kingdom.

I spoke out about the new king's shortcomings at a town meeting one day. This did not bode well. I fled the land and went to a nearby city just outside of my English kingdom's territory. I worried my hometown would fall to ruins with the new regime. Higher taxes by the king often brought even higher taxes in my town.

I spoke to several officials in this neighboring town (outside of the kingdom) to see what action could be done to prevent this disservice to the townspeople. I felt deeply passionate about it. I had seen the plans to collect twice the taxes from the townsfolk. This high tax would bring about an economic downfall in the area.

I stood on a box and spoke in the streets about this issue. I feel like some people looked at me as if I were crazy, but others who had relatives in my hometown were appreciative of the information. Some told me they helped their family move to a new place.

Local supporters would provide me food and shelter. I had no family of my own. My parents were long gone.

About six weeks after I left, guards from the tyrannical kingdom grabbed me from my box and took me back to my old town to be sentenced to death.

According to them, it was treason to speak out against the king."

~ HEALING STEPS ~

Jolene felt a dull pain in her throat when she re-experienced her death in that life. I had her bring her focus on her throat area and to remove any energy of trauma, emotions, and words left unsaid from her throat. Her death formed trauma in her Throat chakra which directly affected the loudness of her voice. We asked for the angels to help with her healing as well.

Her spirit guides said that Jolene needed to practice speaking their truth by saying how she really feels to her girlfriend. This would strengthen her voice. They suggested she repeatedly say the mantra, "I speak clearly."

I guided Jolene to do forgiveness work by forgiving her parents for not listening to her as a child, forgiving herself, and forgiving their voice. I helped her forgive herself in this past life, forgive the king, forgive the guards, and forgive the men who carried out the sentence of death.

~ CURRENT LIFE EXAMPLE: CHLOE ~

Chloe came to me for a reading. She wanted to understand why she could not seem to say how she really felt to her husband of five years. She felt afraid to say anything to him outside of their normal conversations. However, with her friends, she could talk to them for hours about all sorts of subjects. It was confusing to her since her and her husband had a great relationship otherwise. He was not abusive and sounded nurturing. She could not find a cause in this current lifetime.

We asked her spirit guides to show her a lifetime that would help explain to her why she held back conversations with her husband. They showed her she had a history of this pattern with men throughout this lifetime. She asked her spirit guides to show the root cause lifetime to help her heal this Throat chakra issue.

Chloe entered a past lifetime.

~ ROOT CAUSE EXPLORATION ~

"I have lived my whole life devoted to the gods of nature. My husband also believed in this as well, as did both our families growing up. I taught our young daughter to connect to the love radiated by nature, whether it came from the trees, the wheat, or the sun above. In the past few years, there has been a movement to forbid this common belief. I saw no harm in it. Communing with nature united our energies to confirm the interconnectedness of all that is. Connecting to nature enhanced our intuitive abilities.

The push to make this belief punishable by law affected our community too. I heard many died over their beliefs. I was aghast at the thought of anti-paganism. How could the one true God punish anyone with death? It became common knowledge that local authorities and some religious leaders profited from this radical change.

Any information on pagan beliefs, written word, ceremonial objects were buried for safe keeping.

I am outspoken against this change. I do not understand why it was bad to feel love from the plants, trees, and the radiant sun. Some saw this as praying to multiple gods.

Fear spread in our community as many believed the same as me. They said it could be construed as heresy. A militant group came into town to remove all forms of pagan beliefs and objects.

No one wanted to die that day and submissively gave all pagan related items away to the militant group or buried any suspect belongings.

I stood in disbelief near a group who idly watched the proceedings from afar. I started to yell at the group, "We should do something! This is wrong!" The group's fear enticed them to throw stones at me, to stop me from making a scene and attracting attention this way. They said, "Shh! Shut up! Stop! Helen shut up!" My husband heard the ruckus and came out of his butcher shop wielding a knife.

Enflamed in anger by my actions, he said, "I will shut her up!" He took his knife and jammed it down the front of my neck, slitting my throat.

I could no longer speak or breath. The militant group off in a distance looked over this way, but the crowd hid my demise. I saw the militant group turn and continue walking in the opposite direction as my body slumped to the ground. Once the militant group went out of sight, my husband buried my dead body, along with any of our pagan possessions and remnants of my belief in nature's love energy, deep in the nearby woods.

As Helen took her last breath, she saw her spirit guides. They helped her to walk into The Light. Once she entered the greeting room and spoke to several passed over friends and relatives, she was able to work to heal her energy."

~ HEALING STEPS ~

Three healing angels come to greet her and provide healing unconditional love energy to her. One angel uses blue light energy to heal her in the Throat chakra area more precisely.

I guided Chloe to collect and gather any pent-up frustrations, emotions, trauma, resentments, etc. stored in her energy and for her to release it outside, allowing it to go down into the ground so it can transmute back into positive energy. The angels then sent more healing love energy down through her body.

I have her forgive herself, her beliefs, her husband in that past life, the knife, the metal of the knife, the group of people who threw stones at her, the stones, the militant group—and the people who sent them there to her community.

Lastly, I have Chloe send lots of love to her throat to help heal and release her subconscious rule, "I cannot speak my truth to my husband or else I will die." We rewrite that rule with, "I communicate with ease to everyone."

~ AFFIRMATIONS ~

I communicate with ease
I have permission to speak
I speak with clarity
I speak from the heart
The words I say are heard
I speak with ease and grace
I speak clearly and concisely
There is power in my voice
My Throat chakra is healed

Chapter 11

Are You Drained?

Have you ever had a partner where you felt exhausted nearly every time you are around them? Then you go outside, be creative, hang with friends, feel revitalized and then, the moment you are in contact with your partner—even if it is just on the phone—you feel exhausted again. You notice that it is actually more invigorating to do housework than hang with your partner.

So how does this occur and why do you continue to let it happen? Let's start with your partner (keep in mind this could be your spouse, lover, friend, coworker, neighbor, family member, etc.). When they grew up, they oftentimes had one of two common things occur. (There are way more examples, but these two are common ones I have often seen during intuitive readings.)

One, their parent(s) doted on them and gave them attention for everything they did or needed. These poor saps never learned how to raise their own vibration of vital energy within their being. They were taught to run to mommy or daddy for all their emotional needs and never learned how to make themselves feel better. Sometimes they became narcissists.

Two, they might have had a depressed parent or a parent with exceptionally low self-esteem. Negativity ruled in their household. This parent barely took care of themselves and unwittingly never taught their child any coping skills. This person learned victim mode and was taught that someone or something else needed to make them happy.

Now you, on the other hand, have probably been taught to be a giver, nurturer, mothering person, or are naturally helpful in nature. If you were born in the 1980s or before, and especially if you are female, you may already be acutely aware of the social conditioning to be a giver. Watch nearly any of the movies, television shows, or advertisements from the time that radio and television first started airing until at least the 1990s and you will see that nearly all portray women as weak, subservient, helpless, or serve only as caretakers. These leading ladies always decline (with grace and poise) any accolades or reward for their help. These ladies, oftentimes, just do it out the kindness of their heart. Combine that with the rules of religion, which dictate that we must give and give and give, but it is a sin and selfish to receive.

Top all that off with family dynamics of women treated as less than men. Especially if you are an older sibling, it was expected of you to take care of the younger siblings, to help tirelessly around the house, work hard, and more, while the men were permitted to put up their feet and be waited on by the women after they got home from work. Just watch one "Leave it to Beaver" or "I Love Lucy" episode to see this family dynamic portrayed. In the workplace, women today must work harder and prove themselves more often, all while still getting paid less.

Essentially the feeling of being drained can be explained with the visualization of a simple water bottle. First, you must recognize that we are energetic beings wearing a physical 'meat suit' of a body. To sustain this physical and energetic body, your vital energy must be maintained.

For this analogy, the vital energy will be the water and the bottle will be our physical body.

We each must maintain a certain level of water energy in our physical bottle. If the water energy drains all the way down, we become sick. Deplete the water energy completely and we die from exhaustion. We are in a constant state of ebb and flow of vital water energy in and out of our human physical bottle. Raising your vital energy is sort of the same as raising your vibration.

When we spend time in meditation, walk in nature, be creative, sing, immerse in music, or doing something we love, we are essentially raising our vital energy and pouring our water energy into our human bottle. When we give, we are pouring our energetic water out into another person or experience. Sometimes, this is conscious, sometimes it is subconscious. What the draining folks do to those who keep their energetic water levels high, is to literally feed off our energy. Think of them as a syphon, a drain, or an energetic vampire. They may or may not realize they are doing this. I have heard some people actually use the words, "I just called to hear your voice and get some of your good energy." Beware, that is clearly a red flag that they are a draining person.

We commonly use words in everyday life to describe the levels of our vital energy in our human bottle. When you are in love, you are vibrating at the highest level and are often described as: high, on cloud nine, raised up, beaming, etc. When you are vibrating on a low energy level, you are often described as: depressed, low, blue, dark, hit rock bottom, etc.

How do you raise your vibrational bottle of vital energy?

Do things that make you smile. Listen to music you enjoy. Meditate, even for just a few minutes. Spend time enjoying nature. Sing and feel the vibration of the music. Dance and move to the beat. Drive with the windows down in the car with music blaring. Walk, jog, workout—exercise and get your heart pumping. Be creative! Write, paint, sculpt, scrapbook, macramé—create anything! Take time to socialize with your positive loving friends. Consider all the things in your life that fills you with gratitude.

Participate in anything that makes you feel good. When you focus on positive things and feel in complete gratitude, you will continually raise up your vital energy. After focusing on or participating in an uplifting activity, it will feel like you received a surge of positive vibration.

Things that will deplete you include: fear based anything, the news, horror movies, negative people, negative places, negative things, self-deprecation, etc. If you are constantly around people who talk about how sick they are, how sad they are, and/or how much they hate life, this will consistently drain your energy. Do not let negative people, places, or things suck you into their world.

How can you change this? Change your scenery, change who you talk to, redirect the conversation to something positive to break the negative banter. I have even gone so far as to cut off their litany of negativity and ask them, "Can you tell me what made you smile today?" This often changes the mood of the conversation to positive. Sometimes people just get into the bad habit of constantly being negative to play out their victim role often taught to them as the only way to get attention from their parents when young.

Being in a draining relationship is never healthy. It is literally physically, energetically, and mentally exhausting.

Think back, how did you end up in this repeated pattern of giving away all your energy?

Some parents coerced their children to do things for them by guilting them or making them feel like they needed to do something for them in order to win their love and affection—i.e., conditional love.

An alternative outcome of growing up with a depressed, negative, or victim-mode parent, you were taught that when you took care of that parent you were rewarded for what you did for them. Even if it was only a smile or a thank you. Sometimes this was the only attention you received from this parent. People do what they think they need to do in order to get attention in a relationship.

Somewhere, you were taught the pattern that you had to give your energy away to those you love in order to receive love from them. Working on healing your selflove, self-confidence, and increasing your selfcare will help you.

While all patterns could stem from this lifetime, there are definitely types of lifetimes that make this pattern feel comfortable. Some past lives that resonate with the pattern of allowing your energy to be drained include slave, maid, nun, monk, or servant lifetimes. In these types of lifetimes, we were forced to give away our energy or we would be beaten, starved, or killed. Be cautious, these types of lifetimes and feeling this way in this lifetime can cause you to be thrown into victim mode.

~ CURRENT LIFE EXAMPLE: TARA ~

Tara had dated several people so far in her life. During a psychic intuitive reading she was provided the information that nearly every person she dated was draining her energy. Some of these people were even considered psychic vampires (subconscious experts at draining other people's energy).

In this lifetime, she grew up in a devoted religious family. As the eldest of four, she was expected to help take care of her younger siblings each day.

Tara came to the reading appointment looking exhausted. After a review of this lifetime, including the cutting of several cords of attachments, we proceeded to review the lifetimes that could have started the pattern.

The root cause of Tara's pattern of allowing others to drain her started when she was an 8-year-old boy back in Egyptian times in 1200 B.C.

In that lifetime, Tara, as a boy, was sold into slavery along with his parents who could no longer care for him or his siblings because of a debt. His name was Okno. Okno was not used to being a slave—which caused him to receive a lot of beatings. At 18, Okno died due to a wound infection from a beating with a metal barb. He died believing that he was only rewarded for giving his time and energy away, otherwise he would be abandoned or beaten.

~ ROOT CAUSE EXPLORATION ~

"I woke up to hear my parents answer a loud knock at the door of our make-shift home. I peek to watch since people rarely come by to visit.

Our family is extremely poor. I am hoping they are dropping off food. I am only five years old, and I am hungry. We have only had a porridge-like meal once in the last few days.

My parents asked me to come to the door. Two men look at me, lift my arms up, and feel my belly. They turn me around to look all over my body. I feel very confused by the strange rough treatment. The men look at each other and say, "He will work." My mom has tears in her eyes as they tell me to go along with them; at the same time, a small bag is handed to my father.

I have no idea what is happening.

Hours later I am put into a group of other boys in a large room. They shave our heads and have us walk through a large public pool to kill off any bugs like lice. It made us smell medicinal but nice. Getting twenty disillusioned kids to take a bath took a while. They taught us that we had to do this each morning at sunrise.

They then handed us white wrappings to wear and showed us our sleeping quarters. This room was big enough for our entire group. They had us sit against the wall. Two men walk down the row of boys and ask each one of us our name. I say, "My name is Okno," as I shyly stare at the floor while speaking.

I glance at the whimpering boy next to me and try to stay strong.

They began to teach us about our new jobs. Since we were kids, they made it seem like fun jobs which was better than having a group of whiny kids realizing they had just been sold into slavery and would never see their parents again. When someone would ask about their parents, they would respond by saying, "They sent you here to be taken care of better, IF you do your work."

At least they served us two meals a day. A kind lady would drop off our meals outside of the sleeping quarters before and after work.

We were put into groups, determined by our duties, to learn to care for this large mansion. This place was overwhelming; I thought for sure I would get lost.

I finally fully realized I was a slave one day. Exhausted, I stopped working to take a break. I sat down and nodded off, taking a nap. I awoke to being harshly beaten with a switch while hearing them yell, "Wake up slave boy!" My job was to repeatedly dust and clean one long passageway. We never got the chance to play. While cleaning, I would make up stories in my head as I moved down the hallway. Sometimes my stories would include small pieces of lint as characters who helped me clean.

I never adapted well to the life of a slave and would get into trouble often, which would always include a beating of some kind. I tried to escape to no avail. Around the age of ten, I found out that the rest of my siblings and parents were also put into slavery at some other manor. Every day consisted of giving all my energy to my work and my employers. I was mentally, physically, and emotionally exhausted by the end of the day. I was so tired.

My final beating was around the age of eighteen. I had tried to escape for the tenth time and failed. The branding mark, located on my neck, always gave me away. I would be promptly returned for a reward. That night, two caretakers unwittingly punctured my lung while beating me with a metal barb.

I died a few hours later. I never felt like I was allowed to have fun or rest, ever."

~ HEALING STEPS ~

I asked her spirit guides if there were any other lifetimes where Tara was abused in some way for not providing service to others. They showed her a second lifetime, born to a Russian Tzar.

In that lifetime, while she would never be put in power, she was groomed to constantly believe that she was never allowed to do anything for herself. It was ingrained in her that she was born to provide for the people of her nation. She was constantly reminded that she must give her life for the people. She had to behave a certain way, dress a certain way, and speak a certain way. If she would step out of line, she would be severely chastised for it. She was told what to do all day long, even who her friends could be. She was never allowed to speak to or date men. She was unhappy internally but had not been permitted to show any emotions. She often cried herself to sleep. Even though she was the daughter of a great man, she felt enslaved. She died giving up her sense of self.

We worked with the healing angels to provide pure unconditional love energy to Tara. I asked Tara to feel and collect all bottled-up emotions, resentments for enslavement, guilt, anger, and traumas so that she can release them from her energetic being. The angels filled her with the healing energy as she released it all.

She worked to forgive her father, the Tzar. She forgave herself. She forgave the slave owners. She forgave her parents for abandoning her. She forgave those in her current lifetime who made her feel less than or drained. Forgiveness is not saying what they did was ok, but to release you from their draining ties.

I had her re-write her pattern, "I must serve others endlessly;" with "I respect myself, my emotions, and my energy."

We cut cords with anyone and everyone in her current life and anyone who came up in a past life that drained her. I suggested she memorize the mantra, "I only allow mutually supportive and loving connections in my life."

~ CURRENT LIFE EXAMPLE: ISABEL ~

Isabel visited me for a past life regression. She had no particular thing she wanted to focus on but trusted that her spirit guides would lead the way. She explained that she felt tired all the time and wondered if something would come through for that issue.

Isabel was taught to give herself to others as a nun in this past lifetime as Sister Margaret.

As she described her current life, she told me that she grew up in a very strict religious family. She moved out as soon as possible because her mother enforced so many rules, it was exhausting. She still dutifully visited and helped her mother as often as she could, but never had the energy for much more than a few days a week.

Isabel rarely dated and hoped something would help her open her heart to future relationships.

~ ROOT CAUSE EXPLORATION ~

"I see myself as a young girl wearing a loose brown dress. I realize right away that my family is not well-off at all. It is 1565 A.D.

I smile as I sit next to a young boy near some bushes behind my house. We think we are hidden from view. We giggle, flirt, and quietly talk about all kinds of topics.

I blush as he leans over to kiss me as he puts one hand on my cheek. Just as this occurs, my mother comes around the back of the house while chasing a chicken. She quickly stops worrying about the chicken and becomes furious at seeing us kiss.

She grabs the boy by the ears and pulls him to his feet to forcibly walk him away from the house and down the road. I hear her screaming at him and forbidding him to return.

Warm tears run down my face as I watch in disbelief. I stand motionless, not knowing what to do.

My mother returns, beats me relentlessly, and lectures me on the evils of boys and kissing. The next day she grounds me to the house to do a long list of tedious chores while she runs an errand. Later that night, I heard my parents arguing about me.

I quickly find out that my mother went to visit the local church to pray for me and then discuss my chastity issue with a local religious advisor.

A couple days later, I woke up to find my mother packing a few of my things in a bag. She told me to clean up and get ready to leave their house. There was no arguing with my mother.

A few hours later, I stepped foot onto a carriage without even a goodbye. I heard her tell the driver to deliver me to the nunnery located right outside of London, England.

My parents were extremely religious, and any sexually related contact was strictly prohibited; especially at the age of twelve.

I think longingly about my one and only kiss. It will be my last.

The bruises from the beating still burn on my body. Each time the carriage bounces, it hurts. I will never forget the look of rage in her eyes as my mother tried to beat the devil out of me. My mother felt a nunnery would heal me and cure me of the devil's influence. By the end of the severe beating, I believed her.

As the carriage drove up to the nunnery, it appeared even more cold, stiff, and unemotional than I imagined. I step out of the carriage and then watch it slowly drive away. I turn to look at the door to the nunnery. I reluctantly go inside since there was no other place to turn.

I walk into the nunnery alone and sense an unwelcome feeling. I walk down the long, cold, empty hallway. I wait by the main room door. Hours pass.

One nun notices me slumped against the wall. She angrily walks towards me. I stand up quickly and tell her I was sent here to live.

She was appalled at my appearance. She promptly prepares me to meet Mother Superior. She said, "You need to appear proper." She cut my hair extremely short so it could easily be concealed by their head coverings. She shows me no compassion and barely spoke as she dressed me for Mother Superior. She groans and muttered, "Tsk-tsk," at my appearance as she worked to bind my breasts. She tossed my clothes in the garbage. Once she finished, she gave me a plain, long black dress to wear and a large wooden cross pendant that dangled on a piece of leather to hang across my chest. She told me this would be my habit. I had no idea that she meant 'my dress.'

She did tell me that her name was Sister Alice when she handed me a glass of water and a small piece of bread. I sat and waited.

Hours later, I met Mother Superior. She greeted me with the same pithy, repulsed reaction as Sister Alice—even in this attire. I recited a few prayers my parents had taught me to her. That seemed to soften her a bit.

Sister Mary put me right to work in the building. I scrub floors, pray, help prepare food for our meager meals, pray, weed and care for the garden, pray, wash and hang clothes, pray, take care of the chickens, and then pray some more. I went to bed tired and hungry every night. The nuns said this would bring us all closer to God.

I spent a lot of time outside taking care of the animals and the garden. Every other day, a few of us would walk around the land that surrounded the nunnery to harvest berries and gather food. As I looked around the countryside surrounding the nunnery, there was nothing but tree-filled hills and valleys as far as I could see. It is almost as if we were out in the middle of nowhere. Even though there was nothing preventing me from leaving, I had nowhere to go.

Only a few select nuns are permitted to go into town. About once per month, two of them would travel into town to sell their religious embroidery work. They would then purchase supplies for the nunnery. They were always asking for help in exchange for prayers. People would bring us fish and other items for prayers.

One man brought several blankets in exchange for prayers for his wife. We prayed for him and his wife for several weeks that winter.

I feel like an indentured servant. It is only on rare occasions when we share idle conversations and even rarer for somebody to smile. God forbid if you laugh. The silence was deafening.

Years pass by. I became accustomed to living as a nun. They now call me Sister Margaret. I work endlessly and use all my free time to pray for others. It was drilled in our heads that we should never be selfish in any way as it was a mortal sin.

I never heard from nor saw my parents again.

I never left the nunnery and died in my sleep around the age of 56. Mother Superior greeted me in The Light. She had died years ago. We had become close over the years."

~ HEALING STEPS ~

Isabel worked with her spirit guides and angels to forgive her current day mother and her mother in her past lifetime. She forgave the nunnery, the boy she kissed, herself, and the kiss. She symbolically tore down the unseen walls that barred her from leaving the nunnery. These torn down walls became a personal symbol of her venturing out more socially.

Isabel's next step was to learn how to be open to receive in all aspects of her life. Being open to receive strengthens the Solar Plexus chakra by practicing the use of her personal power. Balancing your energy with being open to receive while setting good boundaries on excessive giving can be deeply healing.

In her past lifetime as a nun as well as her current one, Isabel was not allowed or permitted to be herself. She was forced to give her time and energy to others and taught it was unacceptable to receive or be happy.

Her spirit guides requested her to begin by having a loving relationship with herself. She could choose to do this in several ways—one was to be creative. When you take the time to be creative, like when you paint or write, no one can tell you what color to choose or which word to write. You are essentially creating only for you, by yourself. Her spirit guides gave her suggestions on ways to pamper herself.

The most important homework assignment from her spirit guides was to be acutely aware of when others drained her energy. She had to practice saying no to anyone or anything draining. This also gave her the opportunity to learn how to feel when someone or something uplifted her energetically.

This was a major change for her. She told me later that this homework from her spirit guides slowly helped her learn to discern healthy relationship traits and patterns. It is only when you love and respect yourself that others will as well.

~ AFFIRMATIONS ~

I am whole
I am made of love
I respect myself, my emotions, and my energy
My energy is raised up more and more every day
I truly love myself
I respect myself
I love to have fun
Creativity energizes me
I am free
I am a creative being
I love myself
It is safe to set boundaries
I create things for me, and it is okay

Chapter 12

The Victim and the Martyr

We all want love and attention. Some people were raised to believe that attention can only be given to them when under duress. In other words, something negative had to happen to them in order for them to receive attention. Their parent(s) would come to their rescue, showering them with love and affection. Maybe they were too busy otherwise or their parents did not have the emotional wherewithal to be attentive at other times. So, you learn in some weird way that this is how to get love and attention. It is similar to all learning as a child, you continue to do those things that make you feel loved.

A therapist might refer to this habitual need for help and always being in need as victim mode. It can be hard to recognize this in yourself. One clue is that many adverse things happen to you, and you always seem to need help. Yes, sometimes, you do honestly need help. However, if you believe that asking for help is the only way that you can get people in your life to react and care about you, well then, you might be stuck in victim mode.

You may know of someone who is constantly in crisis and always needing rescued emotionally, financially, or spiritually. When your friend constantly talks to you about a litany of issues or problems and rarely talks about the positive aspects of their life, it may be a sign they are in victim mode. They might expect you to stop everything, even if you are at work, to tend to their emotional needs. Some people might even describe themselves as "being needy."

Some take being a victim a step further and become a martyr. These folks actively overextend themselves in a variety of ways and then seek attention for their sacrifices. All with an exhausted smile on their face. These folks often comment how tired they are, their lack of sleep, working until late at night, or rush around trying to do it all.

Someone in victim mode might often say:

- "Woe is me (elaborate problem here)."
- "I can't believe all this (insert trauma here) happens to me all the time."
- "This person or that person is out to get me."
- "My anxiety doesn't allow me to do, be, or have (you name it)"

The person in victim mode might frequently call you during an emotional crisis. Or if you have invited them to a fun social event, you end up spending the entire time talking and working through yet another one of their issues or problems instead of having fun. At some point, the person helping the victim catches on, feels the drain, and stops answering the phone. It is literally exhausting emotionally and energetically.

Now, if you have recognized yourself as someone stuck in victim mode, please seek some help with a good therapist to resolve your need to obtain attention in this way. The root of it is often traced to childhood. While it could definitely be from a past life, this current life has likely compounded it further. It is always healing to take a cold, hard look at your upbringing and to view it objectively, to see how you can heal, notice patterns in behavior, and resolve them in a healthy way. Your parents were doing the best that they could with the skills that they had at the time. Remember, you can choose how you grow from all your experiences.

Doing personal healing work will allow you to be with your friends and lovers in a mutually supportive and loving way. Plus, it allows you to have a fun time together without relying on emotional or other issues to connect with someone.

~ CURRENT LIFE EXAMPLE: SANDY ~

Sandy came to see me for a past life regression. She wanted to find out why she seemed to continuously attract bad situations. She spent the first fifteen minutes of our session going through all the terrible things she had experienced. Right away we talked about victim mode. I talked to her about the law of attraction and learning to rewrite, or only talk about, the kind of life she wanted to have.

Sandy immediately entered a past life where she died believing she only deserved attention if she gave her life for others.

~ ROOT CAUSE EXPLORATION ~

"I am a young 10-year-old girl living on an island.

One morning, a group of eight high priests wander through town looking for a young virgin girl to sacrifice to Pele. The priests chose young girls who have not yet reached puberty. The men belong to a secret society that spoke frequently of the necessity and honor of sacrifice. Men who revealed any aspect of their rituals were killed.

My mom wails when they chose me. She knows she will never see me again. Some parents hid their girls. One priest tells my mother that all the girls descend up to the heavens. They speak endlessly about honor and sacrifice. It feels like brainwashing.

The same day they picked me; they took me to the tall mountain for sacrificing. Some villagers and my mother followed them. At the base of the mountain, they started my preparation. They drugged me with a small green dried plant. They gave me many of these green pea-sized things to eat. The drug made my body feel like jelly. It must be some type of opioid. They brushed my long brown hair and tied it into a ponytail.

It feels damp like it just rained. They put skulls on their heads like masks and begin to chant as they carry me up the mountainside. They warn the villagers they must stay at the bottom to fulfill the wishes of the sacrifice. They strap me to the back of one of the men.

The walk up the mountain takes several hours. We stop halfway. They start to prepare me for the sacrifice by feeding me more little green things. They mash several into a bit of water too. In a drug induced stupor, they remove my clothes and cut my hair. I cry when they cut all my hair off. I loved my long hair. They bind the length of it on the top of a tall stick. They continue carrying me up the mountainside with my naked body exposed. We are so high up; it feels like we have ascended to the heavens.

At the top we come to a small flat, damp area. While they prepare me for the final ritual, they lay me down facing the large gaping hole at the top. I cannot move because of the drugs. I realize the mountain is an inactive volcano. I notice the ghosts of other girls who were sacrificed before me haunting the area. They come near me and express their concern and warn me of danger. I look around at everything and listen to their chatter, as this is the only thing I can do.

I see a large hollow circular opening with sunlight shining through it. I admire the large drawings of a bird-like winged creature decorating the opening. I watch a bioluminescent plant move in the wind.

I hear the men start to chant again. One man roughly picks me up and moves me to a large rock. They pierce my nipples with small sticks. I feel so out of control, the drug made sure I could not fight back or talk. I am held by a few men as they spread my legs and each take turns to roughly impale me. The intent was to rupture me in my crevice of creativity and mix my blood with their jointly deposited semen. Hours passed. They needed the mixture for their ceremony. Completed, they collected the mixture with my hair which is now being used as a paintbrush. They paint it across my face and chest. They paint a star on my stomach with the mixture.

My role has ceased, so they slit my neck to collect more blood. They chant while pouring it down the side of the volcano in hopes that this prevents Pele from spreading lava instead. They plant the stick that holds my hair in the ground nearby. Once my body drains of blood, they burn it unceremoniously. I feel a great deal of anger towards these men. They essentially pick the prettiest girl, rape her, and kill her without any dire consequences."

~ HEALING STEPS ~

To help her heal, I have her offer forgiveness to the men, to forgive her mother for not protecting her. I have her forgive the land and the plants that drugged her.

Several of her chakras were affected by this traumatic experience. Her Throat chakra stored the pattern of, "I have no say." Her Heart chakra stored the energy of parent abandonment. Her Solar Plexus chakra felt depleted of personal power. Her Sacral chakra housed the pattern of, "I cannot trust in relationships." Her Root chakra and Sex chakra contained the sexual trauma energy as well as anger, resentment, and shame. I asked for Archangel Raphael to assist directly with this deep healing. Archangel Raphael uses a specialized healing tool of light that reaches deep within chakras to transmute the negative trauma into healing light.

She died believing she was a victim. This dying thought carried into this lifetime. She received a lot of attention for her sacrifice. She only felt worthy and loved when she was in danger or in some sort of trouble.

Sandy made the recognition that she did not have to give her whole self away to be loved and appreciated. That was a major cathartic healing for her.

~ CURRENT LIFE EXAMPLE: HANNA ~

Hanna came to see me for a past life regression. She constantly got lost each time she drove up towards the top of Mt. Washington, a large hill overlooking Point State Park, a place where the three rivers meet in downtown Pittsburgh, Pennsylvania. She wanted to understand why.

We decided that a past life regression might bring this issue to light. And it did. Here is her past life memory of being in the French and Indian war and her gruesome death on Mt. Washington. This past life helped her heal in many more ways than she would expected.

~ ROOT CAUSE EXPLORATION ~

"I am in the military in the 1750s. I am not a lackey, but a ranking officer. I left behind my beautiful red-headed wife and child in Virginia to fulfill a duty to my government. In reality, it turned out to be an extermination of the American Indians from the land, so we could take it over. I had only been a few places on the east coast as part of my military career.

I was part of a task force to go to Pittsburgh, Pennsylvania to secure waterways to allow westward travel. Many felt that travel would become so much easier with safe water routes.

We eradicated any American Indians we found along the way. It included women and children. I am doing my job, my duty, and at the same time feeling like this was very wrong. I realized the native people were humans and not savages as they were continuously portrayed to the troops. I never let on I felt this way, or it would be like treason. I had men to manage and strict orders to adhere to as well.

The land, now Point State Park, is where the union of the Allegheny and Monongahela rivers create the Ohio River. The area where these three rivers meet is a great military stronghold and trade route. It had already been seized and several men had started building Fort Pitt.

The American Indians were irritated by all our actions. It was their land originally. They were forced to become militaristic to defend and protect the land and their people. Fear prevailed among all tribes. They had seen so many of their friends and family perish.

I am sent by my commander to meet with the American Indians up on the hill of Mt. Washington. He knew on some level that this would be futile and a death wish, but he did not say that at all.

The base of Mt. Washington and its trees had mostly been set on fire by us. This helped us keep an eye on the American Indians up on top of the hill—who were peering back down upon us. We rowed our boat across the river, under the cover of the night, and set fires. This was somewhat of a disadvantage when I took a small group over to see if we could hold peaceful discussions.

We quietly crossed the river. Once moored, the American Indians caught us within the hour. It seemed too easy for them to capture us, as if they knew or watched the whole preparations. We thought of them as stupid and illiterate, but they definitely knew more than we were told. They also knew I was the highest ranked officer of the group, so they forced me to watch each of my men die when they slit their throats. After that spectacle, they strung me up between two trees facing towards the fort's construction. I overheard one say I was a trap to see if more 'white blood' would come so they could be killed too.

I dangled from those trees—stretched out nearly naked and tied up for well over a week. I could see the fort and all the action down below as some watched me via a spyglass. I felt abandoned by them as there was no attempt to save me. The American Indians tortured me by not feeding me or giving me anything to drink. Worse yet, daily they removed long, thin strips of my skin. They would yell at me, spit on me, and throw dirt at my open wounds.

Since my capture, I did not fight back. I felt I deserved the suffering because of all the families that I murdered. I chose to be a martyr. I allowed myself to feel all the pain, even though my spirit could have 'left' my body to avoid that painful death experience. It felt like penance for my sins and for those of my troops.

I died of dehydration. My skin, what is left, was burned by the sun and my open wounds were frequented by birds and bugs. My dead body was left up for many months after I died. Later my body was cut down and let roll towards the bottom of the hillside.

The whole time I endured their torture, I could not shake the feeling that my commander sent me up here on purpose. It is possible he knew, somehow, how I felt about the American Indians and wanted to prove me wrong. He knew I would die. My commander also felt as if he was my ex in my current lifetime, who was equally as spiteful."

~ HEALING STEPS ~

Hanna could not believe this lifetime came up. It explained so many things about her life and some of her unfounded fears. It definitely explained why her subconscious mind would not let her travel to the top of Mt. Washington.

She put her life last and her work first at her current job too. She worked many endless hours, including weekends. All thankless. She recognized that when she put her duty to work first, rather than taking care of herself and her needs, it gave her barely any time for a relationship. She realized she was working towards martyrdom.

She suffered from random painful rashes that the doctors could not figure out in her current lifetime. We hoped this cathartic experience would provide some relief to this health issue. She noticed that the energy of the trauma from this past life still felt like self-punishment as we released it from her spiritual being.

In the healing space, she had seven angels around her to help transmute the trauma energy into love and light.

On behalf of her past life as the military officer, she forgave herself for going against her personal beliefs and not standing up for herself. This strengthened her Solar Plexus chakra. We continued with the forgiveness work as she forgave the bugs for attacking, the commander, any person involved with their torture, the war, and the government. She forgave herself for not speaking up, thus strengthening the Throat chakra.

She asked for forgiveness from the people she killed, which felt like murder to her. She asked for forgiveness from the men in the group, who were also sent to Mt. Washington, who died on this military mission too. She forgave the American Indians for their torture and for starving her in that past lifetime.

I had her release the guilt from leaving her family in that past life. She also released the guilt of causing the death of others, and the grief of all the death.

She had made the vow, "I deserve to suffer," in that past life and died believing she still needed to suffer. We removed the energy of that vow and replaced it with, "I deserve peace and happiness."

While doing her duty to eradicate the American Indians, she shut off her emotions so as not to feel any suffering. Her spirit guides also wanted her to work on trusting again and to open up her feeling sense and emotions more fully. I had her forgive her ex in her current lifetime.

~ AFFIRMATIONS ~

I am healed
I am safe
I overcome obstacles with ease
Good things happen in my life often
I remember to focus on the positive each day
Only uplifting people are in my life
My life is amazing
There are good people everywhere I go
Amazing things happen to me
I see the positive
Great things come to me
I can travel anywhere with ease

CHAPTER 13

MOTHERING A NARCISSIST
I CAN CHANGE THEM. I CAN SAVE THEM

Awwww. They are so sweet; they just need loved. Look how cute they are. I can see the good in them. I can make them happy. I can fix them. I can show them there are good people in the world. I can raise their vibration. I can cure their problems. I can help them. They need me. I can change for them. If I just do this one thing, and this other thing, they will love me. I can take care of them while they sit back and relax. They deserve it. I do not deserve anything in return. I can give up all my hopes and dreams to help THEM.

AAAAAAAAAAAAAAAAAAAAAHHHHHHHHHHHHHHHHH!

Seriously.

It feels like, sometimes, you need to wipe their ass too.

Let's face it, you have had someone in your life like this at one point or another. One that was depressed, lonely, a man-child, broke, distraught, and good at playing that role. They may be a momma's boy or such a good, sweet talker that you did not even notice that they are swindling you and your energy. They make you feel wanted and needed.

You get sucked into their world. In the beginning of the relationship, they make you feel special and wanted. It feels good for a while, but after several months into it, you are so engrained in their life that you do not see an easy way out. Plus, if you mention anything about what you have given up or the extraordinary steps you have taken to help them and all the things you set aside that was important before meeting them, they just make you feel selfish or guilty for even talking about it out loud.

Sorry if men seem to bear the brunt of all this. There are definitely times when a female takes on these traits too.

What is narcissism? I found too many definitions for narcissism to list. It is my opinion that narcissism is when your partner twists your behavior and thinking so much it compels you to compromise or forget about anything that is important to you, including your self-worth, so that their wants and needs become primary. A narcissist twists and turns any issue they have around to make it yours. Narcissists are experts at guilt tripping. They make you feel like you are the only one who can take care of them and do the endless list of things they need or desire. It will never be their fault.

Common examples might be: always doing what they want and never getting around to doing what you want, making dinner for themselves and never thinking they needed to make food for anyone else in the house, taking for granted and expecting you to go out of your way for them and never returning the favor—even if it is something serious like a hospital visit. Or they fall asleep after you get them to orgasm, never even noticing you did not.

You might have had a fantasy of having a relationship where you did everything with your partner, but five years into the relationship you found yourself feeling alone with someone who never took the time to notice you and your needs.

In reality, a narcissist has low self-esteem and in order to hide this fact or to make themselves feel better, they do anything in their twisted mind's power to make you feel less than them.

Only when they first meet you or when they think you are serious about leaving them do they go out of their way to do anything for you. The whole song and dance, or what I like to the call the male peacock display, in the beginning of a relationship with a narcissist is akin to love bombing. They make you feel special until they have you so entangled in their lives that you feel dependent upon them and end up struggling to leave. The relentless love bombing in the beginning that turns into being taken for granted is no different than the fraudulent advertising scheme of bait-and-switch.

Or worse, a narcissist might try gaslighting you. Gaslighting causes you to question your own sanity. Abusers and narcissists use gaslighting to manipulate someone to gain control over them. They lie, call you crazy, and use other controlling tactics, which causes you lose your self-identity and confidence. In severe forms, a victim may question everything, causing them to become dependent upon the abuser which can be a form of Stockholm Syndrome. Stockholm Syndrome occurs when a victim of abuse identifies and attaches in a positive way with their abuser.

When you finally leave a narcissistic relationship, it will be no different than recovering from severe brainwashing. Plus, there is a copious amount of PTSD (post-traumatic stress disorder) to work through to regain your true sense of self back.

Narcissists use people to meet their own needs—they simply do not understand how to have a normal relationship. They cannot comprehend that others need independence and compassion to feel satisfied in a relationship.

Then there are the addicts. Trying to help an addictive person, whether it is drugs, alcohol, sex, gambling, etc. is normally futile, unless they want to truly help themselves. Like narcissists, addictive people turn to the type of person who likes to help—the giver—so they can be enabled to continue their addiction. It is no easy task to help an addict. Professional help is always necessary for them.

The sucky truth of having a pattern of being with a narcissist or an addict, is that you are codependent to them.

A codependent is someone who cannot function on their own accord. A codependent's entire life is structured around another person's wants and needs. Codependents place an extreme low priority on their own needs and become preoccupied with the needs of others. Codependency can be defined as a circular relationship—one person always feels like they need the other person, who in turn, desires the need to be needed.

Codependency is just like addiction. You are addicted to taking care of someone else. Sometimes you become so busy taking care of someone else, that you (conveniently) do not have to deal with your own issues.

Breaking the cycle of codependency begins with setting boundaries and learning a whole lot about selflove. Learning to use your inner personal power from your Solar Plexus chakra will help too.

Oftentimes, abused people describe to me that they feel scattered or all over the place. This tends to be an accurate statement too, especially when that person has been through a lot of different abusive situations and has set aside several pieces of their soul across time and space due to trauma. Parts of their spirit are literally all over the place.

Additionally, people who describe that they feel out of it, often disconnect, or disassociate from their physical body. On an energetic level, they leave their physical body behind and spend a lot of time out of their body. To them, it feels safer. Dissociation is often described as feeling disconnected from thoughts, feelings, memories, and surroundings. It affects who you are and the perception of time. You may literally feel 'out of it.'

Grounding your energy back into your physical body and connecting to all aspects of your surroundings through all of your senses will help.

Some people actually have told me that they leave their body on purpose, so they do not have to feel the pain when they are beaten, whether that abuse is emotional or physical.

How do you break free from the chains of a narcissist? Awareness is always the first step to healing. Taking back control of your needs, finding yourself, reconnecting with the things and the people you love, plus seeking out therapy to help you through it all. As you slowly reclaim what you gave up and start to do the things that you enjoy, even alone, you begin to heal. Remember to nurture yourself throughout this process, you are learning to love yourself again.

While you work on reclaiming yourself and all the things you compromised or gave up, the narcissist will work their covert tactics on love bombing you or guilt tripping you. Please take the time to become fully knowledgeable on how to deal with a narcissist. Having a deep understanding of this type of personality may just give you the advantage you need to help you leave a narcissistic relationship and prevent any continuation of a codependent pattern. Additionally, this knowledge rebuilds your confidence.

Once you continuously react without emotion to the detrimental things they do, this will cause the narcissist to go elsewhere to find someone to use and emotionally abuse. Remember you can never change a narcissist; you can only change how you react to them.

~ CURRENT LIFE EXAMPLE: LIZ ~

Liz came to me for a past life regression to figure out what to do with her relationship. Liz felt as though she had lost herself. It is always interesting to me when someone says something that seems like it would not be literally true but, it is accurate. If someone says they feel lost, they are actually saying they lost their sense of self.

She gave up her wants and needs and saw her boyfriend's needs as more important. This controlling, narcissistic nature squashes your soul. Sometimes it is referred to as compromising yourself. It is extremely hard to see that it is happening when you are involved in any type of emotionally abusive relationship. It is almost as if you need to step outside of your relationship and take a look at it from a third person perspective.

Liz mentioned that her boyfriend did not know she came to see me. I had her put her phone on silence so his texts or calls would not interrupt our two-hour session. As I psychically tuned into his energy, he felt very controlling and abusive. Liz told me she felt he was narcissistic.

To start, I took Liz to the healing space with the angels. I asked them to help her energy fully ground into her physical body and to help her feel safe within it. Next, she entered an abusive lifetime in the early 1800s in Missouri.

~ ROOT CAUSE EXPLORATION ~

"I am an eight-year-old girl, but I feel like I am 30 years old.

I stayed quiet and obedient all the time to avoid a beating. My father is a fire and brimstone preacher with a red-hot temper to match. He forbade me to act like a child.

He beat my mother in the name of Jesus at the slightest infraction. He would yell at her that Jesus made him beat her. She would kneel on the floor and never told him to stop. She was very mousy and did nearly anything to obey him. It appeared as slavery rather than a relationship to me.

He decided we all should go on a mission trip to South America to convert the purported savages to Christianity. He convinced my mother to come since he could not live without their carnal acts.

We traveled for weeks, stopping randomly to preach the gospel of Luke to the locals. He spoke through a Spanish interpreter, but soon learned to speak a few spiritually meaningful phrases in Spanish too. We arrived in Brazil near the Amazon Rainforest. He preached about the bible to those we met and to anyone that would listen.

He had an interesting technique to gather crowds. After we arrived in a new town, Father would make all kinds of racket in the middle of town to get the attention of the villagers. As soon as someone came out of their house, he entrapped them to listen to his sermons. He lambasted those who would leave and return to their home. My father called himself, "the great and almighty preacher, David," in a booming voice.

My father would preach for hours. He expected me to watch my three-year-old brother. Father accepted that my brother could not sit still to listen, so he allowed us to take short walks while he preached. Mother watched Father intently with admiration. She believed in him, but she had given herself up in the process.

It was beautiful here. Everything was so green and uniquely different. My brother and I wandered around looking at things. No one noticed my brother and I walking into the jungle. We walked under a canopy of trees while admiring the lushness all around us. We looked all around in wonder. We admired its intense beauty.

I enjoyed how cool it felt in the jungle. My thickly layered dress caused me to sweat in the hot sun. My father expected women to wear several layers for piousness, to keep women weighted down, and to appear as nonsexual as possible.

We spied a little monkey and followed it throughout the jungle. Soon we found ourselves lost. Unfortunately, we were completely unaware that a pack of black wild dogs followed us. We started to run, but my dress inhibited running. I will never forget the look of horror my brother had on his face when I could not keep up. My brother begged me to hurry. The five dogs ran too fast for us. They attacked us and turned us into their meal of the day.

I died believing my brother would never forgive me for not protecting him. I vowed to do a better job of taking care of others.

I saw my spirit guide immediately as I left my body behind."

~ HEALING STEPS ~

I always appreciate it when spirit guides visit during a past life regression. These beautiful, helpful beings know way more about us than we do. I asked her spirit guide to make sure she saw her brother in spirit. That became a very healing moment when they hugged in spirit, and he forgave her. She released the thought she had failed her brother and herself.

This heartbreaking ending to their lives was really a predetermined exit point in that lifetime for both her and her brother. An exit point is a predetermined point at which you chose to exit from a lifetime. You can include several exit points in a lifetime. Her spirit guide explained that her and her brother's death caused their father and mother to undergo some serious personal healing. This gave her some solace.

The angels helped Liz to clear any pent-up emotions and traumas in her energy and replace them with healing, pure unconditional love and light. The angels worked on her Solar Plexus chakra and Throat chakra to heal them even more.

Her mother taught her the pattern of low self-esteem and to be ok with abuse. We worked to replace the pattern of 'abuse is normal in a family,' with, 'love and respect is normal in a family.'

She cut cords with her mother and father in that past life. She cut cords with her current boyfriend and past abusive boyfriends and family members who were abusive to her. She set the intent to, "Only allow mutually supportive and loving people in my life from this point forward."

She forgave her abusive father, neglectful mother, the dogs who attacked, and herself. She forgave her brother and the resentment of taking over mothering duties to him.

She realized that she had been beaten into silence in that past life and saw the connection to her life now where she felt she could not easily say how she feels.

She often felt as if she was required to be submissive. This connection to her past and current lifetime was cathartic. We talked about the connection of her feelings of being unsupported, unwanted, as well as feeling desperate for love and attention was rooted in this past lifetime. After I brought her out of the regression, I had her say, "My energy is fully grounded, centered, and whole within my physical body, and I can feel it all the way to my toes."

Awareness of any deep underlying issue is always the first step towards healing.

~ CURRENT LIFE EXAMPLE: BAILEY ~

Bailey came to me for a reading, but it soon turned into a past life regression. During the reading, several lifetimes of her mothering over people became apparent.

I asked her if she wanted a glass of water, and it became obvious that it was uncomfortable for her to let me get that for her. She said that she was not used to having someone take care of her. A glass of water was a start. We talked about changing the story she was telling about that and to turn it into, 'I have lots of people who care about me and for me.'

Her spirit guides suggested we do a healing meditation with the angels. This led to her remembering the root cause of her need to mother over people.

~ ROOT CAUSE EXPLORATION ~

"I am a seven-year-old girl wearing a long tan dress in 1851. My little brother and I sit in front of the house we just sold. My parents decided to travel out west for the gold rush. They were excited about the prospect of getting rich. My dad sold most of our possessions and home to buy the covered wagon and supplies. We left Kansas with a large group of others traveling in these wagons.

About halfway there, a traveler in one town warned us about the natives attacking ahead. The traveler said they burned and looted the wagons. Fear abounded. Everyone brought all their possessions.

My dad's temper caused a loud argument with a few others in the group. They disagreed on how to circumvent the attacks. My dad broke away from the group. He did not care that it was unsafe to travel alone. We traveled for days without seeing another person. It was not long before I heard my parents talking about being lost. Somehow, we ended up in what we now call Montana. I do not think they knew where we were.

My mom took care of most everything. Tired from all the travel, we took a break and parked the wagon near a stream. Unfortunately, the giardia tainted water caused my mother to suffer for a week, and die. Incapable of helping her, we painfully watched her die. My dad, now paralyzed in grief, barely moved since we buried her.

I look down at how my dress has grown short; I am due a new one or at least the hem needs let out. I ponder how to sew. My mother did not teach me yet.

Two weeks slowly passed since my mother died. I worry about the dwindling food supply. We were constantly hungry and probably starved at this point. I do not know how to find food. My dad sits there motionless. I tried to take care of my 4-year-old brother and father.

My brother exhausted all his energy. I coaxed him to come with me to go to the bathroom. Shovel in hand, we walked out into the plains area to go the bathroom. Our dad wanted us to go far from the stream and wagon.

As we walked through the grass, a rattler came into our path and we froze, not knowing what to do. The snake bit my brother on his ankle and then slithered away as if nothing happened.

We were nearly dehydrated because my dad did not take the time to boil more water. Our fire blew out two days ago. I wished my mother had showed me how to help more.

My brother did not have the strength to handle a snake bite. I comforted my brother for hours hoping our dad would come. He died in my arms.

I sob, telling him I promise not to leave his side. I cry, "I'm sorry," over and over. I fall asleep in exhaustion. I was afraid to go back to the wagon without him.

Father did not take the time to look for us until late that night. Sitting in the tall grass made it hard for him to find us.

I felt like it was my fault he died and that I could have done more.

I die from dehydration a few days later. In spirit, I watch my distraught father kill himself."

~ HEALING STEPS ~

Bailey, as this young girl from the late 1800s, felt a deep sense of guilt that she personally caused all of the trauma in this past life. In her current lifetime, it felt like she was making up for it all, almost like doing penance. She felt that she had to work hard to take care of everyone so they would not die or abandon her. This past life helped her to see that none of it was her fault.

She forgave her mother for dying, which felt like abandonment. She forgave her father who abandoned her emotionally. She forgave the water for causing all the death. She forgave her father for being so stubborn and hot-headed.

We worked to release her pent-up emotions and trauma energy within her and asked the angels to fill her with pure unconditional love and light.

She recognized that she never got a chance to be a kid and had forgotten how to play and have fun. This knowledge was very cathartic.

We worked to replace her pattern of, "I need to mother over everyone or else they will die," to, "I love myself and love taking care of myself. I appreciate that others are able to learn how to be responsible for themselves."

The next time I saw Bailey, she had gained more confidence and had opened her own online store. She spoke about a new group of supportive friends who celebrated her achievements. She was now ready to remember a true love relationship in a past life to provide a frame of reference to what she desired in a relationship. I hope that the next time I see her she will have met the person of her dreams.

~ AFFIRMATIONS ~

I love myself
I am aware of my energetic exchange
I am an energetic being filled with love
Life is full of miracles
I value myself
I have lots of people who care about me and for me
I set boundaries with ease
I am supported

CHAPTER 14

CHEATERS ALWAYS CHEAT

What happens when you are in a relationship and your partner cheats on you? Does it feel like you always seem to pick a partner that has wandering eyes, hands, and genitalia?

Generally, when one partner decides to include a third party, they are missing some aspect of a need that they cannot fill in their relationship with you. This does not make it okay, for someone who committed to you, to cheat.

Aiden came for a reading to see what to do about his relationship situation. He was married with children, but was in love with another, younger woman too. I knew he was seeking validation, on a spiritual level, for this love triangle. He did not want to lose his wife or the younger woman.

The root cause of his cheating came to light. He and his wife were not able to have intimate conversations. However, he was able to discuss nearly anything with his lover. He could choose to help his wife speak to him more openly and intimately if he desired to save his marriage. His spirit guides said that his best path in this life was to help his wife be open to speaking to him about intimate things. Hopefully, he chose well.

Please note that intimate conversations are not sexting or sexual related discussions. Intimate conversations include topics on hopes, dreams, desires, bucket lists, deepest fears, experiences, and more. These conversations bring you emotionally closer to one another by breaking down walls and heightening vulnerability in each person. Trusting emotional topics with another human being brings you closer on many levels.

This explained why Aidan cheats.

Cheating is still a jerk move, no matter what the reason. Agreed.

This book is to help you, not them.

Sometimes a partner will cheat because, on some level, they know that their current relationship is over. Maybe they are the type of person who does not like to be alone, so they form their next relationship before they get the courage to end the one they share with you.

You might have been aware that your relationship felt off, like a bad roommate or otherwise draining situation, for a few months or even several years. Maybe due to kids or money, you stayed together—way past the point where there was no hope to rekindle the relationship. Sometimes people stay to avoid feeling lonely or refuse to believe that their spouse is no longer committed to the relationship.

I once had someone come to me for a reading and even though they knew their spouse cheated on them regularly, still desperately wanted their spouse to stay with them. She had forgotten how to love herself and had given up her self-confidence during the marriage. I hope one day she realizes she is worth so much more and reclaims herself and her confidence.

Always choose the free will decision of mutual support and love.

Maybe you focused on caring for the kids so much that your partner felt neglected, but they did nothing to rekindle any romance. As the kids reached the independence of high school, you realized you and your partner grew apart. They may have spent several evenings or weekends away participating in a hobby as you turned a blind eye to the potential for them to step outside the relationship and cheat.

So, what is the root cause of staying with someone who no longer feels like your playmate, dinner date, or much of anything?

The most often seen cause is lack of selflove. This is one of the hardest life lessons to learn. Only when you genuinely love yourself, can you be able to feel the love from another person in a relationship.

If you think that you do not deserve their full love and attention, then they will prove to you that you do not. If you believe that you do not deserve someone's love and attention, then you are giving them the permission to prove you right.

What happens when you are dating someone who is involved with someone else? It can be thrilling—the sneaking around is fun and you feel young, like a teenager.

The hardest part is realizing that it is you, not them. You, on some level, are blocking true love from coming into your life if you settle for someone who is not there for you 100% of the time. Maybe you have commitment issues? Maybe you do not want to be hurt again and this feels safe. See "Chapter 5, Closed Heart," on being afraid to allow true love into your life.

If someone wants to date you and they are already in a relationship, they are not ever going to be committed to you completely. Ever. They may bullshit you and sweet talk you and tell you how bad their marriage, girlfriend, etc. is, but at the end of the day, months, or even years later, they continue to give you excuses on why they cannot leave them and commit to you 100% of the time. It is not worth it energetically, emotionally, or physically.

One thing I need to mention is that there are serial cheaters, aka 'players'. These folks are never satisfied no matter what. Some are considered 'bad boys' and there are some ladies who believe they are the ones who will be able to tame their cheating soul. Good luck. Just say, "No." I do not care how much of a smooth talker they are, just say, "No. Hell no."

Then, there are those that are currently looking to jump from one relationship to the next. They may be married and still in a relationship and are unhappy. It sounds like a good idea, but years pass, and they never seem to make any progress on leaving their spouse. The sex is great because you are sneaking around. You feel like a teenager trying not to get caught by your parents. That feeling of getting away with it can be fun, but after a few years it becomes a huge drag and a serious drain on your energy. Trust that old adage: once a cheater, always a cheater. Aside from the fact that you have wasted years of your energy focusing on this person; this relationship also prevented you from being open and available for a mutually supportive and loving person to come into your life.

Think about how nice it would be to regularly crawl into bed with someone, have dinner together, or to openly attend random social engagements together.

You want someone to love you—and only you. Do not settle for anything less than one person devoted to you.

Deep down, players and cheaters have a pattern of not feeling comfortable with just one person so they continue to choose many as a way of life. This way, they do not have to deal with the disappointment that love is not always available or when their partner is emotionally unavailable. Sad, but true.

Remember, a person must want to change—all on their own. You cannot change someone.

So why do you continually choose a cheater? Do you think you can change them? Stop. You cannot. It is impossible to change someone else, you can only change yourself.

Keep in mind that when you first talk to and meet someone, pay close attention to what they say and how they act. They provide telltale signs of exactly who they really are. Most people blow-off those signs as first date chatter, but the real nature of a person comes out. An example would be if someone offhandedly said they hit their dog when it was bad. News flash. If they hit their dog, they would probably not think twice about hitting you. I heard these words on a first date once. I was done with that date in 10 minutes. Ugh. (Sometimes I swear these awful dates were brought to me so I could use them as examples in this book.)

You think you can save them or help them or change them or win them over to just be with you. It is NOT happening. Ever. Please save yourself a ton of grief and stop right now. Sometimes these people come into our lives and seem normal, but then months later, you feel like you need change them in order to help them. Or worse yet, you believe you can be the one to show them deep love. That is not a normal mutually supportive and loving relationship, it became a codependent one. Break it off. It might feel like you are hurting them, but they will just find someone else to feed energy off of and will never, ever change unless THEY truly want to heal.

If you find yourself caught up in the cheater relationship pattern type of cycle, then it is time to nurture yourself. You deserve nurturing. Focus on why you feel that you could not nurture yourself thus far. Someone who dates you and is already in a relationship or cheats on you cannot nurture you. Consider this your wake-up call. Take steps today to nurture yourself and focus on loving yourself more. When you love yourself fully, only those who can love you fully come into your life.

To help you heal from this relationship pattern, let us understand what makes a cheater tick.

Through the information given to me during a reading by others' spirit guides, cheaters generally have had a childhood where they have had to go the extra mile to win the affections from a parent.

Many things can cause someone to cheat on you or with you. Here is a description from a spirit guide I was given during one of my readings. If it is a male cheater, the mother ignored them (and vice versa for a female cheater). They only received a smidgeon of attention from their parent. Maybe their parent had an addiction problem which prevented them from feeling completely loved. It feels like a cheater was abused in some way, physically, mentally, emotionally, or sexually so they always felt half loved and then sought love and attention elsewhere. They have a habit to break. It is like a fear of commitment since their own parent could not commit to love them. They believe if they do not commit completely, they will not get hurt.

~ CURRENT LIFE EXAMPLE: ADAM ~

Adam came to me to try to understand why he kept having relationship issues repeatedly. He told me that he seemed to go from girlfriend to girlfriend, afraid to commit to any of them. He described himself as a bit of a player. I could feel intuitively that he habitually dated several women at once.

After we talked for a bit, I helped him go into a relaxed, meditative state to regress him into a past life. I had him describe what he was wearing to ground him into a past life memory. Adam remembered a past life as a young boy who learned to sweet talk mother-like figures in his neighborhood so he could have food. His rarely saw his mother in this lifetime.

~ ROOT CAUSE EXPLORATION ~

"I am wearing a tan leather short boot-like shoe that laces up. Kind of like a Robin Hood shoe. My dark brown pants come to midcalf.

I am sitting on a chair in my house. My mother gives me directions on what to do and what not to do while she is gone again today. I just turned eight. I sit and listen quietly while worrying about where I will find lunch today. I feel a rush of air as she walks out the door.

I never know where she goes. An older kid in the neighborhood told me my mother works as a whore. My mother always avoids answering my questions on who my father is too. She has only provided me the vague answer, "He lives somewhere in England."

I feel lonely and sad all the time. Per my mother's firm instructions, I stay in our meager house alone most days.

Sometimes I walk next door to visit our neighbor. She often saves me a bit of food leftover from her lunch. She does not spend a lot of time with me, but I appreciate her loving consideration in the rare moments I do share with her. I feel more love and care from her than my mother provides me.

Now that I am 10 years old, I muster the confidence to venture out of the house more. My mother rarely comes home, therefore food rarely makes it into my house. My mother never worries or wonders how I eat. She seems happy to see me and treats me with kindness when she shows up at our home.

I learned survival skills to find food. I walk for hours scoping out the neighborhood and use my sense of smell to discover food. It feels like I won a prize when I find a morsel of something.

Once I was caught taking a meat pie from a windowsill but was able to talk my way out of being accused of stealing by telling them that I was saving their food from an animal invasion. I eagerly took the prize of a few pieces of pie for my gallant help.

Today, I walk up to a home where I smell sweets baking. My stomach growls as I ask the owner of the house if she has any odd jobs I can do in exchange for the delicious treats I smell baking. I shower her with compliments since I learned early on how incredibly well they work. I work hard for her, and she notices. She also noticed I was hungry too. That evening, she fed me what I considered a big dinner and then gave me a few small cakes to take home. Even though they look delicious, I tell her I will save them for breakfast. I walk home, smiling all the way. I think, "This was a good day." I add her to my mental list of places to get nourishment."

~ HEALING STEPS ~

In his current lifetime, Adam's mother worked several jobs and was not available to care for him. One of his teachers would help him after school and that filled some need for attention.

Basically, we all want love and attention, and we will seek this out however we can.

His spirit guides showed him how he affected many of the women in his life by not giving them 100 percent and how he missed out on several very loving relationships. The angels helped him remove blocks from his Heart chakra. One was the feeling that he did not feel safe to love. They told him to say the mantra, "It is safe to love," every day.

Adam was eager to find someone to be with him in a committed, long-term relationship. His spirit guides said, he needed to spend some serious time learning to love himself more deeply first. Sometimes it is best to take a break from dating in order to truly heal.

~ CURRENT LIFE EXAMPLE: AMY ~

Amy seemed to continuously meet men who were already dating or married but would sweet talk her into being in a relationship with them on the side. She was approaching thirty and wanted to have children. These relationships with non-committal men kept her from having the meaningful relationship she deserved in order to have a family. We decided to see if we could find the root cause in a past life.

Amy entered the lifetime feeling seasick and as though she was on a boat. I took her back to an earlier time in that life to get more of an understanding about this past lifetime.

~ ROOT CAUSE EXPLORATION ~

"I grew up in Wales, Great Britain, in a small farming community. Most people considered me shy.

So many awful things were happening all around us these past few years. The Plague took the life of my father and several other close relatives and friends. I counted my blessings every day that my husband, myself, and my mother did not get sick. Social unrest prevails in every city. Several normal items became scarce fast.

My husband convinced me and my mother to move to the Colonies across the ocean to get away from it all. "Not much remains here for us," he said.

I have been married to Percy for five years. I think he married me for convenience. We live with my mother. I never thought I would get married. My mother thought he was a good catch. He was a sweet talker and liked to make her laugh.

I recently learned about two of his girlfriends he keeps in town. My heart breaks. This knowledge influenced my decision to agree to move to the new land. My low self-confidence prevents me from telling Percy how I feel.

After looking at maps and talking with a few people who knew about moving to the Colonies, we decided to go for it. A few weeks later, I found out that I was pregnant with our first child. We pushed the trip out a year. They did not let pregnant women go on this journey.

We sold the farm and most of our belongings for money for the big move. They limited the number of items we could bring anyway. Jacob turned eight months the week we packed and left Wales behind. It took us three long days to travel to the seaport. The baby fussed the whole time causing us to stop more often than necessary. Percy had no patience for the child. His anger did not help. I prayed the boat ride would be more soothing to him.

That summer of 1667, we set sail on the ship, The Queen Mary.

The first week on the ship felt exciting—the view of the water so serene. By week three, everyone on board knew one another. They limited the capacity to one hundred people, yet still, the living arrangements were small and not private. The rationed food usually tasted stale or disgusting. Many folks tried to find some solace in singing. Most were exhausted from the lack of good rest and the boredom of being trapped on this large wooden ship. It felt like we were on Noah's ark with all the animals some days.

I recognize that my mother in this past lifetime is my mother again in my current lifetime. My mother and I watch the baby while my husband flits around chatting to other passengers, often offering unwanted advice.

I speak of my husband's infidelities to her, hoping she would offer guidance. My mother responded by flippantly saying, "That is normal for a man. Indiscretions happen and you have to accept that."

(My mother gave similar advice in this current lifetime when I was with a man who cheated on me. She said, "You have to work it out no matter what." It seemed like my happiness and safety did not matter to her.)

As we landed in Maryland, even though exhausted, all the passengers cheered. Jacob cried from all the noise. The last two months were the longest of my life.

Percy found a place for us to live in a small settlement south of Baltimore. A week after we settled into our new home, we celebrated Jacob's first birthday and the fact that we survived the trip. Fresh water and bread were welcome treats. Everyone in town seemed so nice and helpful.

Within the year, my husband resumed his habit of flirting with women. The townspeople knew he flirted with nearly every woman. I suspect he did more than flirt. I turned a blind eye to all his indiscretions; one could not live on their own here in the Colonies.

If I mentioned anything to Percy about all the women he would reply in a condescending voice, "Now, Caroline Stryder, that is none of your concern," and dismiss it all with a wave of his hand in the air. I never pressed the issue further; this avoided a beating.

One lady's husband punched him in the eye for openly flirting with his wife. He told me a different story, but I had already heard the news. It made me smile. Bastard.

By the time my son turned eight, my husband had given me a venereal disease. Percy had turned to traveling for his job where he could access a variety of indecent women. My doctor just shook his head. He knew the source but could offer me no cure.

I continuously felt depressed by my circumstances. There was nothing I could do except to focus on Jacob and tending to the house. I recognize this as a repeated pattern in my current lifetime too.

My mother helped with the chores and regularly taught Jacob and a few of the neighbor children what she remembered from the schooling she received as a child.

I died young in that lifetime because I did not learn my life lesson. I recognize that am definitely in victim mode in that past life and in this current lifetime."

~ HEALING STEPS ~

Amy's biggest lesson in her current life and in her past life is to work on raising her self-confidence. On some level she did not feel she deserved to be loved and cherished by a man. The mother repeatedly gave her the rule that her wants and needs were not important. This became engrained in her.

The lesson to learn self-respect and self-worth was not learned in that past lifetime. She can work on this life lesson by learning to say, "No," when enough is enough, to stand up for herself, and to basically speak her truth. We worked on strengthening her Solar Plexus chakra by asking the angels to remove the rules her mother imposed upon her of, "Always put others' needs above your needs," with, "I am worthy of care and consideration of my needs."

We had the angels send healing love energy down through her as she released any pent-up resentments and emotions from this life and this past life. One angel stood in front of her with a yellow Solar Plexus energy to focus on healing that area more precisely.

We did forgiveness work. She forgave her mother, her husband in her past life, herself for feeling she was not worthy of one person's full attention, and all the attached men in her current life. We cut cords with all of these men and her mother too.

She came out of the past life regression feeling very empowered to stand her ground and feeling very worthy of a meaningful, faithful relationship.

~ AFFIRMATIONS ~

I love my body
I love my mind
I love my soul
I am confident
I love myself
I deserve deep love
I am worthy of a faithful relationship

Chapter 15

Chakras—How I See Them

The chakras. They are a beautiful set of colorful energy centers that spin with deep meaning. There are copious books on the subject, but I felt that I needed to include a brief overview of them for you.

As a psychic intuitive, I psychically see the chakras a little different than some, so I will describe how I see them in my readings.

I see the usual seven chakras normally shown in pictures and described in most books. They are Root, Sacral, Solar Plexus, Heart, Throat, Third Eye, and Crown. They are represented by the vibrational colors of the rainbow, with the Root being red, Sacral orange, etc.

These core seven chakras are connected to the major glands in our physical bodies. The Third Eye chakra is associated with the pineal gland. An interesting example, the Eye of Horus, is a representation of what an actual cross section of the brain and pineal gland looks like. The Eye of Horus is the ancient Egyptian representation of an all-seeing viewpoint. The Third Eye features the psychic ability to see visions.

I have been repeatedly shown an Orange-Red chakra when someone has sexual trauma. I have not found consistent information on this chakra, but sometimes it is referred to as the Sex chakra. I would agree with that name.

I also see numerous chakras that extend up beyond the Crown chakra through all the dimensions above as well as numerous chakras extending beyond the root chakra down through all the dimensions below. This entire system of chakras extends through all dimensions in both directions connecting our entire soul, typically called the higher self.

We are energetic beings having a human existence. This human life we are experiencing is where we are currently putting our attention at in this moment.

All the chakras have a beautiful flow of energy connecting them together. They are individual and connected at the same time. For example, if you want to tell someone how you really feel about something you need to express, you are using your Throat chakra and your Solar Plexus chakra together.

Chakras beyond the Root chakra extend all the way down through all the dimensions below us and connect to the center of the Earth.

The red Root chakra is located at the base of the spine and connects us to our basic needs, the 'root' of our life. Home life, parents, nourishment needs, etc. Mantra for healing the Root: "I am grounded. I am."

The orange-red Sex chakra is located in the groin area. It is sexual energy and holds any sexual trauma from this lifetime or past lives. Mantra for healing the Sex: "I am safe."

The orange Sacral chakra is located just below your belly button and is the center for relationships and creativity. Having a relationship with yourself is vital too. Mantra for healing the Sacral: "I am creative. I feel."

The yellow Solar Plexus chakra is located just above your belly button. It is the main source of your personal power. Mantra for healing the Solar Plexus: "I am strong. I do."

The green Heart chakra is located in your heart center. The Heart chakra holds love for others and grief when they pass. Mantra for healing the Heart: "I am Loved. I love."

The pink Higher Heart chakra is located above and behind the Heart chakra. This is the space for unconditional love for others and yourself. Mantra for healing the Higher Heart: "I am love."

The blue Throat chakra is located in the throat. It is the communication specialist that helps you speak your truth and listen with clarity. Mantra for healing the Throat: "I am expressive. I speak."

The purple or violet Third Eye chakra is located a little above the area between your eyes. It houses your intuitive senses such as seeing, hearing, knowing, feeling (clairsentience, clairaudience, clairvoyance, and empathy) of which are enhanced by your other chakras as well. Mantra for healing the Third Eye: "I am connected. I see."

The luminescent iridescent Crown chakra raises up like a literal crown reaching out from the top of your head upwards to the other side. The Crown chakra is your connection to your spirit guides, angels and passed over loved ones. It appears iridescent since all chakras within your body spiral up through the Crown chakra. Some see this as indigo. Mantra for healing the Crown: "I am divine. I understand."

Chakras directly above the crown appear to me as silver, then gold, then crystalline—beyond that, the rest seem hard to explain in words. These chakras become illuminated when you start to awaken to the knowledge that we are more than just this human existence. Some might refer to you as 'awakened' or 'enlightened.' If your spirit guides show me this chakra illuminated, I know you connect deeply to your true spiritual self.

Chakras extend up, connecting us through all the dimensions above us, ultimately connecting us to Source, which is pure unconditional love.

Chakras extend down, connecting us through all the dimensions below us, ultimately connecting us to the center of the Earth, grounding us in this Earth plane. The center of the Earth emanates the energy of the root of creativity bringing manifestation. This makes complete sense to me since the Earth is constantly renewing itself allowing for new growth.

CHAPTER 16

TOOLS TO HELP YOU HEAL

There are so many ways you can heal. From my psychic intuitive perspective, they all are essentially the same—you are healing an energetic aspect of your soul. How you get there is purely up to you.

I have learned about, tried, and have been given guidance during readings and past life regressions on a variety of ways we can heal on a soul level. It is now your turn to pick and choose what works best for you to help bring you closer to loving yourself fully. That is truly the key to healing. True love comes from truly loving yourself. Healing is selfcare and selflove.

As I mentioned in the introduction, in all healing modalities the bottom line is that you are releasing the dark, grey energy of patterns, traumas, or emotions and replacing it with pure unconditional love. I have included lots of other energy healing modalities in addition to past life regression.

We are energetic beings having a human existence. Everything in the Universe is comprised of atoms in a constant state of motion or vibration.

The energetic part of us is incomprehensibly large. This energy part of us, essentially our whole soul, extends throughout many dimensions or planes of existence. The whole soul part of us is often called our higher self. One small piece of our whole soul resides in our human body here in this Earth plane or dimension. Today, you are here, living in the Earth plane of existence because this is where you have chosen to focus your conscious attention.

The highest plane of existence, the highest vibration, is Source or God. It is comprised of healing pure unconditional love. We can consciously connect to or raise our energy to this higher vibration through gratitude and positive affirmations. The healing energy of love is available for everyone, anytime, and anyplace.

When I psychically see a trauma or pent-up emotion in someone's energy, it appears as a dark or grey area in an otherwise radiant, resplendent, translucent energy. This dark area prevents your whole soul energy from easily flowing and can cause blocks or patterns in your life and in your love life.

You might feel comfortable with Reiki after trying a past life regression. You might resonate with EFT or recognize that you need a soul retrieval healing. Try them too. Try several. You must pick what works for you. In this chapter, I am only providing a truncated, basic understanding to most of these modalities. Ask your spirit guides to bring you more information on a modality you would like to try.

As we heal, our energy becomes more whole, vibrant, and loving. It is at that point when we attract someone as equally healed and vibrant. When you love yourself and respect yourself, other people in your life have no choice but to reflect that love and respect back to you. The more you love yourself, the more you open the door for someone else to love you fully.

You picked this book because you chose to love yourself. I know how many years and how many modalities it took for me to get to where I am today. Be patient and kind with yourself. You can heal too.

~ REMEMBER A PAST LIFE ~

Of course, the main essence of this book is to heal your relationship patterns and traumas through past life regression. My hope is that the examples contained within this book will inspire you to feel comfortable healing through catharsis via remembering a past life. See, "Chapter 3, How to Remember a Past Life," for more specific information.

~ FORGIVENESS ~

Forgiveness is a HUGE key to healing. When you forgive, you release your conscious or subconscious connection to the issue. Forgive every single aspect of it. Forgiveness can heal PTSD (post-traumatic stress disorder) too. Forgiveness rewrites the energetic coding that was written in your energy as the trauma occurred. Forgiveness is NOT saying what happened was ok, it merely releases you from it.

Forgiveness is essential to healing. When we forgive someone, we release an unseen tether of attached emotion to that person. From this perspective, forgiveness heals everyone involved.

Again, forgiveness is not saying that it is okay that something happened, but that you are releasing your attachment to it—whatever that may be.

At the end of each past life regression, mentally review each harmful act. Send forgiveness to what or whoever harmed you or caused your death directly or indirectly. You heal spiritually, emotionally, and physically each time you offer forgiveness.

Each injurious act may have contributed to an emotional or physical pain in your current lifetime. By acknowledging it, you release it from your being. Usually, a particular place in your body correlates with the pent-up pain from a past lifetime. Sometimes trauma from a past life can physically appear as a birthmark, literally marking the place where that energy is stored in your body. Each time you release the bottled-up energy from a past life experience or death, from wherever it was stored in your body, your health could improve in that area.

Some of these bottled-up emotions have been stuck inside of you for thousands of years. They are long overdue for their release!

For example, during one regression I released the pain and any associated emotions from the slice of a sword to my back. I use a visualization process to release the stuck emotions. I visualize pouring the painful energy from where it was stored in my body into the dirt of the Earth outside. I fill this void in my energy with unconditional love (the highest form of positive loving energy) and visualize sealing the opening shut.

To complete forgiveness work, send love to anyone or anything you affected. Offer forgiveness to people, happenings, and things. Most importantly, forgive yourself so healing on a deeper level can occur.

Forgiveness is necessary to continue the soul's development and growth. Unseen weights on your shoulders detach each time you forgive, helping you feel lighter and less burdened.

Forgiveness can set you free.

When a relationship is over you can say, "I love you for the lesson. I leave you in forgiveness."

Forgiveness can help you with PTSD (post-traumatic stress disorder) too. If you cannot forgive the entire experience all at once, focus on each smaller aspect of the trauma. Take your time; be gentle with yourself.

~ REPLACE PATTERNS WITH POSITIVE ONES ~

When you recognize a pattern that you would like to replace, choose a new, positive version of how you would like to see yourself. Read through, "Chapter 17, Making True Love Affirmations," for inspiration.

Alternatively, find a past lifetime or a time and place before the root cause, trauma, or pattern to your relationship issue occurred. Then bring that healed, loving, confident feeling forward to help heal the energy of the trauma or pattern by replacing it with the re-remembered, renewed feeling of knowing there is security in loving and receiving authentic love.

For example, true love with mutual respect, support, and intimacy—is a positive, loving pattern. Allow yourself to take that pattern, feel it and see it integrate it into your energy in your lifetime, now. Bring it forward completely to the present moment and send it fully into your body, integrating it with emotions and feelings, and asking the angels to help you continue to integrate it, continue to manifest it, to keep it flowing into your future plus future lifetimes.

~ FUTURE LIFE STATEMENT ~

State: "I ask to bring forward all my current skills, knowledge, and healing into all future lifetimes."

~ CONTRACT/VOW RELEASEMENT ~

Sometimes we unwittingly make a vow or a contract that we really did not mean to keep throughout several lifetimes. Sometimes we create these vows near our death in a past life. These rules we created energetically no longer serve us. You can release those now. It is as if you are putting your foot down and cancelling all vows through all time.

Owen Waters said it best. The following is an excerpt from Owen Waters' book, *Love, Light, Laughter: The New Spirituality*.

"Sooner or later, all obsolete vows need to be released in order to set yourself free from the invisible chains of self-imposed limitation. Any vows taken in past lives with no expiration date are typically inappropriate in the way they affect later lives. The circumstances that made a past life vow appropriate at the time no longer exist because every life is a different adventure in a different setting.

In order to develop your own potential, you need to be free of obsolete, past-life obligations. Only you can develop your potential. No one else can do it for you. This life is your adventure, and it is your time to either grow to realize your true potential or to be hobbled continually by blockages that slow everything down.

If you suspect that your subconscious mind may be harboring inappropriate vows, you can release them quite simply by conscious effort. Here is how to set yourself free with your own personal Declaration of Independence:

Enter a quiet state and make this necessary and long-overdue statement:

"I now renounce and release all vows that I have taken which have outlived their purposes and which now limit my potential for growth. I reclaim my personal freedom and declare such vows renounced and released as of now. I replace old vows with the knowing that I am loved and that I am Love."

For best effect, repeat it two or more times, adding feeling and meaning each time. Continue to revisit the statement until you feel truly liberated and able to move forward to grow and naturally prosper in these, the dawning days of The Spiritual Age."

~ CUT THE UNSEEN CORDS ~

How do you cut energetic cords?

So, you recognize that you had a few icky or emotional relationships? I suspect some of them still weigh on your mind. They might even make you cry.

Why does this still affect you? Each person that you encounter connects energetically with you, normally in your Solar Plexus and Sacral chakra area located on your stomach and lower abdomen. From my perspective, there is an etheric cord (also called a string, rope, wire, cable, filament, strand, etc.) of energy that connects from you to them.

It is as if your energy reached out and connected to them when you met. It is one way we connect as beautiful energetic beings. Interestingly, we do not even have to be physically next to that person for this to occur. (This can include online friends and people you chatted with on dating sites.) There is a connection that runs from you to each and every person you meet.

Some of them are positive loving connections. This mutually supportive connection is the goal. Some of them are negative and will absolutely drain your energy like a psychic vampire. Your energy and theirs should flow nearly equally back and forth every time you interact with them in any type of way—including texting. You form these cords with lovers, neighbors, family members, coworkers, acquaintances, and even random people you meet during your normal, daily life. Some are thick cords, and some are very thin. Thicker cords tend to be a stronger relationship. Thinner cords tend to be an acquaintance. The people that affect you negatively can often create a spiderweb of cords attached to you.

Ask the question in each relationship: Is this draining? Is this mutually supportive?

Is a Relationship draining me?

You might ask, "How does all this drain me?" Think of yourself as a bottle of water. When it is filled completely, your vital energy is at its highest. You maintain this level of vital energy by doing things you love. Participating in anything that makes you feel good, (whether it is exercise, painting, walking in nature, singing, socializing, focusing on positive things or feeling gratitude) will continually raise your vital energy up, like a positive vibration jolt. When you surround yourself with people who are draining you, the cords actually become siphons connected to your bottle that drains all the water (energy) out therefore draining your vital energy. This starts a cycle of constantly trying to find ways to raise your energy. If you do not, then you will get sick.

Abusive and narcissistic relationships will have hidden or multiple cords in many places on your body. Sometime these abusive connections can actually cause pain. Sometimes they twist and wind around your body like an etheric captured bug wrapped in a spider's webbing.

Is a relationship mutually supportive?

You probably would not be reading this book if you found a mutually supportive romantic relationship. How can you tell if a cord you have made with someone is a positive, mutually supportive, and loving connection? It is easier than you think. Remember when you were chatting with someone and you felt like you were raised up, positive, happy, comfortable, or joyful while interacting with them? You both leave happy—sometimes with a smile on your face. They are absolutely a positive connection, and your vibration was heightened.

Think of someone who makes you feel sad, exhausted, worn out, fatigued, drained, spent, or depleted when you interact with them. They are actually draining your vital energy.

When someone is giving all the energy in a relationship, there is co-dependency occurring. This is especially clear and true when one person is a nurturer and a giver, and the other is narcissistic or a controller in a relationship. Please be aware that this will drain the nurturer to the point of depletion thereby potentially causing depression and sickness.

Now, with the understanding of how we can be very connected to one another, we can disconnect energetically. When you disconnect from a bad relationship, it will help you to heal from that relationship. They can no longer drain your energy because you have put your foot down and raised your personal power quotient. You are taking charge of your vital energy. You are strengthening and healing your Solar Plexus chakra.

The goal is a mutually supportive and loving relationship that connects on all levels.

We live in this Earth plane that has the strict rule of free will. It is our own free will that consciously allows another person to connect to us. It is our free will decision to allow the connection to continue or to sever it. Remember, your energy flows wherever your attention goes.

Selfcare is not selfishness, it is selflove.

You can cut ALL cords and start over. This technique is adapted from Ho'oponopono, a Hawaiian practice of reconciliation and forgiveness.

I recommend taking a moment right now, close your eyes and relax, and visualize the people you want to include in this cutting the cords ceremony.

You can pick one person or form groups of people from your life: your neighbors, your family, friends, old friends, schoolmates, acquaintances, coworkers, lovers, past relationships, (friends and relatives of your friends and past relationships,) and people you see randomly—like the dentist, doctor, etc. Start with an easy group, such as your neighbors. Visualize each group standing in front of you. If you connected to someone that negatively impacted your life, I recommend focusing on just that one person.

Choose your weapon—anything that cuts. Pick out something that makes you feel powerful and slices well. I personally utilize a flaming chainsaw. I visualize the smoke coming from the chain as I start the engine. Then, I light it on fire as I imagine flames spewing as it spins. People have picked anything from an exceptionally large pair of scissors to a laser to a sword. I like to make sure these tools are on fire so that the cords can be cauterized and therefore cannot easily reattach.

Visualize or feel the individual or group standing in front of you. Then:

1. Thank them for being part of your life.
2. Tell them you love them. (Note: if that is hard, remember that on a soul level you love everyone.)
3. Forgive them (not saying what they did was ok, but to release you).
4. Say you are sorry (If you feel you need to do so).
5. Visualize or feel the cord(s) connecting you to them.
6. Visualize a sharp cutting instrument of any kind. Set it on fire. Cut it.
7. Set the intent: I only allow mutually supportive and loving connections with you.

Beware—they may contact you to reconnect this severed cord. Cut again.

What do you do with family members that you feel obligated to include in your life? You can still cut the cords, but then set the intent, "From this point forward; I only allow a mutually supportive and loving connection."

Now, ask for the angels to heal you where it has been severed. Visualize and allow all your energy to be returned to you and then send any of their energy back to them.

You can also use this cord cutting to help heal from situations that have caused PTSD (post-traumatic stress disorder) issues.

1. Each time you are reminded of the issue in even the smallest of ways, start by thanking the universe for bringing that trigger to your attention.
2. Send love to the situation (which is actually sending love to you and giving love to it all—remember, it is something that made you who you are today).
3. Forgive anything involved with it.
4. Cut the cords.

This exercise helps to teach you about your energy. You might start to notice that when you feel drained after talking to someone, you become aware that you must cut cords with them and disconnect. After a while, it becomes quite obvious who drains you.

~ RAISE YOUR VIBRATION & VITAL ENERGY ~

Essentially the feeling of being drained can be explained with the visualization of a simple water bottle. First, you must recognize that we are energetic beings wearing a physical 'meat suit' of a body. To sustain this physical and energetic body, your vital energy must be maintained. (From "Chapter 11, Are You Drained?")

For this analogy, the vital energy will be the water and the bottle will be our physical body.

We each must maintain a certain level of water energy in our physical bottle. If the water energy drains all the way down, we become sick. Deplete the water energy completely and we die from exhaustion. We are in a constant state of ebb and flow of vital water energy in and out of our human physical bottle. Raising your vital energy is sort of the same as raising your vibration.

Raise your vibration by spending time in meditation, walking in nature, creating, singing, immersing in music, etc. By doing something we love, we are essentially raising our vital energy and pouring our water energy into our human bottle. When we give, we are pouring our energetic water out into another person or experience. Sometimes, this is conscious, sometimes it is subconscious. What the draining folks do to those who keep their energetic water levels high, is to literally feed off our energy. Think of them as a syphon, a drain, or an energetic vampire. They may or may not realize they are doing this. I have heard some people actually use the words, "I just called to hear your voice and get some of your good energy." Beware, that is clearly a red flag that they are a draining person.

We commonly use words in everyday life to describe the levels of our vital energy in our human bottle. When you are in love, you are vibrating at the highest level and are often described as: high, on cloud nine, raised up, beaming, etc. When you are vibrating on a low energy level, you are often described as: depressed, low, blue, dark, hit rock bottom, etc.

How do you raise your vibrational bottle of vital energy?

Do things that make you smile. Listen to music you enjoy. Meditate, even for just a few minutes. Spend time enjoying nature. Sing and feel the vibration of the music. Dance and move to the beat. Drive with the windows down in the car with music blaring. Walk, jog, workout—exercise and get your heart pumping. Be creative! Write, paint, sculpt, scrapbook, macramé—create anything! Take time to socialize with your positive loving friends. Consider all the things in your life that fills you with gratitude.

Participate in anything that makes you feel good. When you focus on positive things and feel in complete gratitude, you will continually raise up your vital energy. After focusing on or participating in an uplifting activity, it will feel like you received a surge of positive vibration.

Things that deplete you include: fear-based anything, the news, horror movies, negative people, negative places, negative thoughts, self-deprecation, etc. If you are constantly around people who talk about how sick they are, how sad they are, and/or how much they hate life, this will consistently drain your energy. Do not let negative people, places, or things suck you into their world.

How can you change this? Change your scenery, change who you talk to, redirect the conversation to something positive to break the negative banter. I have even gone so far as to cut off their litany of negativity and ask them, "Can you tell me what made you smile today?" This often changes the mood of the conversation to positive. Sometimes people just get into the bad habit of constantly being negative to play out their victim role often taught to them as the only way to get attention from their parents when young.

~ ASK YOUR SPIRIT GUIDES OR ANGELS FOR HELP ~

You must ask your spirit guides and angels for help with anything. We live in a free will world; they cannot interfere with our lives unless we ask. Please ask for a specific sign, answer, help, etc. They love us all in a deeply indescribable way.

Ask for help to raise your vital energy. Ask for clarity on an issue. Ask for guidance to find the root cause. Ask for healing.

**Always thank your spirit guides, the angels, and Archangels for their wonderful guidance and inspiration.

Also, please note that angels are neither male or female, so you might see them either way and that is totally acceptable.

There are so many more amazing angels that you can work with during your healing journey. There are all types of angels too. Here are some of the archangels in addition to Michael and Raziel. Archangel Metatron—awakens people, often shows me a Merkabah (translates literally to light, spirit, body) symbol that is sort of like a 3D intersecting star. Archangel Raguel—helps with justice, paperwork, and court related things. Archangel Jophiel—seen often during a near-death experience, brings joy. Archangel Raphael—amazing expert in healing.

~ ASK ARCHANGEL MICHAEL ~

I have been guided repeatedly to ask Archangel Michael to help me and to ask for his assistance in helping others as well. Archangel Michael is the epitome of strength. If you need strength, please ask Archangel Michael to help provide you with the strength you need to get through it.

I have an amazing Archangel Michael example of strength. While walking back to my car after teaching a class late one night, I started to feel nervous walking towards the alley where my car was parked. I asked Archangel Michael for help with strength. Immediately after asking, I swear I felt him with his wings outspread walking directly behind me. He felt immense, oozing strength and love. It was an awe-inspiring experience. I remember it like it was yesterday, even though it was many years ago and probably one of the first times I asked him for help.

When it comes to removing any attachments of other peoples' words, actions, emotions, energy of any kind, my 'go to' is Archangel Michael. I have been guided to say these words when helping others. You can do this now. Say it out loud.

Archangel Michael, I ask you please, to remove any and all attachments of any kind, through all time, space, and dimensions, known or unknown, conscious or unconscious, from all of me and throughout my entire energetic being. Please remove any cords, vows, contracts, ropes, strings, threads, and any other connections of any kind, seen or unseen, known or unknown, through all time, space and dimensions, throughout my entire energetic being. Thank you.

Some people ask for both Archangel Michael and Saint Germain to help. That is up to you. The point is that you are taking charge of your own energy by making this stance and asking for help. This is also an immense help for empaths who feel everything from others and may personally absorb others' emotions (consciously or subconsciously).

~ ASK ARCHANGEL RAZIEL ~

Call upon Archangel Raziel to help you remember lessons and experiences from past lives which have had an impact upon your current life. Ask them to help you understand and heal from issues that you faced during any of your past lives. Ask Archangel Raziel to show you any blocks to your intuition.

Visualize yourself surrounded in all the colors of the rainbow. Ask him to guide you to recognize and release all that no longer serves you in this life.

With love, offer forgiveness, release the energy connected to whatever was shown to you, and ask for healing from it all.

When I first saw Archangel Raziel many years ago, I saw rainbow colors all over him. Ever since then, I have called him "razzle dazzle Raziel." He is so kind and loving.

~ WORK WITH YOUR HIGHER SELF ~

Your higher self is your entire soul aspect of you that is connected through all dimensions. Your higher self can tap into the knowledge found in Universal Consciousness and Universal Knowledge. It is an amazing experience to meditate and go to this higher knowledge place.

~ GET OUT INTO NATURE ~

Being in nature is inherently healing. Surrounding yourself with a cool breeze, the warm sun, the gentle splash of water, the rustling of leaves, feeling the sand or grass between your toes—all can ground you and provide healing.

Being in nature raises your vital energy. Spend some honest time in nature and really feel it all around you.

Meditate in nature. Allow yourself to feel the pure loving energy oozing from all that is around you. It is possible to experience feeling all the energy connecting to and through nature and into your energetic being.

~ BE CREATIVE ~

Paint. Draw. Write. Sculpt. Sing. Dance. Explore new ways to create something. This opens your chakras to healing on a deep level.

Plus, you can rekindle selflove by being creative. When you create, you are the one directing what you ultimately design. Creating art of any kind is like having a relationship with yourself. This aids in healing your Sacral chakra plus as a side benefit, it helps other relationships.

~ PROTECT YOURSELF ~

If you feel you need protection, you can try this. Each day visualize a shield of white or golden light around you. Say, "The golden light surrounds and protects me. No harm can come through my light, only goodness." You can ask Archangel Michael to help with this too. Remember, you are from and of this light. You are a light being.

~ REIKI OR OTHER ENERGETIC HEALING TREATMENTS ~

Reiki is a type of energy healing. It is amazing. Basically, a Reiki practitioner connects to the energy of Source and allows that energy to channel through their hands and onto you. This helps transmute your energy back to positive.

There are so many kinds of energy healing work available, and more and more practitioners get trained in it every day. Find an energy healing modality that resonates with you and give it a try. There are many loving, kind healers who can help you. It feels wonderful.

~ BE INSPIRED ~

Tap into the knowledge of some great metaphysical teachers. There are too many to name. Find a topic that resonates with you and see if you can learn more.

~ UNDERSTAND THE LAW OF ATTRACTION ~

Learn more about the teachings on the Law of Attraction. The Law of Attraction is like the Law of Gravity. It is very real. The Law of Attraction is the ability to manifest or attract anything in your life. It does not mean just attraction of another person.

It is fun to play with the Law of Attraction. Start with something simple, like saying, "I always get that parking spot right in front of the store," or "I always get the green lights." Simple fun helps you trust and validate that you can, in fact, manifest things in your life. It is as if you are asking the universe for what you want in life.

A key to using the Law of Attraction is to formulate what you want in your life using only positive words while acting as if it is already happening. Negative words do not seem to be heard.

Say, for example, you want more positive people in your life. If you say, "I don't want negative people in my life." The universe hears this as, "I want negative people in my life." A final affirmative statement would be, "I only have positive, loving people in my life."

Another example, "I want to bring love into my life." Here, you are asking for love to be brought into your life at some future point. If you say this for years, that future point will never come. Instead say, "I have love in my life now." Own it. Act as though you already have love in your life.

Law of Attraction exemplifies why it is so vitally important to always focus on the positive things in your life. Make every effort to only use positive words when describing yourself, strive for positive experiences, watch positive videos or movies, hold positive conversations, associate with positive people, etc. Surrounding yourself with all good, positive things does make an impact on your life in a positive way.

Sure, we all have bad days, but with a positive attitude, you will endure. That has been proven scientifically.

~ VISION BOARD—VISUALIZE THE NEW YOU ~

Make a vision board. Essentially, it is a poster collage filled with things you want to see in your life. If you are a visual person, this is a great reminder of what you want out of life. It is fun to do.

I add items to mine all the time. You can make a paper one with pictures clipped from magazines or do a quick search online for anything you desire and print them out. Or you can copy pictures and paste them on a document you keep on your computer. The more you look at the vision board, the better. When you see it, you start to believe it is part of your life.

~ GROUND WITHIN YOUR BODY ~

Have you ever felt unsettled? Scattered? Or cannot think clearly? Try grounding yourself.

Grounding your spiritual aspect of you back into your physical body is a fantastic way to feel more connected to your human body again. You feel more settled, and this allows you to think more clearly.

I encourage people to say, "I am fully grounded, centered, and whole within my body, all the way to my toes."

Other grounding techniques include running down a mental list of all five senses: sight, sound, smell, taste, and touch. Start with feeling the air of each breath going slowly in and out of your chest to relax you. Sight: look around you to see and acknowledge anything, even the blue sky, the white clouds, and the green leaves rustling in the tree nearby. Sound: listen to whatever sounds are nearby you. Smell: smell the air to see what you can sense, or smell something like a candle or essential oil. Taste: enjoy the taste of a cool drink, even water. Touch: feel how the clothes you are wearing lie against your skin or wiggle your toes and feel them hit against your socks and shoes.

You can also ground by simply walking outside in nature and even touching their bare feet in grass, sand, or dirt.

~ WRITE A JOURNAL ~

Writing down your daily wins, positive experiences and anything that makes you smile in a journal helps you remember that good things do happen in your life.

Write down every time you smile. Write down every positive thing that happens to you. Write just to write. Write and ask your spirit guides for inspiration and messages. Write for fun. Then, when you have a bad day, open your journal and read the positive entries to easily raise up your vibration and lift your spirits.

~ ON LOVING YOURSELF ~

Another way to begin to love yourself is to actually say that you love yourself every day. Say that you love all aspects of your body, mind, and soul.

If you have a hard time doing that, just start with something easy—like your pinky toe. Say, "I love you, my sweet little pinky toe." Then, reflect on and love as many parts of your body that you can until you can love it all.

I love you, pinky toes. I love you, big toes. I love you, feet. I love you, ankles. I love you, calves. I love you, knees. I love you, thigh. I love you, hips. I love you, buttocks. I love you, stomach. I love you, back. I love you, chest. I love you, throat. I love you, neck. I love you, shoulders. I love you, arms. I love you, elbows. I love you, wrists. I love you, fingers. I love you, face. I love you, hair. I love you, brain. I love you, spirit. I love you, my body. I love you, intuition. I love you, my chakras. And on and on.

You are so much more than your body; love all aspects of you.

~ ONLY POSITIVE LOVING WORDS ~

It starts with positive self-talk. That means that you only say and think positive self-image words and thoughts about yourself. Remember, thoughts are things, so if you look in the mirror with disgust for your body, you are sending negative vibrations to your body. If you say, "I am so stupid," then you are sending negative vibrations to yourself. It is actually hurting your energy.

It is the same when your knees hurt and you are constantly saying, "I hate my knees," or any such thing. You can actually cause more pain to your body with all the negativities. Self-deprecation is always a bad energetic idea.

Visualize it this way: it is similar to sending beautiful kisses to your body when you love and cherish it and sending painful daggers to your body when you degrade it.

Self-deprecation sucks. No, it is not funny at all.

Calling names do hurt—especially as a child. Once you learn how bad harsh words hurt on so many, many levels, you will strive to maintain a positive loving attitude towards yourself and others.

I recommend the book, *Hidden Messages in Water*, by Japanese scientist Masaru Emoto. He proves how the influence of our thoughts, words, and feelings on water can impact everything, including our bodies.

Emoto experimented with water crystals. He exposed water to harsh words and the crystals became mangled. He exposed the water to loving words and it formed beautiful crystals. Think about it, we are made up of over 60 percent water. The Earth is made up of 71 percent water. What kind of water crystals are forming in your body?

Think of what this does to you, yourself. Reconsider any harsh things you say to anyone, especially children. When I do readings, I often find trauma from childhood created by what a parent said to them as a child. Energetically, the yelling, screaming and harsh words appeared like a baseball bat hitting their energy and permanently bruising it—or worse—hitting a piece of their soul out of them.

Do one quick internet search and you will find that many people have done their own experiments with positive words vs. negative words and the impact they have on plants, rice, flowers, etc.

I challenge you to try this experiment at home too. I have two easy ones.

RICE EXPERIMENT

Make a 1 cup of cooked rice all in the same pot. Divide the rice into two separate sealed plastic baggies. Label one with 'love' and other positive affirmations. Label the second one with 'hate' and other negative words. I put these little baggies inside a larger one, just in case it leaks. Lay them separately up on a high shelf out of the way. Then every day for a month, just think about these two bags. Send love to the first one and send mean words to the other. When I did this, the loved rice was still white, and the hated bag of rice had turned brown and gross. It left me speechless.

ROSE EXPERIMENT

My good friend tried a similar experiment but used roses she received from her son. Every morning on her way to work, she stopped by her bouquet of roses to kiss and say, "I love you," to one particular rose. After a week, all the other roses drooped and died, but the one she kissed and spoke loving words to was still vibrant and healthy.

~ WRITE OR TELL THE STORY YOU WANT TO HEAR ~

Focus on you. Write down how you want your life to be. Include things that only state the positive - use NO negative words/thoughts. For example: Say, "Only loving people are in my life." Do not say, "Keep all the men who attach to me out of my life." Say, "I know what I want in my life." Do not say, "I am a lost soul."

The reason I tell you this is because: the story you tell about you, becomes you. Tell the story you want to have in your life (even if it sounds crazy or outrageous now).

Here are some story openers:

- "I have lots of friends who love and respect me."
- "There are nice people everywhere."
- "People do nice things for me every day and I accept them with gratitude."
- "The men I meet love and respect me."
- "I am confident in everything I do."
- "I have courage."
- "I am open to receive."

You could start your story like this:

- "I opened my heart to love. It felt scary at first since I had to remember how to feel love. I have done a lot of forgiveness work as well as healed many things. I enjoy being with others and know I have love in my life."

~ STATEMENT TO CLEAR YOUR BLOCKS TO YOUR HAPPINESS ~

Here is a way to clear any blocks you may have by Joe Vitale. It is excerpted from his audio recording, *The Missing Secret*. Fill in the blanks with your new positive loving patterns. Say it with emotion and feelings so it resonates throughout your entire being.

"Spirit, Superconscious, please locate the origin of my feeling, thoughts of _____.

Take each and every level, layer, area and aspect of my being to this origin.

Analyze and resolve it perfectly with God's truth.

Come through all generations of time and eternity.

Healing every incident and its appendages based on the origin.

Please do it according to God's will until I am at the present, filled with light and truth, God's peace and love, forgiveness of myself for my incorrect perceptions, forgiveness of every person, place, circumstances, and event which contributed to these feelings and thoughts.

With total forgiveness and unconditional love: I allow every physical, mental, emotional, and spiritual problem and inappropriate behavior based on the negative origin recorded in my DNA to transform.

I choose _____ (What you want to be) _____.

I feel _____ (what you want to feel) _____.

I am _____ (what you want to be) _____.

It is done. It is healed. It is accomplished now."

~ SOUL RETRIEVAL ~

Soul retrieval is the act of bringing a piece of your spiritual being back to your whole soul. Bringing this piece back to you helps you to become more whole. Soul retrieval was extremely healing for me, so I share it here with you.

You are a large, beautiful, energetic being having a human experience.

How does a piece of your spirit disconnect from your soul? Trauma is the short answer.

When you experience a trauma, whether it is this lifetime or a past lifetime, a piece of your spirit breaks off and stays stuck in time and space wherever the trauma occurred. You subconsciously set aside a small part of your energetic self.

People who have been through a lot of traumas often say the words, "I feel scattered," or "I feel all over the place," because some of their soul literally has been left all over the place.

When a trauma occurs, highly charged emotions can be so overwhelming that your subconscious reacts by preserving a piece of you for later healing. This separation of a piece of your soul happens because there is so much energy to the event that it is impossible to store it within your body, so it—sort of—explodes off you to be stuck in time and space.

Sometimes these pieces include a talent, part of your chakra health, a creative ability, or a certain aspect of themselves. For example, personal power to stand your ground as part of the Solar Plexus chakra, ability to express as related to the Throat chakra, leaving behind a creative ability like painting or writing, or setting aside the ability to enjoy life, even a simple sunset. There are lots of examples.

A soul retrieval might be necessary when you recognize that you have given up something you once enjoyed, right around the time of a traumatic experience. This can be something minor like being yelled at as a child, or a hard event like a car wreck, a breakup, death of a loved one … really anytime that there were a lot of emotions on a particular day in your life. Normally a person might have otherwise stuffed the hard emotions down inside.

First you have to recognize that there is a part of you set aside due to a particular trauma. Then, once you have forgiven the trauma, you need to agree on a spiritual, emotional, and energetic level that you are okay with that piece to come back to you. When the piece comes back, you will need to deal with the emotions that you could not work through on the day of the trauma.

Angels can help reconnect lost parts of your energetic being to be reconnected and reintegrated into you. Just ask for them to help you. You can also work with someone to help you with this or ask for healing during a meditation.

~ EFT (EMOTIONAL FREEDOM TECHNIQUE) TAPPING ~

Tapping, also known as EFT (Emotional Freedom Technique), is a re-programming technique that stimulates and balances the body's energy flow. Gary Craig developed EFT in the early 1990s. There are a tons of books, videos and more available online but here are the basics.

EFT focuses on the meridian points (energy flow areas in your body) to restore balance to your body's energy. If you can restore your energy flow by releasing the blocked emotional energy stored there, it can alleviate an issue. Some examples are PTSD (post-traumatic stress disorder) symptoms, release a negative experience, rewrite a pattern, or release stored emotions.

The meridian endpoints tapped on your body are the same ones used in acupuncture. The idea is that if you can stimulate the area associated with a specific body part, which is in turn connected to a specific emotion, then you can remove a block in your energy flow and neutralize the emotional charge stuck there. It is like removing a large stone from the flow of water in a stream.

To perform it, you tap specific parts on your body in a particular order while saying several phrases, to basically reprogram subconscious rules within you.

Start by identifying and stating the issue out loud. Then anything that comes up, you repeat the tapping—until you have taken the original statement and end with replacing it with a new, positive statement. This might take 5 minutes or 30 minutes.

Create your statement. Here is an example: "Even though I feel _____ about _____, I deeply and completely accept myself."

Tap on the side of hand point (sometimes called the karate chop area) while repeating this initial statement three times.

Tap on the meridian endpoints (below, 1-8) while repeating a shortened phrase that summarizes the issue.

If you use the right hand, then you will tap the left side of your body and vice versa.

Here are the meridian/energy flow areas to tap. Tap each about three times lightly with two fingers, in this order:
1. Top of the head
2. Center of forehead near or on eyebrow
3. Side of the eye on temple
4. Under the eye on cheekbone
5. Under the nose, in the center
6. Chin, in the center
7. Collarbone
8. Under the arm (about four inches down from armpit)

Some example statements are:

Even though terrible things may have happened to me, and my instinct may be to suppress unwanted thoughts, emotions, or bodily sensations, I am loveable, and I accept myself.

Even though I may feel devalued by traumatic occurrences, I know at my core that I am whole and good, and I now choose to lovingly create that as my truth.

Even though I feel unworthy of a loving relationship, I deeply love myself and I completely accept myself.

~ HUMAN RIGHTS IN INTIMATE RELATIONSHIPS ~

By Leslie Cantrell, *Into the Light: A Guide for Battered Woman.*

- The right to share equality with your partner in all decisions and responsibilities related to your relationship, children, home and finances.
- The right to share equally with your mate in all financial decisions.
- The right to grow and explore your potential without feeling guilty, selfish, or afraid.
- The right to have friendships with both women and men outside of your relationship as long as you do not violate the privacy of your relationship with your partner.
- The right to express your opinions and have them given the same respect and consideration as those of your mate.
- The right to have and express your sexual needs and desires without feeling like you are selfish, demanding or aggressive.
- The right to have your emotional, physical, and intellectual needs be as important as the needs of your mate.
- The right to expect your mate to give 50% to resolve difficulties in your relationship.
- The right to hold your mate responsible for their behavior rather than assuming the responsibility yourself.
- The right to seek professional help with your relationship.
- The right to NEVER be physically attacked or psychologically degraded by your mate and the right to terminate the relationship if either occurs.
- The right to expect significant behavioral changes rather than apologies and promises from your partner if a single battering incident occurs.
- The right to not blame yourself if the relationship in which you have invested so much love and effort, ends.

~ BILL OF PERSONAL RIGHTS ~

by Edmund J. Bourne, Ph.D., *The Anxiety and Phobia Workbook*

1. To express my feelings and wants
2. To be treated with respect
3. To change my mind
4. To make mistakes and be responsible for them
5. To experience the consequences of my own actions
6. To say "No" without feeling guilty
7. To say "I don't know" or "I don't understand"
8. To do as I choose without justification
9. To receive what I contract or pay for
10. To be my own judge
11. To take risks
12. To ask for information
13. To do less than my best
14. To have privacy
15. To choose my companions
16. To control my own body

~ THINKING ~

A poem by Walter D. Wintle, first published in 1905 in *Unity*.
I like this truncated, unisex version of Wintle's poem that I call, "Think Positive." This poem was inspirational to me.

If you think you are beaten, you are
If you think you dare not, you don't
Success begins with your own free will
It's all in your state of mind
Life's battles are not always won
By those who are stronger or faster,
Sooner or later, the person who wins
Is the person who thinks they can!

~ MY DECLARATION OF SELF ESTEEM ~

by Virginia M. Satir (1916 - 1988) Author, Psychotherapist

Virginia Satir originally wrote this poem for a thirteen-year-old girl. A poster entitled "I AM ME" was produced by Celestial Arts in 1975. The poem was published in her book, *Self-Esteem*, in 2001.

I Am Me

In all the world, there is no one else exactly like me
Everything that comes out of me is authentically me
Because I alone chose it—I own everything about me
My body, my feelings, my mouth, my voice, all my actions,
Whether they be to others or to myself—I own my fantasies,
My dreams, my hopes, my fears—I own all my triumphs and
Successes, all my failures and mistakes Because I own all of
Me, I can become intimately acquainted with me—by so doing
I can love me and be friendly with me in all my parts—I know
There are aspects about myself that puzzle me, and other
Aspects that I do not know—but as long as I am
Friendly and loving to myself, I can courageously
And hopefully look for solutions to the puzzles
And for ways to find out more about me—However I
Look and sound, whatever I say and do, and whatever
I think and feel at a given moment in time is authentically
Me—If later some parts of how I looked, sounded, thought
And felt turn out to be unfitting, I can discard that which is
Unfitting, keep the rest, and invent something new for that
Which I discarded—I can see, hear, feel, think, say, and do
I have the tools to survive, to be close to others, to be
Productive to make sense and order out of the world of
People and things outside of me—I own me, and
therefore, I can engineer me—I am me and
I AM OKAY

CHAPTER 17

MAKING TRUE LOVE AFFIRMATIONS

Reading, writing, speaking, and listening to positive affirmations is a powerful tool to your healing. It rewrites negative programming.

Read through this entire list of affirmations for a really uplifting, vibration-raising time. You will feel amazing!

Use this list to help you find the positive loving pattern to replace one of your old, outdated patterns.

Try incorporating one or more of these to use as your daily mantra. My favorite is: I only allow mutually supportive and loving people and experiences in my life.

~ HEART CHAKRA MEDITATION USING POSITIVE AFFIRMATIONS ~

Do you want to go one step further with affirmations? (This is based on a class I taught in a past life. I talk about it in *Life Is Just Another Class—One Soul's Journey Through Past Life Regression*.) Get a group of your friends together, sit in a circle, hold hands, take turns reading one affirmation at a time. Really feel the affirmation within. Include any positive experience you want to describe too. Go around the circle, taking turns, in a clockwise fashion. These affirmations open you heart energy. Direct your heart chakra energy into the center of the circle. You can light a candle in the center to help you. It really opens your heart. A beautiful ball of love energy actually forms in the center that will grow and expand as you continue speaking and feeling each affirmation.

These affirmations raise your vibration up so high; some people have had angels and spirit guides come through with messages. It is like you are raising your vibration to meet these higher vibrating beings on a higher dimension. You can start with the list of affirmations provided in, "Chapter 17, Making True Love Affirmations."

Whew. This is a super powerful experience. When I have led this meditation, participants always come to me later and remark that they felt like they were 'high' for days afterwards from their powerfully raised vibration. This experience is more healing than words can describe. Read about the Maharishi Effect for a deeper dive on how this works.

All my relationships support me in my lesson of learning deep love, support, and trust
Amazing things happen to me
Being touched is safe
Creativity energizes me
Deep, mutual love is here for me
Emotions are the language of my soul
Enjoying naked time with myself and others is healthy
Every part of my body is beautiful
Feeling pleasure is good
Good things happen in my life often
Great things come to me
Happiness is mine for the claiming
I choose happiness now
Hope, faith, and love brightens the light within
I allow myself to experience pleasure
I always feel safe in a relationship
I am
I am a creative being
I am a powerful, loving being
I am a sexual being
I am allowed to feel pleasure
I am allowed to relax
I am at peace
I am at peace with myself
I am beautiful and young at heart and I express my beauty from the inside out
I am brave
I am capable
I am capable of being loved and giving love
I am complete
I am confident

I am creative
I am doing the best that I can, and it is enough
I am empowered
I am enough
I am free
I am free to choose in any situation
I am free to love anyone
I am good enough
I am happy
I am healed
I am in control of my life
I am lovable and worthy of receiving love
I am love
I am loveable
I am loved
I am made of love
I am made of pure unconditional love
I am more aware of my energy expenditure every day
I am my own person
I am open to experiencing the present moment through my senses
I am open to new experiences
I am open to receive
I am open to receive help
I am open to receive in all ways
I am open to receive pleasure
I am open to the fullness of my power
I am open to touch and closeness
I am passionate
I am proud of my achievements
I am safe
I am secure in the knowledge that I love myself
I am strong
I am treated with respect every day
I am valued
I am wanted
I am wanted and loved
I am whole
I am worthy
I am worthy of a faithful relationship
I am worthy of amazing love
I am worthy of deep, long-lasting love
I am worthy of love
I am worthy of receiving

I am worthy of respect
I am worthy of true love
I appreciate a positive energetic exchange
I appreciate and celebrate my purposeful relationship
I attract love into my life
I believe compliments
I can be with anyone
I can do anything
I can do anything I set my mind to do
I can express my thoughts and feelings with ease to anyone
I can go anywhere
I can travel anywhere with ease
I choose to rejoice
I commit to being the change
I commit to being the witness of my own healing
I communicate with ease
I create things for me, and it is okay
I delight in weaving the creative tapestry that is my life
I deserve deep love
I enjoy being playful, loud, and frisky
I feel pleasure and abundance with every breath I take
I feel pleasure and it is okay
I genuinely love myself
I have healthy boundaries
I have healthy, nourishing relationships
I have love in my life
I have loving people in all aspects of my life
I have permission to speak
I have the power to manifest my dreams
I have true love with mutual respect, support, and intimacy in my life
I honor the power within me
I know how to take care of my needs
I learn from everything that I do
I let my soul guide me to my soulmate and trust it knows the way
I live my life with integrity
I love and enjoy my body
I love everything about me
I love my body
I love my mind
I love my soul
I love myself
I love myself more every day

MAKING TRUE LOVE

I love to have fun
I love what I do
I make my own choices
I nourish my body with healthy food and clean water
I only allow a healthy, loving relationship
I only allow mutually supportive and loving connections
I only allow mutually supportive and loving experiences in my life
I only allow mutually supportive and loving relationships in my life
I only allow mutually supportive and loving people and experiences in my life
I only allow mutually supportive people in my life
I only allow truth in my life
I open my heart to myself, and I trust that true love will follow
I open my heart to receive love
I overcome obstacles with ease
I raise my vital energy more every day
I release all blame and guilt
I release whatever is standing in the way of love
I remember to focus on the positive each day
I respect myself
I respect myself and honor my emotions
I respect myself at all times
I respect myself, my emotions, and my energy
I say goodbye to the wrong relationships and say hello to true love
I say what I feel
I see the positive
I speak clearly
I speak clearly and concisely
I speak clearly and with confidence
I speak from the heart
I speak with clarity
I speak with ease and grace
I take care of myself in every way
I take good care of my physical body
I touch myself with ease
I treat myself as if I am my own soulmate
I truly love myself
I trust in my own perfection
I trust
I value and respect my body
I value my energy
I will never settle for less than what my heart and soul desire
I'm learning how to give and receive love and it is okay

It is my life, and I can bring what I desire to me
It is safe to love
It is safe to love again
It is safe to set boundaries
Masturbation is selflove
My body is my own
My Crown chakra is healed
My energy is raised up more and more every day
My Heart chakra is open and healed
My heart is open to love
My intuition guides me in all that I do
My intuitive abilities get better and better each day in every way
My life is amazing
My Root chakra is healed
My Sacral chakra is healed
My sexuality is sacred
My Solar Plexus chakra is healed
My soulmate is attracted to my joy
My spirit guides support me in all that I do
My Third Eye chakra is open and healed
My Throat chakra is healed
My time has come. Love is in the air. I breathe it in and embrace it as my own
Only uplifting people are in my life
Others' hear what I am saying
Relaxing is fun
Rest and relaxation are beneficial to my health
Sex is fun
Sex is natural
The angels support me in all I do
The energy I give is valuable
The words I say are heard
There are good people everywhere I go
There are many soulmates out there for me
There are many people who love me
There is power in my voice
To be loved and give love is rewarding
Whatever I do is more than enough

CHAPTER 18

WARNING! DANGER! SIGNS OF ABUSIVE RELATIONSHIPS

This chapter is the most important chapter in this book.

I do hope you read through these lists and find some insight in, hopefully, a past relationship. Essentially, I want to help you become acutely aware of abusive relationship warning signs.

If you are in an abusive relationship currently, I hope this motivates you or inspires you to find the courage to stand your ground, take your confidence back, and leave.

Many of the following series of lists were provided to me by the sweet ladies at a woman's shelter in Texas.

The author of some of these lists were not provided, but if found can be included in future versions of this book. I thank the authors in advance for their dedication to providing resources to help prevent and teach about signs of abuse.

~ CHARACTERISTICS THAT MIGHT IDENTIFY A POTENTIAL BATTERER ~

From a project conducted by SAFE House in Michigan

1. Does he/she report having been physically or psychologically abused as a child?
2. Was his/her mother battered by the father?
3. Has he/she been known to display violence against other people?
4. Does he/she play with guns and use them for protection against other people?
5. Does he/she lose his/her temper frequently and more easily than seems necessary?
6. Does he/she commit acts of violence against objects and things rather than people?
7. Does he/she drink alcohol excessively?
8. Does he/she display an unusual amount of jealousy when you are not with him/her? Is he/she jealous of significant other people in your life?
9. Does he/she expect you to spend all of your free time with him/her or to keep him/her informed of your whereabouts?
10. Does he/she become enraged when you do not listen to his/her advice?
11. Does he/she appear to have a dual personality?
12. Is there a sense of overkill in his/her cruelty or in his/her kindness?
13. Do you get a sense of fear when he/she becomes angry with you?
14. Does NOT making him/her angry become an important part of your behavior?
15. Does he/she have rigid ideas of what people should do that are determined by male or female sex-role stereotypes?
16. Do you think or feel you are being battered? If so, the probability is high that you are a battered person and should seek help immediately.

These clues are certainly not definite signs that a man or woman is a batterer, only that he/she has the potential to become one.

~ QUESTIONS TO ASK YOURSELF: WARNING SIGNS OF ABUSIVE PERSONALITIES ~

Anonymous

1. What do they do when they get angry? ... with things? ... with animals? ... with people? (Threats, break things, throw things?)
2. Are they cruel to animals?
3. Do they resent sharing the decision making?
4. Do they want the final say?
5. Do they blame others for their problems?
6. Do they resent or feel threatened by your goals, successes?
7. Do they recognize your right to privacy and alone time to use as you choose?
8. Do they object to you having your own interests?
9. Do they discourage you from seeing others and want you 'all to themselves' ... are they jealous?
10. Do they treat you like a doll, a sex object, a child, a servant, or a possession?
11. Do they use you as the brunt of jokes?
12. Do they save up gripes to vent at home?
13. Were they physically or sexually abused as a child?
14. Did they witness abuse as a child?
15. Do they or did they abuse their partner or children from a previous relationship? Do they say anything constructive or good about them?
16. Are they cruel to their parents, grandparents, or other family members?
17. Are they anti-feminist, chauvinist, anti-men, or generally resentful of women, especially in the workplace?
18. Are they unreasonably uncomfortable with others' expressing emotions?
19. Do they or did their parents have a problem with alcohol and/or other drugs?
20. Have they ever hit a former partner?
21. Do they insist on always knowing your whereabouts? (i.e., mileage checks, frequent or unexpected phone calls, curfews, limiting phone use, controlling access to money, transportation, etc.)
22. Do they seem to have no sense of others' comfort levels or personal boundaries, pressuring an unwilling partner for favors or compliance?
23. Do they claim not to feel guilt or other 'weak' emotions?
24. Do they believe in harsh discipline?
25. Do they have a low tolerance; are they easily angered?

26. Do they have poor impulse control?
27. Do they threaten suicide if deserted?
28. Are they subject to depression?
29. Are they very 'now' oriented; a poor planner and do not want to wait for pay-offs?
30. Do they have low self-esteem?
31. Are they prone to sabotage success or unable to accept success?
32. Do they tend to be a loner, yet claims great closeness with victim?
33. Do they have poor social skills, or believe they do?
34. Do they have unrealistic standards?
35. Are they hypercritical of others and/or self?
36. If their 'play' is rough, and you call for a halt, do they cooperate?
37. What is their attitude about you working? (Forbid it, sabotage it, are they unsupportive, negative, or do they try to control your decisions about work or education?
38. Do they spend your money?)
39. How are they in competitive situations?
40. How are their communication skills? Do they downplay what others have to say, ignore others' comments, depend on defensive or offensive remarks, take control of conversations, or do they converse at all?
41. Are you afraid to talk to them, or to express an opinion?
42. Are there subjects that are off limits, or that they have an extreme attitude about, and about which there is no discussion?
43. Are they undependable; seem unconcerned when they don't follow through on plans?
44. Do they resent expectations that they must follow through?
45. Do they neglect themselves?
46. Do they expect others to tend to their needs?
47. Do they have extreme mood swings in a short space of time?
48. What are their morals? Are they consistent or do they downplay thievery, lying, condone killing, violence, or bigotry?
49. Do they have unrealistic or fanatical expectations, judgements, plans?
50. Do they seem to live in a fantasy world?

~ TRAITS AND CHARACTERISTICS OF VIOLENT OFFENDERS ~

Prepared by Supervisory Special Agent Alan C. Brantley of the Critical Incident Response Group's National Center for the Analysis of Violent Crime. It is intended to serve as a guide when conducting assessments of subjects suspected or known to be dangerous. The items included on the checklist were selected primarily on the basis of both law enforcement and mental health experience with violent offenders.

Alan C. Brantley, *Traits and Characteristics of Violent Offenders*, FBI Academy.

1. Low Frustration Tolerance—Reacts to stress in self-defeating ways, unable to cope effectively with anxiety, acts out when frustrated. Frustration leads to aggression.
2. Impulsive—Is quick to act, wants immediate gratification, has little or no consideration for the consequences, lacks insight, has poor judgment, has limited cognitive filtering.
3. Emotional Liability/Depression—Quick-tempered, short-fused, hot-headed, rapid mood swings, moody, sullen, irritable, humorless.
4. Childhood Abuse—Sexual and physical abuse, maternal or paternal deprivation, rejection, abandonment, exposure to violent role models in the home.
5. Loner—Is isolated and withdrawn, has poor interpersonal relations, has no empathy for others, lacks feelings of guilt and remorse.
6. Overly Sensitive—Hypersensitive to criticism and real or perceived slights, suspicious, fearful, distrustful, paranoid.
7. Altered Consciousness—Sees red, "blanking," has blackouts, de-realization/depersonalization. ("It's like I wasn't there" or "It was me, but not me"), impaired reality testing, hallucinations.
8. Threats of Violence—Toward self and/or others, direct, veiled, implied, or conditional.
9. Blames Others—Projects blame onto others, fatalistic, external locus of control [belief they have control over their destiny], avoids personal responsibility for behavior, views self as "victim" instead of "victimizer," self-centered, sense of entitlement.
10. Chemical Abuse—Especially alcohol, opiates, amphetamines, crack, and hallucinogens (PCP, LSD), an angry drunk, dramatic personality/mood changes when under the influence.
11. Mental Health Problems Requiring In-Patient Hospitalization—Especially with arrest history for any offenses prior to hospitalization.

12. **History of Violence**—Towards self and others, actual physical force used to injure, harm, or damage. This element is the most significant in assessing individuals for potential dangerousness.
13. Odd/Bizarre Beliefs—Superstitious, magical thinking, religiosity, sexuality, violent fantasies (especially when violence is eroticized), delusions.
14. Physical Problems—Congenital defects, severe acne, scars, stuttering, any of which contribute to poor self-image, lack of self-esteem, and isolation. History of head trauma, brain damage/neurological problems.
15. Preoccupation with Violence Themes—Movies, books, TV, newspaper articles, magazines (detective), music, weapon collections, guns, knives, implements of torture, S & M, Nazi paraphernalia.
16. Pathological Triad/School Problems—Fire-setting, enuresis, cruelty to animals, fighting, truancy, temper tantrums, inability to get along with others, rejection of authority.

~ WARNING SIGNS TO LOOK FOR IN A BATTERING PERSONALITY ~

Prepared by the Project for Victims of Family Violence, Fayetteville, Arkansas.

Source: *Dating Violence: An Anti-Victimization Program*, Texas Council on Family Violence and The National Center for Victims of Crime/Dating Violence Project.

Many are interested in ways that they can predict whether they are about to become involved with someone who will be physically abusive.

Below is a list of behaviors that are seen in people who beat their partners. If the person has three or more of the following behaviors, there is a strong potential for physical violence. The more signs a person has, the more likely the person is a batterer. In some cases, a batterer may have only a couple of the behaviors, but they are very exaggerated (e.g., will try to explain the behavior as signs of their love and concern, and the partner will be flattered at first) but as time goes on, the behaviors become more severe and serve to dominate and control the relationship.

Jealousy—At the beginning of a relationship, an abuser will always say that jealousy is a sign of love. Jealousy has nothing to do with love; it is a sign of possessiveness and lack of trust. The abuser will question the partner about who they talk to, accuse them of flirting, or be jealous of the time they spend with their family, friends, or children. As the jealousy progresses, the abuser may call frequently during the day or drop by unexpectedly. The abuser may refuse to let the partner work for fear they will meet someone else, or even do such strange behaviors such as checking the car mileage or asking friends to "watch" them.

Controlling Behavior—At first, the batterer will say this behavior is because they are concerned for the partner's safety, the need to use their time well, or the need to make good decisions. They will be angry if the partner is "late" coming back from the store or an appointment, will question closely about where they went and who they talked to. As this behavior gets worse, the offender may not let the partner make personal decisions about the house, clothing, going to church, and may keep all the money or even have the partner ask permission to leave the house.

Quick Involvement - Many victims of domestic violence dated or knew their abusers for less than six months before they were married, engaged, or living together. The relationship starts like a whirlwind, with claims such as, "you're the only person I've ever been able to talk to," or "I've never felt loved like this by anyone." There will be pressure to commit to the relationship in such a way that the victim may feel very guilty or that they are "letting the other person down" by wanting to slow down or break off the relationship.

Unrealistic Expectations—Abusive people will expect their partners to meet all their needs: they expect the partner to be the perfect spouse, parent, lover, and friend. They will say things like "If you love me, I'm all you need and you're all I need."

Isolation—The abusive person tries to cut the person off from all resources. If, for instance, the abusive person is a male and his partner has male friends, he might say that she is a "whore" and if she has female friends, she is a "lesbian." The abusive person accuses people, who are supportive of the partner, of "causing trouble." They may try to keep the partner from having a phone, car, or they may try to keep them from working or going to school.

Blames Others for Problems—They may feel that others are always doing them wrong or are out to get them. They may make mistakes and then blame the partner for upsetting them and keeping them from concentrating on the task. The abuser may tell the partner that they are at fault for almost anything that goes wrong.

Blames Others for Feelings—An abuser may tell the partner, "You make me mad," or "It's your fault that I hit you."

Hypersensitivity—An abuser is easily insulted. They claim their feelings are "hurt" when really, they are very mad. They take the slightest setback as personal attacks. They will "rant and rave" about the injustices of things that have happened; things that are really just part of living, like being asked to work overtime, getting a traffic ticket, being told some behavior is annoying, or being asked to help with chores.

Cruelty to Animals or Children—The abuser is a person who punishes animals brutally or is insensitive to their pain or suffering. They may expect children to be capable of doing things beyond their ability (e.g., spanking a two-year-old for wetting a diaper) or they may tease children until they cry (60% of abusers also beat the children in the same home). They may not want children to eat at the same table or expect them to stay in their rooms all evening while they are home.

Verbal Abuse—In addition to saying things that are meant to be cruel and hurtful, the abuser can be degrading, vulgar and running down the partner's accomplishments.

Dr. Jekyll and Mr. Hyde—Many partners are confused by their abuser's "sudden" changes in mood—they may think the abuser has some special mental problem because one moment they are nice and the next they are exploding. Explosiveness and moodiness are typical of people who beat their partners, and these behaviors are related to other characteristics like hypersensitivity.

Applies mostly to male abusers:

Playful Use of Force in Sex—This type of abuser may like to throw the woman down and hold her down during sex, he may want to act out fantasies during sex where the woman is helpless, letting her know that the idea of rape is exciting. He may show little concern about whether the woman wants to have sex and uses sulking or anger to manipulate her into compliance. He may start having sex with the woman while she is sleeping, or demand sex when she is ill or tired.

Rigid Sex Roles—The abuser expects a woman to serve him; he may say the woman must stay at home, that she must obey in all things—even things that are criminal in nature. The abuser will see women as inferior to men, responsible for menial tasks, stupid, and unable to be a whole person without a relationship.

The following are red flags that victims often fail to identify as being the beginning of physical abuse:

Past Battering—This person may say that they have been involved in domestic violence in the past but that the victim "made them do it." The partner may hear from relatives or ex-spouses/partners that the person is abusive.

Threats of Violence—This could include any threat of physical force meant to control the other person such as, "I'll slap your mouth off," or "I'll kill you," etc. Most people do not threaten their mates, but an abuser will try to excuse threats by saying, "Everybody talks like that."

Breaking or Throwing Objects—Breaking a loved one's possessions can be used as punishment, but mostly it is used to terrify the partner into doing what they want. This demonstrates a sign of extreme emotional immaturity, but there is also a great danger when someone thinks they have the "right" to punish or frighten their partner.

Any Force During an Argument—This may involve taking car keys, barring the person from leaving the room, physically restraining, or any pushing or shoving. The man may hold the woman against a wall and say, "You are going to listen to me!"

~ WARNING SIGNS OF DOMESTIC VIOLENCE ~

By the National Domestic Violence Hotline. This project was supported by a grant from the Administration on Children, Youth and Families, Family and Youth Services Bureau, U.S. Department of Health and Human Services.

It is not always easy to tell at the beginning of a relationship if it will become abusive.

In fact, many abusive partners may seem absolutely perfect in the early stages of a relationship. Possessive and controlling behaviors do not always appear overnight, but rather emerge and intensify as the relationship grows.

Domestic violence does not look the same in every relationship because every relationship is different. But one thing most abusive relationships have in common is that the abusive partner does many different kinds of things to have more power and control over their partner.

Some of the signs of an abusive relationship include a partner who:

- Tells you that you can never do anything right
- Shows extreme jealousy of your friends and time spent away
- Keeps you or discourages you from seeing friends or family members
- Insults, demeans, or shames you with put-downs
- Controls every penny spent in the household
- Takes your money or refuses to give you money for necessary expenses
- Looks at you or acts in ways that scare you
- Controls who you see, where you go, or what you do
- Prevents you from making your own decisions
- Tells you that you are a bad parent or threatens to harm or take away your children
- Prevents you from working or attending school
- Destroys your property or threatens to hurt or kill your pets
- Intimidates you with guns, knives or other weapons
- Pressures you to have sex when you don't want to or do things sexually you're not comfortable doing
- Pressures you to use drugs or alcohol

You may be experiencing physical abuse if your partner has done or repeatedly does any of the following tactics of abuse:

- Pulling your hair, punching, slapping, kicking, biting or choking you
- Forbidding you from eating or sleeping
- Hurting you with weapons
- Preventing you from calling the police or seeking medical attention
- Harming your children
- Abandoning you in unfamiliar places
- Driving recklessly or dangerously when you are in the car with them
- Forcing you to use drugs or alcohol (especially if you have had a substance abuse problem in the past)

You may be in an emotionally/verbally abusive relationship if your partner exerts control through:

- Calling you names, insulting you or continually criticizing you
- Refusing to trust you and acting jealous or possessive
- Trying to isolate you from family or friends
- Monitoring where you go, who you call, and who you spend time with
- Demanding to know where you are every minute
- Trapping you in your home or preventing you from leaving
- Using weapons to threaten to hurt you
- Punishing you by withholding affection
- Threatening to hurt you, the children, your family, or your pets
- Damaging your property when they're angry (throwing objects, punching walls, kicking doors, etc.)
- Humiliating you in any way
- Blaming you for the abuse
- Gaslighting - abuse that causes a victim to question their own feelings, instincts, and sanity
- Accusing you of cheating and being often jealous of your outside relationships
- Serially cheating on you and then blaming you for his or her behavior
- Cheating on you intentionally to hurt you and then threatening to cheat again
- Cheating to prove that they are more desired, worthy, etc. than you are

- Attempting to control your appearance: what you wear, how much/little makeup you wear, etc.
- Telling you that you will never find anyone better, or that you are lucky to be with a person like them

Sexually abusive methods of retaining power and control include:

- Forcing you to dress in a sexual way
- Insulting you in sexual ways or calls you sexual names
- Forcing or manipulating you into to having sex or performing sexual acts
- Holding you down during sex
- Demanding sex when you're sick, tired or after hurting you
- Hurting you with weapons or objects during sex
- Involving other people in sexual activities with you against your will
- Ignoring your feelings regarding sex
- Forcing you to watch pornography
- Purposefully trying to pass on a sexually transmitted disease to you

Sexual coercion

Sexual coercion lies on the 'continuum' of sexually aggressive behavior. It can vary from being egged on and persuaded, to being forced to have contact. It can be verbal and emotional, in the form of statements that make you feel pressure, guilt, or shame. You can also be made to feel forced through more subtle actions. For example, an abusive partner:

- Making you feel like you owe them—ex. Because you are in a relationship, because you've had sex before, because they spent money on you or bought you a gift
- Giving you drugs and alcohol to "loosen up" your inhibitions
- Playing on the fact that you're in a relationship, saying things such as: "Sex is the way to prove your love for me," or "If I don't get sex from you I'll get it somewhere else."
- Reacting negatively with sadness, anger, or resentment if you say no or don't immediately agree to something
- Continuing to pressure you after you say no
- Making you feel threatened or afraid of what might happen if you say no
- Trying to normalize their sexual expectations: ex. "I need it, I'm a man"

- Even if your partner is not forcing you to do sexual acts against your will, being made to feel obligated is coercion in itself. Dating someone, being in a relationship, or being married never means that you owe your partner intimacy of any kind.

Reproductive coercion

Reproductive coercion is a form of power and control where one partner strips the other of the ability to control their own reproductive system. It is sometimes difficult to identify this coercion because other forms of abuse are often occurring simultaneously.

Reproductive coercion can be exerted in many ways:
- Refusing to use a condom or other type of birth control
- Breaking or removing a condom during intercourse
- Lying about their methods of birth control (ex. lying about having a vasectomy, lying about being on the pill)
- Refusing to "pull out" if that is the agreed upon method of birth control
- Forcing you to not use any birth control (ex. the pill, condom, shot, ring, etc.)
- Removing birth control methods (ex. rings, IUDs, contraceptive patches)
- Sabotaging birth control methods (ex. poking holes in condoms, tampering with pills or flushing them down the toilet)
- Withholding finances needed to purchase birth control
- Monitoring your menstrual cycles
- Forcing pregnancy and not supporting your decision about when or if you want to have a child
- Forcing you to get an abortion or preventing you from getting one
- Threatening you or acting violent if you don't comply with their wishes to either end or continue a pregnancy
- Continually keeping you pregnant (getting you pregnant again shortly after you give birth)
- Reproductive coercion can also come in the form of pressure, guilt, and shame from an abusive partner. Some examples are if your abusive partner is constantly talking about having children or making you feel guilty for not having or wanting children with them—especially if you already have kids with someone else.

Economic or Financial Abuse

Economic or financial abuse is when an abusive partner extends their power and control into the area of finances. This abuse can take different forms, including:
- Giving an allowance and closely watching how you spend it or demanding receipts for purchases
- Placing your paycheck in their bank account and denying you access to it
- Preventing you from viewing or having access to bank accounts
- Forbidding you to work or limiting the hours that you can work
- Maxing out credit cards in your name without permission or not paying the bills on credit cards, which could ruin your credit score
- Stealing money from you or your family and friends
- Using funds from children's savings accounts without your permission
- Living in your home but refusing to work or contribute to the household
- Making you give them your tax returns or confiscating joint tax returns
- Refusing to give you money to pay for necessities/shared expenses like food, clothing, transportation, or medical care and medicine

Digital abuse

Digital abuse is the use of technologies such as texting and social networking to bully, harass, stalk, or intimidate a partner. Often this behavior is a form of verbal or emotional abuse perpetrated online. You may be experiencing digital abuse if your partner:
- Tells you who you can or cannot be friends with on Facebook and other sites
- Sends you negative, insulting or even threatening emails, Facebook messages, tweets, DMs [Direct Messages] or other messages online
- Uses sites like Facebook, Twitter, Foursquare, and others to keep constant tabs on you
- Puts you down in their status updates
- Sends you unwanted, explicit pictures and demands you send some in return
- Pressures you to send explicit videos
- Steals or insists on being given your passwords

- Constantly texts you and makes you feel like you cannot be separated from your phone for fear that you will be punished
- Looks through your phone frequently, checks up on your pictures, texts and outgoing calls
- Tags you unkindly in pictures on Instagram, Tumblr, etc.
- Uses any kind of technology (such spyware or GPS in a car or on a phone) to monitor you

You never deserve to be mistreated, online or off. Remember:
- Your partner should respect your relationship boundaries
- It is ok to turn off your phone. You have the right to be alone and spend time with friends and family without your partner getting angry
- You do not have to text any pictures or statements that you are uncomfortable sending, especially nude or partially nude photos, known as "sexting"
- You lose control of any electronic message once your partner receives it. They may forward it, so do not send anything you fear could be seen by others
- You do not have to share your passwords with anyone
- Know your privacy settings. Social networks such as Facebook allow the user to control how their information is shared and who has access to it. These are often customizable and are found in the privacy section of the site. Remember, registering for some applications (apps) require you to change your privacy settings
- Be mindful when using check-ins like Facebook Places and Foursquare. Letting an abusive partner know where you are could be dangerous. Also, always ask your friends if it is ok for you to check them in. You never know if they are trying to keep their location secret
- You have the right to feel comfortable and safe in your relationship, even online

~ RELATIONSHIP SPECTRUM ~

Prepared by the National Domestic Violence Hotline. This project was supported by a grant from the Administration on Children, Youth and Families, Family and Youth Services Bureau, U.S. Department of Health and Human Services.

All relationships exist on a spectrum from healthy to abusive with unhealthy somewhere in the middle. Check out the Relationship Spectrum below to see where your relationship falls.

GREEN GO. A healthy relationship means that both you and your partner(s) are:

- Communicating: You talk openly about problems and listen to one another. You respect each other's opinions.
- Respectful: You value each other as you are.
- Trusting: You believe what your partner has to say. You do not feel the need to "prove" each other's trustworthiness.
- Honest: You are honest with each other but can still keep some things private.
- Equal: You make decisions together and hold each other to the same standard.
- Enjoying personal time: You enjoy spending time apart, alone, or with others. You respect each other's need for time apart.
- Making mutual sexual choices: You talk openly about sexual and reproductive choices together. All partners willingly consent to sexual activity and can safely discuss what you are and are not comfortable with.
- Economic/financial partners: You and your partner have equal say with regard to finances. All partners have access to the resources they need.
- Engaging in supportive parenting: All partners are able to parent in a way they feel comfortable with. You communicate together about the needs of the child(ren), as well as the needs of the parents.

YELLOW CAUTION. You may be in an unhealthy relationship if **one** or more partners is:

- Not communicating: When problems arise, you fight, or you don't discuss them at all.
- Disrespectful: One or more partners is not considerate of the other(s).
- Not trusting: One partner does not believe what the other says or feels entitled to invade their privacy.
- Dishonest: One or more partners tells lies.

- Trying to take control: One partner feels their desires and choices are more important.
- Only spending time with your partner: Your partner's community is the only one you socialize in.
- Pressured by the other into sexual activity: One partner uses pressure or guilt on the other to have sex or do anything sexual at any point.
- Ignoring a partner's boundaries: It is assumed only one partner is responsible for making informed decisions.
- Unequal economically: Finances are not discussed, and/or it is assumed only one partner is in charge of finances.

RED STOP. Abuse is occurring in a relationship when one partner:

- Communicates in a way that is hurtful, threatening, insulting, or demeaning.
- Mistreats the other: One partner does not respect the feelings, thoughts, decisions, opinions, or physical safety of the other.
- Accuses the other of cheating or having an affair when it's not true: The partner who accuses may hurt the other in a physical or verbal way as a result.
- Denies that the abusive actions are abuse: An abusive partner may try to blame the other for the harm they are doing or makes excuses for abusive actions or minimizes the abusive behavior.
- Controls the other: There is no equality in the relationship. One partner makes all decisions for the couple without the other's input.
- Isolates the other partner: One partner controls where the other one goes and who they talk to. They may isolate their partner from family and friends.
- Forces sexual activity or pregnancy: One partner forces the other to have sex or do anything they do not want to do sexually at any point. In relationships where pregnancy is a physical possibility, one partner may force the other to become pregnant.
- Exerts economic control: One partner controls the money and access to resources. Having an open dialogue about finances is not an option. This may include preventing a partner from earning an income or not allowing a partner access to their own income.
- Engages in manipulative parenting: One partner uses the child(ren) to gain power and control over the other partner, including telling the child(ren) lies or negative things about the other partner.

CHAPTER 19

INSPIRATION FROM ARCHANGEL CHAMUEL ON SOULMATES & TWIN FLAMES

Archangel Chamuel enjoys serving as the angel of soulmate connections. Making connections with the love-of-your-life makes a whole lot more sense when you recognize that the greater number of connections, the greater the chance that you found your best match.

During an experience to practice channeling in 2018, I channeled Archangel Chamuel. I had never heard much about this angel before and had not previously spoken to him during one of my readings.

Earlier that same day, in the midst of texting my friend about the class, my phone autocorrected 'channel' to 'Chamuel.' I typed in Chamuel again, it came up as a misspelled word. I knew then it was a sign from spirit.

Right away I did an online search of Chamuel which stated that he was an archangel and that his specialty was soulmates! My friend and I agreed, he must be the one I am meant to channel. (Channeling is the ability to allow a spiritual being to talk through you—I personally only channel higher vibrating beings.)

I loved every minute of class that night. I will not ever forget the experience. It was amazing to feel so close to an angel. I swear I could see and feel his wings. I would not have been surprised to find feathers afterwards. Channeling always feels healing and uplifting to me.

Archangel Chamuel said, "Each and every person we meet is our soulmate, because on a soul level, because ultimately, we are one, as well as unconditionally loving spiritual beings. It is our human existence that creates blockages to remembering this deep connection."

It is all about the percentage of connections we have with another person. There are many ways to connect. For example, if we have a high number of open, healed, clear connections, we will not resonate with a person who has not done any personal healing; we might even be repelled by them.

As the percentage of connections increase with a person, the more we relate to, get along with, and really like that other person. This can be friends or lovers. I like to call it the Chamuel Scale.

Archangel Chamuel gave me a visual to explain what he meant by a connection. (You might have to do an internet search to understand this more fully, but I will do my best to explain this to those of you who have only ever used a cellphone.) He showed me an exceptionally large telephone switchboard operator panel.

In the late 1800s, telephones were brand new. All phones were connected by telephone wires. In order to connect one person's phone to connect to another person's phone, an actual human—the switchboard operator—would have to make the connection. If you wanted to make a call, she would see a light near your specific plug receptacle on a large pegboard-like panel in front of them. It would light up once you picked up your landline phone. She would then take a cord (that has a jack at both ends) and plug one end into the receptacle opening by your light. Then, after speaking to you to find out who you wanted to talk to, she would plug the other jack into the receptacle of your friend to connect the two phones. The connection would be made, and you two could talk.

It is the perfect analogy. As you read on, you will understand.

Since we are spiritual beings having a human experience, we need to relate to each other as humans, here in this human experience on Earth. While each person may be our soulmate on a higher vibrational level, it is not often we can maintain a meditative state all day to be aware of this deep spiritual connection we all share.

During the years we live in this human experience, it is the higher overall percentage of connections that brings us closest to our true love. Archangel Chamuel said, "When we attain a high percentage of connection—somewhere between 85%-95%, then it is true love. It all starts with loving yourself in all ways."

Think about any relationship you have formed. You, no doubt, met because you shared an interest—like art, dancing, wine, work, or anything. You name it. You formed that first connection by a shared interest. As you continue to visit and talk to this person, you realize that you share many more connections. As these shared experiences are consciously and subconsciously recognized and tallied, then you start to feel more at ease with this person. You may become friends or even lovers.

Think about your coworkers. You may get along famously while at work, but in social situations, you find that you only seem to have the topic of work in common.

People often connect via sexual attraction first. That can be fun, but many soon realize that sexual compatibility cannot sustain a true relationship if no other connections are found.

If you start connecting with someone on a variety of ideals and experiences, you might start to think about this person as a mate.

When we are aware that there are hundreds of ways to connect to someone in a mutually supportive and loving way, we begin to be more discerning in partner choices.

So, what makes a connection? Notice how many synchronicities, meaningful coincidences, bonding experiences, ties to similar ideals, comparable likes or dislikes, parallel beliefs, healing experiences, emotional intelligence, etc. you share. Additionally, there may be even more on a subconscious level or in one or several past lives. These correlations plus other normal things in common, can link you together for a deep soulmate connection. It may feel like you actually resonate with one another. This makes complete sense when you realize that you are just energy vibrating—just like on the atomic level. When frequencies match, they resonate together just like tuning forks do.

Sure, you hit it off chatting online or meeting randomly at a store. You connect in some basic way as you continue to talk, meet, and learn about one another. As you get more comfortable and open up to each other, you grow closer, maybe even forming a type of bond.

It goes deeper than that. Let me explain.

First, visualize or feel that you are covered with ethereal plugs that are waiting to connect to another person. Thousands of these connections layer over your whole being because you are a multi-faceted human with a plethora of experiences. This includes anything from this life, past lives, other dimensional experiences, and more. Each aspect of you that is open and clear (i.e., healed and illuminated) will connect to another person if they match or vibrate on that same level. The connections that are closed due to trauma, past lives, fear, etc. will inhibit a connection. The more you heal yourself, you increase the number of connections you have available to bring true love into your life.

If the commitment plug is filled with the connection to another, there is no room for you. When you learn that the other person is in a committed relationship, then this primary plug is not open to you, no matter what. While some may attempt to participate as a third person in a relationship, you are a third wheel and will only ever get a trickle of a connection from this plug. There will not ever be enough to sustain the connection of devotion that you deserve.

Let us say you meet someone. You first connected because both of you enjoy traveling. You talk and realize you both have been to Paris—one connection. Both of you have a parent that passed over—another connection. Both of you enjoy snow—connection. Both of you enjoy past life research—connection. Both of you choose not to smoke or gamble—connection, connection. As you continue to learn about the other person, you form many connections and your heart warms to the potential of a relationship blossoming. All of this forms a deep bond.

During the first few dates and conversations, people weave in things they like, just to see if the other person responds in the same excited way about what they love. They do not like to play board games—failed connection. They say they do not like to dance—failed connection. They say they have no interest in traveling—failed connection. When you meet someone who constantly responds with disinterest to the things you adore, they soon depart from being part of your life. If you are desperate for any relationship, you might compromise by giving up one or more things you love for that relationship. However, if they, instead, are open to trying something new or supporting you in the things you love, then it could work.

It is the connections that are subconscious that become a bit harder to acknowledge or notice right away. Some of them might include: ability to move through grief, thinking positively on a daily basis, released fear of flying, healed their Heart chakra from past relationship hurts, being awakened, enjoying the little things in life, supported each other in a past life, capable of intimate conversations, and more. Spiritually or energetically, each of your chakras may connect as you talk to someone you are trying to get to know.

These connections are all on a subconscious or energetic level. You might feel these connections first and it may be these unseen bonds that draw you to talk to a stranger and seek more obvious connections. You may experience these subconscious connections when you get an amazing feeling about someone you have never met. This feeling may come from your gut, your Sacral chakra. It is your intuition making you aware of your subconscious energetic connection.

I have experienced a missed opportunity of a deep connection. There is no other way to explain it. A very long time ago, I was walking through a

Dallas, Texas mall. I passed by a man on my way to find a particular store. We exchanged glances and probably a smile. I did not know him, but something was different—what exactly, I did not know. I talked myself out of turning around and making conversation. I continued to the store, shopped, but could not get him out of my mind. I immediately walked back to where I saw him last and waited about an hour in the hopes he would come back past. I actually cried when I left the mall—sad that I missed the chance to meet this man. I still think about that experience today. I am told by my spirit guides that he was a person who would have been an important part of my life had we met. Who knows, we may still meet; I have a lot of life left. Chamuel says he had an 87% connection with me. If only I knew then what I know now. Life continues to be all about the learning.

The ultimate goal is to feel a high percentage of connections with another person.

I really believe that when you meet someone for the first time AND there is an instant attraction beyond the sexual, then the only explanation can only be the subconscious energetic connections. If you go on a first date to meet someone and feel no connection, no spark, no sense of comfort, that equals an exceptionally low percentage of connections.

Here is an anecdotal story that many will appreciate. I met someone online, we chatted via text, and then spoke on the phone. He had all the basics, plus he was cute, had a decent job, and said he cared about his parents. The next logical step was to meet. As we spoke and spent time together that evening, it became acutely apparent that he was clearly only interested in sex. He was very closed off emotionally and it became obvious he needed a lot of deep healing on several levels based on a few things he mentioned during our conversations. He seemed very professional on the phone, but in person he appeared as more of man-child. It was a very frustrating first date with zero chance of a second date.

Two days later, I received all the information from Archangel Chamuel regarding soulmate connections and how the percentage of connections help determine the potential for deep, true love.

As one should for most anything, I asked. I asked for help from my spirit guides and Archangel Chamuel to determine what the bad date experience was supposed to teach me. The sole reason for this date was so that he could be the inspiration for one of the chapters in this book. More importantly, I asked him, "What was the percentage of connections to this person?" Chamuel responded, "17%." (Can you hear my groan?)

It is only through these tough experiences that we learn the most. (Second loud groan.)

What is true love? Genuinely loving yourself to care deeply enough for yourself to heal. Others can only love you as much as you love yourself.

Common questions are, "How will I know they are the right person?" or "Where is my soulmate?" When you have chosen to do the healing work on yourself, and you have removed any blocks to receiving, feeling worthy and more, then you will start to resonate with those with which you will have the most meaningful connections.

Archangel Chamuel is not saying that you must meet someone who is exactly like you in all aspects, but someone that exhibits a lot of beliefs, healing attributes, and openness to your wellbeing. Allow someone who cherishes you in all ways to come into your life. You deserve it.

Trust your intuition. If you wonder what your percentage of connection is with a particular person, then ask. Archangel Chamuel will provide the answer.

Interestingly, if you meet someone who has connections with you on a lot of things, you can both continue to heal emotionally and spiritually to open yourself to more connections between the two of you. Or not. Here is one example.

~ CURRENT LIFE EXAMPLE: NANCY ~

When Alex and Nancy met, they found they connected on some common things. However, Alex enjoyed shooting guns at the firing range. He spoke passionately about guns and even worked in the police force for a short while. Nancy, however, had a fear of touching guns that started during childhood. She could talk about guns but did not want to touch them or shoot them.

When someone is passionate about a particular subject matter, this cord of potential connection becomes very large and necessary for that person to connect with their true match. Nancy realized this would be an issue with their relationship and looked deep within to see if there was something she could do to resolve her fear.

Nancy came to me for a past life regression. We talked beforehand about the gun issue. She could relate it to her use of a BB gun as a young teen when she tried to shoot a bird. The whole experience made her uncomfortable. She sought a deeper answer and felt past life regression therapy could help. During her session, she remembered a lifetime during the Civil War.

~ ROOT CAUSE EXPLORATION ~

"I am a young man of about twenty-five. I recently found out my wife and I are expecting a baby! She glows when we talk about the baby. I love her so much. The Civil War just started, so we thought it remained safe to visit her favorite aunt in Virginia to share the news. It is the summer of 1861 A.D.

We believed in President Lincoln and felt he was doing right by all the people in the states.

As we prepared to leave Virginia, we heard there were troops in the area looking to kill Northerners. Unfortunately, they raided my wife's aunt's house whilst I ventured out to try to find out what was really happening. They slaughtered my wife and unborn child. I found her laying on the settee bleeding out of her mouth and stomach areas. I spotted a large open wound, as if someone sliced down her center—probably with a bayonet.

Overcome with grief, I made the decision to fight for the north to help stop this madness. I felt this heinous act was unforgivable and took up arms to fight for Lincoln. I did not have to go far to join 'the cause' since a northern group was said to be passing near this area. I am a learned, professional man with management experience from training in business.

I eventually joined the 151st Regimen and stayed with them for about four years. I fought many battles. In that time, I killed 54 men and boys. The hardest being the 12-year-old boy that was doing his best for his Pa. I did not realize he was so young until I rolled him over to check his neck for a pulse. He was barely twelve. I heard of young boys joining the war with their fathers or joining because they had lost their mothers. I cried like a baby that night. That could have been my child.

They soon gave me the supposed honor to oversee about forty men. Sometimes I had thirty, sometimes I had 50. Men would die, more would join. It always fluctuated. Either way, they would line up to hear their daily orders for the war from me.

I thought about my wife and baby every single day. This ignited my fire to push forward in battle. I became emotionally immune to all the death around me. I was a very good shot with a long gun, but I preferred my pistol.

One of the battles of my group occurred in Gettysburg, Pennsylvania.

I came upon a scruffy-faced man in his thirties already wounded from battle. I was under directive to not let one Southerner live. He looked filthy, as were all of us, and dressed in tattered clothes. The smell of gun smoke, decaying bodies, and blood surrounded me and the battlefield. The smoke that billowed up in the air made the sky blackened. The moans of the dying could be heard for miles. The man reached out to me, begging for his sorry life. He reminded me of the men who killed my wife and unborn child, so I grit my teeth, aimed my gun, and shot him in the chest, then moved on to continue my mission.

Later, I joined a few of the men—5 of them—on a mission to locate scouts sneaking into our camp looking for intel. We found three of them. A fourth got away. After we beat some information out of these men, I had them kneel before me, their hands tied behind their back, and their mouth gagged. I shot them, point blank, between their eyes. Three shots for three men. I confidently held the gun with one hand. I did not waste one bullet. My anger and sadness from the loss of my wife and child filled each bullet I shot.

After the war ended, I could not remove the image of my dead wife and child from my mind. I missed them constantly. I had no place to go and no family left. I drank to forget and to drown my emotions of sadness. I drank hoping to remove it all from my memory. It never did leave. The moment I would forget my wife, the people I shot in the war would come flashing in front of my eyes. I felt haunted by them. The post-traumatic stress of the war enveloped my whole being.

I literally drank myself to death within two years after I left the war.

My wife and child greeted me with open arms in The Light. It was only then that I knew it was going to be okay."

~ HEALING STEPS ~

We work on healing at the end of this session. It includes working to forgive themselves, the war, the gun, the bullets, the alcohol, the people who killed his wife and unborn child, and more. It is not saying what they did was okay, but to release any energy, conscious or subconscious, that is attached to these things or experiences.

This also helped with any PTSD (post-traumatic stress disorder) that resulted from this lifetime.

We asked the angels to provide pure unconditional love energy to raise her vital energy and provide healing on an energetic level. We asked that they remove any pent-up or stored emotions from her energetic being and replace it with love and light.

We asked the angels to help with retrieving any parts of their soul that they set aside for later healing. We asked that any parts of their soul be returned to them and to help them reintegrate within them through all time, space, and dimensions and to continue to integrate now and into the future.

Remembering this lifetime helped to resolve her fear of war and guns. This past life was the root cause of the current life's fear of holding a gun. The gun represented unresolved guilt, grief, and sadness from the horrific experience during the Civil War. These emotions became equated with guns.

She also shut off any emotions in the Civil War lifetime. This prevented her from feeling empathy in the current lifetime. This could prevent her from fully opening up emotionally to someone in this current lifetime too.

One of Nancy's potential connections to Alex was the love of guns and shooting. Clearly Nancy was good at using a gun, but even though she healed her fear of guns, plus so much more, the relationship dissolved. You cannot base a relationship on one connection. The Archangel Chamuel percentage of connection was 48—not strong enough for a true love soulmate connection.

~ WHAT ABOUT TWIN FLAMES? ~

I channeled Archangel Chamuel again in May of 2021, not long before publishing this book. A friend and I wanted to understand the difference between a soulmate and a twin flame connection.

Archangel Chamuel said, *"So, you want to know more about soulmates? I am at your mercy and joy. When you meet someone that opens your inner spark, that is congruent to what you refer to as the twin flame.*

Our inner light being, the conscious part of us, has an inner doorway which is opened by someone who ignites your inner flame.

This inner doorway of connection can be opened by many, not just one. You must know that. Through many lifetimes, over time, many aspects of your inner soul are opened in this way. Twelve times it must occur. Sometimes many lives will pass. It will not be the same each time. [Archangel Chamuel showed me an image of a pie, sliced into twelve pieces.] Wedges of time. This connection awakens that aspect of you that has been closed, like a rebirthing. Inner knowledge and expansion is all part of soul growth. They open yours; you open theirs. That is why it is twin.

It has nothing to do with commingling. Meeting during a lifetime is the key that unlocks the door. This key opens that port, that inner flame. You open theirs; they open yours. It does not mean a relationship must be had.

Soulmates are much different than this. It is a completely different, separate thing.

Twelve times it must happen to complete the cycle to move to the next level. If you need reminded to remember... If you do not find it in other Earthly ways, then this being will come to you to help unlock and open that aspect of your inner soul.

If you are lucky, you find one in a lifetime. Some have found two but that is rare. The soulmate is what you aspire to find.

The flame opener—they come when you need ignited—opened up. They ignite the flame within; a spark that pushes you to the next level. That is what it is about.

The chemistry between two people keeps the flame lit, the door open. Pushing your soul growth. The love that you feel for the other person is a soul level love connection based on many lifetimes and soul encounters on the other side. All of this is pre-arranged and pre-determined beyond this Earth experience.

This intense soul growth, is for the betterment of 'The All.' Knowledge is the key to expansion."

Meeting a 'flame opener'—a twin flame—is a catalyst for deeper soul growth.

Then he said to me, "That is all for now."

BIBLIOGRAPHY

Bourne, Ph.D., Edmund J. *The Anxiety and Phobia Workbook*. Oakland, CA: New Harbinger Publications, 1990. Print.

Bowman, Carol. *Children's Past Lives*. New York: Bantam, 1997. Print.

Cantrell, Leslie. *Into the Light: A Guide for Battered Woman*. Edmonds, WA: C. Franklin Press, 1986. Print.

Emoto, Masaru, *The Hidden Messages in Water*. Hillsboro, OR: Beyond Words Publications; 2004. Print.

Ferster, Charles B., and Skinner, B. F. *Schedules of Reinforcement*. B. F. Harvard University. Office of Naval Research. Appleton-Century-Crofts, New York. 1957. Print.

Ghost Inside My Child. Dir. Sandra C. Alvarez. Prod. Amanda Spain. Los Angeles, CA: A&E Television Network/LMN, TV Series. 2013, 2014. Television.

Kubicko, Karen A. *Life Is Just Another Class—One Soul's Journey Through Past Life Regression*. Natrona Heights, PA: Karen Kubicko, 2014. Print. Electronic. Audio.

Lipton, Bruce H. *The Biology of Belief*. Carlsbad, California: Hay House, 2008. Print.

National Domestic Violence Hotline. "*Warning Signs of Domestic Violence*." www.thehotline.org. Austin, Texas. National Domestic Violence Hotline. n.d. Web. 7 Nov. 2018.

National Domestic Violence Hotline. "*Relationship Spectrum.*" www.thehotline.org. Austin, Texas. National Domestic Violence Hotline. n.d. Web. 7 Nov. 2018.

SAFE House in Michigan. *Characteristics that Might Identify a Potential Batterer.* Ann Arbor, MI. circa 1990. Print-1 page.

Satir, Virginia M. *I am Me.* Berkeley, Calif: Celestial Arts. 1975. Poster. Print. Satir, Virginia M. Self Esteem. Berkeley, Calif: Celestial Arts. 2001. Print. Virginia Satir Collection. HPA Mss 45. Department of Special Collections, Davidson Library, University of California, Santa Barbara. Donated by Virginia Satir, ca. 1987 and by the Avanta Network, 1991. Poem.

Scarr, Sandra, and Zanden, James Vander. *Understanding Psychology.* New York: Random House, 1984. Print.

Stevenson, Ian. *Reincarnation and Biology*: Birthmarks. Volume 1 & 2. Connecticut: Praeger, 1997. Print.

Tennyson, Alfred Lord. *In Memoriam* A.H.H. OBIIT. MDCCCXXX111:27. London: E. Moxon, 1850. Poem. Print.

Vitale, Joe. *The Missing Secret.* Wheeling, IL: Nightingale-Conant. 2014. Audiobook.

Water, Owen. *Love, Light, Laughter: The New Spirituality.* Delaware: Infinite Being Publishing, LLC, 2010. Print.

Wintle, Walter D. *Thinking.* Missouri: Unity, 1905. Poem. Print.

INDEX

abuse traits, 3
abuse-love cycle, 66
abusive behavior, 3, 203
abusive patterns, 13, 38, 71
affirmation, xiv, xix, 181
aided hypnosis, 25
Akashic Records, 58, 71, 86
Alfred Lord Tennyson, 59
American Indians, 127, 128, 129
angelic healing, 5, 6, 61, 101
angels, vii, xvii, xix, xx, 2, 8, 23, 24, 27, 29, 31, 32, 33, 35, 45, 46, 49, 53, 54, 58, 59, 61, 62, 63, 68, 70, 71, 75, 82, 85, 92, 93, 95, 98, 101, 105, 110, 111, 118, 121, 128, 135, 136, 137, 139, 146, 149, 152, 158, 162, 165, 181, 186, 212, 221
anorexia, 40, 41
Archangel, x, 8, 31, 32, 70, 126, 165, 166, 167, 205, 206, 209, 210, 213
Archangel Chamuel, x, 205
arranged marriage, 47, 82, 83, 85, 86
asthma, 4, 5, 12
baby spirits, 63
birthmark, 27, 157

boundaries, 3, 78, 81, 121, 122, 133, 139, 184, 186, 189, 201, 203
Brian Weiss, 4, 221
cake, 39
chakra, xv, xviii, 4, 7, 13, 24, 29, 30, 31, 32, 37, 39, 40, 45, 46, 48, 49, 53, 55, 59, 61, 75, 77, 81, 82, 86, 90, 93, 108, 109, 110, 111, 112, 121, 126, 128, 133, 136, 146, 149, 151, 152, 153, 160, 161, 167, 174, 181, 186, 208
Channeling, 205
class of life, xiv
codependency, 39, 133
compromising, 66, 77, 134
computer programing, 24
conscious, xiv, 30, 31, 32, 33, 41, 71, 87, 114, 155, 157, 159, 163, 166, 212, 213
cut cords, 75, 118, 136, 149, 163
depression, 49, 52, 54, 57, 62, 79, 161, 190
Digital abuse, 200
dimension, xiv, 155, 182
DNA, 24, 173
Domestic violence, 196

Earth, xiii, xiv, xv, 27, 30, 52, 53, 54, 67, 98, 152, 153, 155, 157, 161, 171, 206, 214
energetic vampire, 114, 163
energy healer, xix
Eye of Horus, 151
feather, 55
Financial Abuse, 200
Forgiveness, 26, 27, 38, 45, 71, 118, 157, 158
free will, xiii, xv, xvii, 63, 86, 142, 161, 165, 178
Free Will, 52
God, xv, 2, 6, 78, 85, 110, 120, 121, 155, 173
Greece, 83
guided meditation, 61
Heaven, xiv, 6, 53
Hedonistic, 38
higher self, xiv, 151, 155, 166
hormone, 36
human bottle, 114, 163, 164
human existence, xviii, 63, 151, 153, 155, 205
hypnosis, 4, 25
hypnotherapist, 4
hypnotic state, 5, 6, 25
icing, 39
incarnate, xiii
induction script, xvi, xviii, 29
Induction Script, 29
intent, vi, xiii, xiv, xvi, xvii, 13, 14, 15, 25, 26, 27, 29, 38, 69, 109, 125, 136, 162
intimacy, 24, 158, 184, 199
Intimate conversations, 141
intuition, 5, 6, 8, 25, 71, 166, 170, 186, 208, 210
intuitive abilities, 5, 46, 53, 110, 186
intuitive senses, xviii, 152
kissing, 1, 20, 40, 104, 119

Law of Attraction, 2, 168
Law of Gravity, 52, 168
learning lessons, xiii, 14
Lena, 3, 5, 6, 12, 27
lessons, xiii, 19, 67, 85, 142, 166
Life Is Just Another Class—One Soul's Journey Through Past Life Regression, 5, 13, 55, 77, 82, 181, 221
manifestation, xv, 30, 53, 153
masturbation, 35, 36, 38, 42, 48
Masturbation, 36, 49, 186
Meditation, 25
metaphysical, 3, 4, 5, 7, 88, 167
metaphysics, 7, 221
miscarriage, 37, 63, 89
modality, 25, 156, 167
molestation, 36, 37, 40
Mt. Washington, 126, 127, 128, 129
multi-dimensional being, xix
narcissist, 36, 37, 38, 132, 133, 134
near-death experience, 3, 8, 63, 165
New York, 215
open to receive, 24, 33, 40, 46, 49, 95, 105, 121, 172, 183
orgasm, 36, 38, 40, 42, 46, 89, 132
padding of protection, 40
past life, xiv, xv, xvi, xvii, xviii, xix, 1, 2, 4, 5, 6, 7, 11, 12, 13, 14, 15, 17, 18, 25, 26, 27, 29, 32, 33, 35, 36, 40, 42, 46, 47, 51, 53, 54, 55, 56, 59, 62, 69, 71, 79, 81, 82, 86, 89, 93, 98, 99, 101, 108, 109, 110, 111, 118, 119, 124, 126, 128, 129, 134, 136, 137, 138, 139, 145,

146, 148, 149, 155, 156, 157, 159, 181, 208, 210, 212, 221
past life regression, xiv, xvi, xvii, xviii, xix, 4, 5, 6, 12, 13, 15, 25, 26, 27, 29, 35, 40, 42, 46, 47, 53, 59, 62, 69, 71, 79, 99, 101, 109, 119, 124, 126, 134, 136, 137, 149, 155, 156, 157, 210, 221
pent-up emotion, xix, 156
Perfectionism, ix, 97
PFA, 67
physical touch, 39, 40
Pittsburgh, v, 101, 126, 127
privacy, vi, 44, 105, 177, 178, 189, 201, 202
programming, 13, 38, 70, 107, 108, 175, 181
psychically, xv, xix, 2, 38, 40, 41, 135, 151, 156
PTSD, 3, 37, 46, 68, 133, 157, 158, 162, 175, 212
Queen Elizabeth, 80, 81
red flag, 37, 39, 66, 78, 80, 87, 90, 114, 163
Reiki, xix, 5, 71, 156, 167
Reproductive coercion, 199
RICE EXPERIMENT, 171
root cause, xiii, xvi, xvii, xviii, 7, 8, 28, 33, 35, 36, 41, 42, 45, 52, 55, 56, 59, 68, 69, 71, 79, 90, 91, 93, 97, 110, 116, 137, 141, 142, 146, 158, 165, 212
root causes, xiv, 7, 25, 27
ROSE EXPERIMENT, 171
selfcare, xx, 78, 88, 98, 116, 155
self-hypnosis, 4, 25
selflove, xii, xvii, xx, 12, 36, 41, 49, 67, 75, 98, 116, 133, 142, 155, 161, 167, 186

Sex, ix, 35
Sex chakra, 40, 126, 151
sex equals love, 39
sexual abuse, 39, 46
Sexual coercion, 198
sexual issues, 35, 36, 37, 40, 47
sexual pleasure, 42, 48, 49
sexual trauma, 3, 35, 36, 37, 40, 42, 45, 126, 151, 152
shelter, vii, 2, 3, 67, 68, 109, 187
Solar Plexus, 29, 67, 75, 77, 81, 82, 86, 90, 93, 121, 126, 128, 133, 136, 149, 151, 152, 160, 161, 174, 186
soul level, xiii, 26, 55, 62, 70, 155, 162, 205, 214
soul retrieval, xix, 7, 92, 156, 174
Source, xv, 8, 30, 153, 155, 167, 193
spirit guide, 5, 6, 8, 9, 12, 27, 33, 58, 71, 75, 86, 90, 91, 136, 144
spirit guides, vii, xvi, xvii, xviii, xx, 3, 5, 7, 8, 12, 13, 27, 28, 29, 31, 32, 35, 45, 46, 53, 54, 55, 59, 62, 63, 71, 82, 85, 93, 95, 99, 102, 105, 110, 111, 118, 119, 121, 122, 129, 136, 137, 141, 144, 146, 152, 153, 156, 165, 169, 181, 186, 209, 221
spiritual being, xv, xviii, 26, 31, 32, 67, 75, 128, 174, 205
spiritual beings, vii, 3, 55, 63, 205, 206
spiritual healing, 5
subconscious level, 41, 51, 52, 98, 207
Suicide, 5
telepathy, 6, 53

Telepathy, xv
The Light, 5, 8, 23, 45, 58, 60, 70, 75, 81, 85, 105, 111, 121, 212
theta state, 26, 107, 108
Third Eye, 3, 29, 151, 152, 186
Throat chakra, 7, 29, 45, 47, 108, 128, 136, 174
unconditional love, xi, xii, xv, xix, 21, 23, 27, 30, 31, 45, 64, 66, 67, 68, 71, 75, 95, 111, 118, 136, 139, 152, 153, 155, 157, 173, 183, 212

unresolved issue, 41
vibration, xiv, xv, xviii, 113, 114, 115, 131, 155, 160, 161, 163, 164, 169, 181, 182
vibrational, xiv, 115, 151, 164, 206
victim mode, 67, 113, 116, 123, 124, 148
visualization process, 27, 157
vital energy, 31, 67, 88, 95, 113, 114, 115, 160, 161, 163, 164, 165, 167, 185, 212
weight, 36, 40, 41

ABOUT THE AUTHOR

Karen Ann Kubicko is a past life regressionist and intuitive psychic reader passionate about teaching and helping others heal through working with their spirit guides, angels, and the patterns found in their own past lives. Since 2004, the study of all spiritually healing concepts and modalities, angels, spirit guides, reincarnation, and past life regression has been her passion.

Karen completed the Past Life Therapy Professional Training course with Carole and Dr. Brian Weiss in 2007. She has personally remembered well over 150 past lives and has helped numerous others remember their own past lives.

Karen utilizes her intuitive skills to help others realize that their angels, spirit guides, and passed over loved ones deeply love them and are always with them, helping them, and supporting them.

Devoted to creating, she is an avid writer, speaker, and artist. She also enjoys mixing science with metaphysics and understanding the why behind it all. Karen loves being the mother of her two beautiful children and enjoys traveling the world.

Karen has been featured on several internet radio interviews. Karen, supporting her youngest child, can also be seen on the LMN television show *Ghost Inside My Child* (S2 E1, 2014).

Follow Karen's work, ask questions about how past life regression can help you, or schedule a session with her. Her first book, *Life Is Just Another Class—One Soul's Journey Through Past Life Regression*, is available on Amazon.

For more information on how to schedule with Karen, please visit www.KarenKubicko.com.

CONNECTING

Website: www.KarenKubicko.com
YouTube: Karen Kubicko
Instagram: Karen Kubicko
LinkedIn: Karen Kubicko
Facebook: www.facebook.com/KarenAKubicko
Twitter: www.twitter.com/KarenKubicko
Pinterest: www.pinterest.com/karenkubicko
Redbubble: Karen Kubicko

Made in the USA
Middletown, DE
26 May 2022